✳

Making Waves

Fernand Braudel Center Series
Edited by Immanuel Wallerstein

Alternatives: The United States Confronts the World
by Immanuel Wallerstein

The Modern World-System in the Longue Durée
edited by Immanuel Wallerstein

Overcoming the Two Cultures: Science versus the Humanities in the Modern World-System
Richard E. Lee and Immanuel Wallerstein, coordinators

Making Waves: Worldwide Social Movements, 1750–2005
William G. Martin, coordinator

✶

Making Waves

Worldwide Social Movements, 1750–2005

William G. Martin, coordinator

with

Tuba Agartan
Caleb M. Bush
Woo-Young Choi
Tu Huynh
Fouad Kalouche
Eric Mielants
Rochelle Morris

Paradigm Publishers
Boulder•London

Copyright © 2008 by Paradigm Publishers

Published in the United States by Paradigm Publishers, 3360 Mitchell Lane, Suite E, Boulder, Colorado 80301 USA.

Paradigm Publishers is the trade name of Birkenkamp & Company, LLC, Dean Birkenkamp, President and Publisher.

Library of Congress Cataloging-in-Publication Data

Making waves : worldwide social movements, 1765–2005 / William G. Martin, coord., with Tuba Agartan ... [et al.].
   p. cm. — (Fernand braudel center series)
   "This is the first of three inter-related books (in a project directed by Immanuel Wallerstein) whose overall objective is to provide an alternative account of contemporary developments of globalization. Current events can only be understood within the historical development of the capitalist world-economy. Authors will explore the three interrelated loci of action within the system — the structural trends in the capitalist world-economy, the categories of social knowledge, and the waves of antisystemic movements. Each book will investigate each of these sectors worldwide for long historical periods (two to four centuries) to discern what is special about the current period, and to seek to understand why we are nearing a crisis-breakpoint of the historical system in which we live today" — Provided by the publisher.
   Includes bibliographical references and index.
   ISBN 978-1-59451-480-7 (hardcover : alk. paper) — ISBN 978-1-59451-481-4 (pbk. : alk. paper) 1. Social movements—History. 2. Social conflict—History. 3. Capitalism—History. 4. Globalization—History. I. Wallerstein, Immanuel Maurice, 1930– II. Martin, William G., 1952– III. Agartan, Tuba.
   HM881.M34 2007
   306.3′420903—dc22

2007020034

Printed and bound in the United States of America on acid-free paper that meets the standards of the American National Standard for Permanence of Paper for Printed Library Materials.

Designed and Typeset by Straight Creek Bookmakers.

11 10 09   3 4 5

＊

Contents

✳

Foreword

The Fernand Braudel Center, somewhat dismayed by the ahistoric analysis of the contemporary world that has been occurring in much of the literature that parades under the rubric of globalization, decided to launch a three-part investigation of what we think are the three major pillars of the existing world-system—the systems of production, the knowledge systems, and the antisystemic movements. Each was to be analyzed in historical depth and worldwide, permitting a reasoned assessment of what actually has and has not changed in the last third of the twentieth century and the beginning of the twenty-first.

This volume is the first of the three to appear. It is, we believe, the first attempt to look globally at social movements of all types since approximately 1750, to see their interconnections, their strong points and strong moments, and the forces they confronted. The basic assumption is that there were a series of waves of such movements, each worldwide, each different. But there has also been a cumulative story, which enables us to look intelligently at what may be coming in the next thirty years or so.

Immanuel Wallerstein

✳

Acknowledgments

This project was a collaborative one, engaging many persons and much support. Our research and writing were formulated and guided by discussions among members of the Fernand Braudel Center's Research Working Group on Antisystemic Movements. The Group's membership included Tuba Agartan, Caleb M. Bush, Woo-Young Choi, Melvyn Dubofsky, Tu Huynh, Fouad Kalouche, Richard Lee, Eric Mielants, Rochelle Morris, Immanuel Wallerstein, and William G. Martin as coordinator.

Special thanks are due to Patrick Bond, Ravi Palat, and Michael West, who critically reviewed first findings at a March 2004 workshop. Support from the World Society Foundation underwrote our workshop review and allowed us to bring our work to a timely conclusion, for which we are very grateful. Special thanks are due to Susan Thornton, who provided copyediting support. Finally, it was only the consistent support of the staff at the Fernand Braudel Center, including Becky Dunlop and particularly Donna Devoist, who made our work possible year after year.

*

Introduction

The Search for Antisystemic Movements

William G. Martin

Over the course of the past decade, radical protest activity has exploded across the world-economy, stretching from Chiapas to Chicago, from Prague to Porto Alegre, from Seattle to Sandton, South Africa. Appearing as it does long after the demise of the 1960s movements and the pacification of the movements that toppled dictatorships during the 1980s, the current outbreak is quite remarkable. Two signal aspects stand out: First, it exhibits a stark anticapitalist character. Second, the new movements consciously and increasingly operate through transnational and transcontinental alliances.

For most observers in the North these features prefigure a dramatic new era of "antiglobalization" movements, emblematic of a new era marked by a remarkably integrated global culture and global economy. This project proposes a quite different, historical understanding of this new wave of what we would call *antisystemic* movements. Our previous work in very different fields suggested a very different hypothesis than those most commonly encountered; namely, that for at least several hundred years there have been successive waves of movements that have attacked and destabilized the capitalist world-economy, its hegemonic powers, and dominant geocultures, and yet, at the same time, have come to provide legitimacy and the foundation for a new ordering of accumulation and political rule on a world scale. Seen from this perspective, present movements potentially take on a very distinctive meaning within a family of world movement moments, and pose for us quite different possible futures than those most commonly charted.

The aim of this introductory essay is to set the stage for the following world-epoch studies that carry the body of our collective argument. This ground-clearing proceeds in three parts. First, I set out the concerns and conceptualizations that generated our endeavor and frame our ongoing research. Second, I outline our research steps and missteps. Third, I sketch a series of leading questions and conclusions, focused particularly on the future of world movements and the world-economy. Consideration of this last item suggests that contemporary movements pose radical challenges to the existence of capitalism on a world scale, and, at the same time, point to the possibility that these challenges could lead to the creation of a stable, postliberal, capitalist world-economy. Almost all of these points, from conceptions of "antisystemic movements" to conclusions on contemporary movements, remain subject to vigorous debate among research working members—as will become evident in the epoch studies to come.

Movement Studies and Movement Anomalies

The current outbreak of "antiglobalization" movements has not only challenged states and capital and international institutions all across the world, but fundamentally called into question the last generation of social movement research. In part, the state of movement research reflects the fate of the new social movements of the 1960s and 1970s, as scholars in the richer zones of the world-economy concentrated on how these movements became part of the institutional landscape of advanced capitalist societies and states. Thus, many North American and European studies in the 1980s and 1990s stressed the demise of the revolutions and violent protests that defined the old and new Left, and focused instead on the rationalization, normalization, and institutionalization of protest activity. Labor, civil rights, feminist, and Green movements in the North, and nationalist and national liberation movements in the South, had been transformed and incorporated, we were told, into everyday institutions, particularly political parties and the state. By the mid-1990s this work coalesced into a dominant paradigm in North America, the "political process" school. The radical anticapitalist, utopian, or materialist movements and revolutions of the first two-thirds of the twentieth century were thus increasingly seen by scholars as historical artifacts.

The development of movement studies along these lines in the last half of the twentieth century served to further entrench conceptions and replicable narratives of the so-called nation-state. Movements were studied as national movements, leading to the formation of nation-states within which they would be encapsulated. In such a framework it was almost impossible to conceive of long-term, transnational relationships among movements. As in other areas the North and the West would guide the South, and show the Third World its future: successful movements achieved independence, confirming the state-centric focus of analysts and activists alike. If 1968 was a shock from this perspective, it could at least be explained as the outcome of wealth and post-Fordist, consumption-oriented, societies. The steady institutionalization and normalization of protest activity in succeeding decades thus led, in Tarrow's trenchant phrasing, to a "social movement society" (e.g., Tarrow 1994: 193–98; Meyer and Tarrow 1998: 4–6). Demonstrations and protests, when they took place, were cast as events executed by calculating organizations: orchestrated, media-attuned, nonviolent, and nondisruptive (McPhail 1991).

The new movements of the last decade constitute anomalies to such perspectives: as noted they have been highly confrontational, anticapitalist, and antistate. They have flourished, moreover, outside the European Union and North America, making the application of models developed in the North less and less viable. The relocation in the 1970s and 1980s of wage-labor movement militancy from core to semiperipheral areas of the world-economy provided an early sign of these trends, as in the role of trade unions in the overthrow of a series of dictatorships from Poland to Brazil to South Korea to South Africa. More recent and even more unexpected, however, has been the rise of activity ranging from riots to organized movements attacking poverty and state policy even in the formally democratic regimes that emerged in the 1980s—ranging from protests against privatization and the WTO to demands for radical land reform, public goods (housing, food, electricity, health care, water), and social and racial justice. The Zapatista rebellion, launched by design on the first day of the North American Free Trade Agreement (NAFTA), exhibited all these anomalies; subsequent rebellions and meetings suggest a new, long wave of antisystemic activity.

The accelerating international coordination of this movement activity poses even greater anomalies for prevailing paradigms. Signs of such linkages abound, ranging from the creation of global support via the Internet for movements in specific locales, as in Chiapas, through the coordination of international protest events in Seattle, Genoa, Prague, Sandton, and Geneva to the emergence of worldwide networks linking local indigenous, land, reparations, women's, and environmental movements and the formation of the World Social Forum in Porto Alegre and regional fora elsewhere. The studied distance from the pursuit of state power, so evident in Chiapas and the relative exclusion of political parties from the World Social Forum, also marks a clear break from the expected institutionalization and state-centered activity of past movements and movement studies. In short, fewer and fewer movements can be neatly encapsulated in the models that came to focus upon national, normative, and institutionalized movement activity and organizations.

Attempts to inflate dominant nation-state models to cover disruptive, noninstitutionalized, and transnational movements have flourished, but with mixed success at best (McCarthy 1997; Tarrow 2002).

A New Global Age and Global Movements?

For many, these anomalous phenomena herald a new age, marking the impact of economic and informational globalization. Globalization is indeed the buzzword of our period. Anthony Giddens's (1990: 64) definition posed it as "the intensification of worldwide social relations which link distant localities in such a way that local happenings are shaped by events occurring many miles away and vice versa." Equally common is an emphasis on space-time compression and a global consciousness, as in Roland Robertson's early definition of globalization as "the compression of the world *and* the intensification of consciousness of the world as a whole" (1992: 8, emphasis added). The common key note is economic and technological, pinpointing an accelerating global flow and coordination of finance, trade, and technology, and especially, cultural flows; for those stressing media and information technology the focus often becomes the emergence of a global culture, multiple diasporas, and a new cosmopolitanism. In the face of these flows the boundaries and territories of the modern age purportedly collapse: states, oceans, and continents give way to the rise of a networked, yet still diverse, worldwide culture and economy.

If one turns to the many analyses that link economic globalization and social movements, one can see the difficulties "globalization" poses for studies of modern social movements. As the global system theorist Leslie Sklair suggested in a review essay in the mid-1990s, "There have been few, if any, examples of successful movements against the global capitalist system, which is not very surprising. As Charles Tilly and others have argued, most social movements have developed in relation to the nation state. If we are, indeed, entering a phase of global capitalism we might expect this to change" (1995: 3).

By the late 1990s a whole series of works did begin to link a new global phase of capitalism with new global social movements. Hence, for example, the influence of analyses stressing the emergence of a global networked society and movements as in Castells's work (1997), or the new, boundary-less form of empire and new movements of Hardt and Negri (2000). As Hardt and Negri forcefully and fancifully phrase it, "We have witnessed an irresistible and irreversible globalization of economic and cultural exchanges. Along with the global market and global circuits of production has emerged a global order, a new logic and structure of rule—in short, a new form of sovereignty. Empire is the political subject that effectively regulates these global exchanges, the sovereign power that governs the world" (2000: xi). While "empire" has been called into being by past proletarian and international struggles, today's movements remain, they tell us, localized, unconnected, and ineffective in coalescing any challenge to empire (2000: 55–58).

As Arrighi (2002) has convincingly pointed out in his review of *Empire* (2000), there is more metaphor than material evidence that a new, de-centered and de-territorialized age of empire and cosmopolitanism is upon us. By many indicators world commodity, migration, and capital flows were greater, for example, at the end of the nineteenth century than at the end of the twentieth century. Thus Arrighi and Silver (1999: 8–9) approvingly cite fellow globalization debunkers Hirst and Thompson (1996): "If the theorists of globalization mean that we have an economy in which each part of the world is linked by markets sharing close to real-time information, then that began not in the 1970s but the 1870s." Others such as Wallerstein (1976) have long pushed the claim of a global market, linked by multinational corporations and transnational flows, back to at least the period of Dutch hegemony, while yet others trace globalization back to earlier and competing Asian world-economies (Abu-Lughod 1989; Frank 1998).

More difficult to dispense with are more concrete studies that stress the formation of new global action networks, including transnational networks operating through social movement and civil society organizations, usually NGOs (e.g., Keck and Sikkink 1998; O'Brien et al. 2000). This case for a new age of linked social movements, particularly those studies that empirically tackle the rise of networked movements within a structured world society, is strong. Yet here the notion of globalization, while proclaiming a new age, usually remains moored to past conceptions. As the editors of *Globalizations and Social Movements* admit in their introduction, "Globalization ... refers primarily to the 'modernization' of the non-Western world" (Guidry et al. 2000: 4). Thus most of these accounts stress the emergence, for the first time, of coordinated global activity as protest activity in the "Third World" expresses modernity and is finally linked to movements in the North. While globalization and global social movements are supposed to mark a rupture in the fabric of human history, these conceptions nevertheless remain tethered to a series of stages from national movements to a global one, largely based on the experiences and models of "modern" Western states.

For those who know world history, this is fundamentally shortsighted: as any account of abolitionist, labor, anticolonial, nationalist, or antiwar movements would reveal, transcontinental movement linkages have a very long history indeed. Similarly, radical anticapitalist activity, so much at the heart of anti-WTO, anti–structural adjustment, antiprivatization, and antisweatshop protests, is hardly new. All these features do of course challenge the post-1968 thesis of the terminal institutionalization of social movements within bounded nation-states. Yet from a long-term perspective contemporary movement phenomena should not surprise us. What we critically need to understand, and what we are so ill-equipped to determine, is whether, and if so how, current radical movements once again pose a real challenge to the capitalist world-economy as a whole. Here we simply lack the world-historical and theoretical materials by which to understand anticapitalist, world-oriented protest.

Why our conceptual tools and historical analyses are so badly suited to understand these movement conjunctures is not a topic we can pursue here at any length. In the broad sweep of the structures of knowledge, we might simply note that the liberal, developmentalist paradigms that underpinned post–World War perspectives have collapsed in the past twenty-five years, ushering in a period of postliberal, worldwide uncertainty. What is clear is that we lack substantive studies of movement activity across the capitalist world over long periods of time. Radical and world-systems scholars have in the past twenty years paid far more attention to matters of hegemony and accumulation, for example, as might be expected given successive world-economic crises and the dangerous collapse of U.S. hegemony. Existing theoretical and historical scholarship also provides little guidance. While political economists and historians turn to Marx, Weber, and Schumpeter, for example, there are few parallel authorities for movement scholars, much less a significant body of work on world-scale movements. If we thus seek to place current movements within historical patterns and discern future possibilities, we face considerable difficulties. Are present movements substantially different from earlier movements? Do they pose fundamental challenges to the capitalist world-economy? We do not know.

Mapping Movement Waves

It was to explore these questions that in late 1999 we came together and formed the Research Working Group on Waves of Antisystemic Movements at the Fernand Braudel Center at Binghamton University. Our aim was to pick up the challenges posed, but left relatively unpursued in the following decade, in the slim volume of essays produced by Giovanni Arrighi, Terence K. Hopkins, and Immanuel Wallerstein in the 1980s on antisystemic movements (1989).[1] We set ourselves a bold task: to collect and analyze historical data on movement activity over several centuries.

We have cast our conceptual net widely in one direction and narrowly in another. We use the term "movements" to encompass broadly not just organized, normative, and institutionalized collective activity as commonly defined, but disruptive, momentary, and noninstitutionalized collective action. This captures phenomena, for example, from seemingly spontaneous outbreaks (e.g., food riots, as in contemporary Latin America and elsewhere) through organized movements (e.g., from historical trade union formations to the World Social Forum) to classic state revolutions (e.g., the American, French, and Haitian revolutions of the late eighteenth and early nineteenth century to twentieth-century revolutions in Mexico, Russia, China, etc.). A narrower focus is suggested by the adjective "antisystemic": we are primarily concerned in activity and movements that engage and oppose dominant capitalist forces and processes; conceptually, antisystemic movements are thus relationally composed.

In so proceeding we have been particularly concerned to incorporate and relate clusters of movement activity outside core European and North American zones. The aim here is not simply to counter past conceptions and models built on national Northern models and applied elsewhere, but to uncover worldwide conjunctures of movement activity as well as relations—antagonistic as well as reinforcing—among movements across the world-economy. Indeed we have been especially concerned to unearth unusual clusters of movement activity on a world scale. While there are many studies of movement waves over time in national locales, (such as strike waves and protest cycles) (Shorter and Tilly 1974; Tarrow 1998: 141–60), and waves of feminist or, more rarely, black nationalist movements (West 1999), we have few that attempt to relate these episodes to each other, much less to chart movements over time and on a world scale (e.g., see Silver and Slater 1999; Frank and Fuentes 1990; Silver et al. 1995; Silver 2003).

There is little long-term data that speak to the issue of movements that cluster or operate on a world scale, either in organizing across national boundaries or in targeting global political or economic actors. While we have studies of such global phenomena prior to the present period (e.g., the antislavery movement, the international socialist and labor movements, Pan-African, and anticolonial movements), the historical data on local movements are much richer, as may be expected by the national compartmentalization of the historical social sciences. Yet even these data have not been substantively coalesced and analyzed to discern the extent and timing of the eruption of movement activity on a world scale, the character and depth of transnational linkages among local movements, or long-term shifts in movement strategies and modalities of organization. As noted, movement activity outside Europe and North America is rarely accounted for by existing models or chronologies, leaving us with very partial accounts.

Data collection on these areas formed a first, central task, and one that required us to make a further and critical methodological choice: whether to examine movement types over time or examine all movements within specific periods. The research team first sought to discern, on the basis of group members' own past work and surveys of secondary historical studies, whether worldwide waves of activity were evident for *specific* movements over the *longue durée*.

This attempt to chart global movement activity by type of movement failed. Our research quickly revealed (1) the limited number of overall movements types we could examine, since few spanned long periods of time, thus leaving out large central movements; (2) too heavy a dependence on core-centric movements, models, and literatures; and (3) the necessity to redefine and even recategorize activities under examination as they mutate across world-historical epochs and various movement forms (e.g., feminism in abolitionist and nationalist movements). This does not mean studies of specific movements over long periods cannot be carried out (e.g., Martin 2005). To address, however, our concern here—successive world waves of anticapitalist movements over time—required us to turn to different research tactics, methods, and data collection.

Rather than tackling specific movements, we radically shifted research strategies to observe world epochs, and then sought to locate central outbreaks of movement activity across the world-economy within these space-time frames. This allows us to analyze relationships among movements, and the collectivity of movements as a whole for different world periods. The resulting construction of a historical geography of movements is a crucial procedure, one that enables the exploration of whether and why there have been different patterns at different conjunctures. As we move toward the present, for example, this should permit us to see whether a decisive break with past patterns is occurring, and where new forms of antisystemic activity are emerging.

More concretely, we aimed to chart movement waves, and the linkages among movements, within and then across four periods: 1750–1850, 1848–1917, 1917–1968, and 1968–2005.[2] Each of these time periods is loosely bounded by a well-known outbreak of movement activity and by transitions in the world-economy and interstate system. Such a procedure permits ascertaining relationships among movements, changing movement strategies and organizational forms, and the evolving processes of the world-system as a whole. We naturally expected fuzzy edges and variations in different zones of the world-system.

The primary sources of data were historical records and surveys on social movements, sometimes by continent but often by country. For each time period we first established the central systemic characteristics of the world-economy and the interstate system at the beginning and end of the period. These features include: phases of global expansion and depression, spatial expansion of the boundaries of the world-economy, forms of capital and production, major modes of labor control, the key markers of the interstate system (hegemony/rivalry, colonial empires), and the geoculture.

Against these features we have then sought to chart wherever possible: (1) the key movement clusters of the period (in terms of mobilization, impact, and the fears of the ruling strata; (2) the social bases and geographic locations of these clusters; (3) movement organizational types and targets; and (4) the relationships of the various movements to each other: across space for the same kind of movements, and among the kinds of movements that existed (in each zone and worldwide).

We expected this research to reveal whether and to what extent antisystemic activities across the many different spaces of the capitalist world were common and connected phenomena. This led to further questions: Did movement activity appear in clusters across core, semiperipheral, and peripheral zones of the world-economy? Was movement activity differentiated by zone, nationality, or state, or heavily segmented by time and place? To what degree and manner were relationships among movements evident, and in what periods and locations over the past two and one-half centuries?

Our leading hypothesis was straightforward: significant clusters of movement activity existed across zones of the world-economy from at least the eighteenth century. How these were expressed and how they served to shape the world-economy and subsequent movements remained, however, very much open to investigation. It is to these deliberations we now turn.

Notes

1. See Amin et al. (1990) as well as the few but exceptional world-scale movement works cited below.

2. We originally designed the study to begin much earlier, in 1450 or 1650, but had to abandon this effort for practical reasons. Considerations of movements against the expansion of the early capitalist world-economy, as well as early movements from within and along the boundaries of the world-economy are, however, covered in the first epoch study (chapter 1). See, for example, the discussion there of "transformative" movements.

*

Chapter 1

The Transformation of the Capitalist World: 1750–1850

Tuba Agartan, Woo-Young Choi, and Tu Huynh

Our thesis is simply stated: multiple modes of resistance against European culture and capitalism stood at the heart of the incredible transformation of the world-system and its global competitors in the long eighteenth century (1750–1850). From the worldwide organization of and rewards to labor and capital through the vastly expanded boundaries of the capitalist world-economy to the emergence of new hegemonic order, it was acts of resistance, and not solely the power of European capital and states, that shaped the modern world. We refer to these diverse acts of resistance as "transformative movements," and this chapter traces their historical contours.

Our argument proceeds in three parts. We first briefly lay out our framework for examining "transformative" movements and the hallmark features of this critical epoch. Second, we present selected instances of movement activity to illustrate the different articulations of key political and economic processes operating across the world in this period. Finally, rather than tallying achievements and failures of world movements, we demonstrate how the uneven responses generated to European capitalist expansion fundamentally refashioned the structure of the modern world-system and rival societies by the mid-nineteenth century. As we shall see in succeeding epoch studies, the new forms of life and governance brought into being by "transformative" movements often became pillars of a new phase of accumulation on a world scale—and targets for subsequent antisystemic activity.

Transformative Movements and Epochal Transformations

This period is generally known among scholars as the "Age of Revolutions," marked as it is by the iconic French, British, and American revolutions. From these spring, we have conventionally been told, capitalism, modernity, and the struggle for "liberty, equality, and fraternity." We aim to provide, however, a broader historical account and theoretical analysis of the transformation of the whole of the capitalist world-system as well as of social worlds that existed beyond the reach of capitalism's eighteenth-century boundaries. For this purpose our primary attention is directed toward neither state-bounded "revolutions" in Western Europe and the United States, nor the nascent "social movements" that confronted one another within the European nation-states. Our view is instead often directed elsewhere, to areas often deemed unrelated to Western, state-bounded revolutions: the "transformative" movements that were imbricated with Western Europe's territorial, political, and economic expansion overseas.

The term "transformative movements" is not intended to substitute one category, "antisystemic movements," of resistant activities for another. We use the term "transformative movements" to encompass the diverse forms of resistance during the long eighteenth century—e.g., maroonage, millenarian revolts, slave revolutions, peasant rebellions, wars by indigenous communities, mutinies and piracy, and so forth—that shared a systemic quality but appear to historians and social scientists as unrelated or unsystematic. In large part this draws upon recent work by scholars who, in retrieving the histories of resistance in Asia, Africa, and the Americas, have sought to escape the limits of residual, primordial categories that serve to exclude acts of resistance from the history of the capitalist world (e.g., "primitive," "precapitalist," "primary," "peasant.") Such neglected accounts offer us, as we shall see, revolutionary accounts of the Haitian revolution and the development of Atlantic capitalism, or the impact of modern, yet millenarian resistance in Asia both to local states, empires, and world-economies as well as to early European capitalist intrusions.

To state this differently, acts of resistance are often cast as unorganized and unrelated, making it unthinkable to conceive of them as part of a larger "movement" with any "revolutionary" influence. Such a judgment often arises from the claim that these forms of resistance were far from being progressive in the modern sense since they drew upon, for example, mythical pasts, millenarian claims, or messiahs to create an alternative existence. Yet the material conditions that brought together groups of people in these activities were often absolutely new and products of capitalism, leading to improvisation in the process of seeking the transformation of an oppressive new world.

These transformative movements moved, moreover, parallel to the development of the European capitalist world-system that was still in a nascent and transformative condition itself. The contours of this world-system were in the process of being shaped as it was evolving, with seemingly local forms of resistance outside Europe also transforming Europe in ways that have yet to be adequately studied. Our view is accordingly aimed to bring into focus what has often been overlooked: a diverse set of resistance activities that occurred beyond the boundaries of Europe and the nation-state and that exhibited themselves through a nonlinear temporality.

The "transformative" movement as a concept thus has three advantages. First, it allows us to encompass and link a broad range of direct assaults against elite groups that dominated land, labor, and capital within and across the capitalist world-economy. Second, it also allows us to explore parallel and often overlapping forms of resistance by those most negatively affected by Europe's expansion and economic crises, including the peoples of the Ottoman, Chinese, and Mughal empires. Third, we use the word "transformative" to capture these diverse acts of resistance as interrelated, oppositional forces that generated the systemic transition of the modern capitalist world-system in this early (but not earliest) period of its existence. As we shall see, the effort to open up the study of protests and movements in this period allows us to push forward our argument that collectively organized acts of resistance over the course of the eighteenth century transformed not only local relations but also the shape of the capitalist world to come.

World Integration and Transformation

To assert that transformative movements are interrelated historically and globally suggests that some manner of the integration of the world must have occurred. The outline of an increasingly powerful European world-economy over the course of 1750–1850 is easily constructed along the following lines from conventional world-historical accounts. In the mid-eighteenth century the European world-system was a dominant but not hegemonic social world on the planet. Having suffered a long period of stagnation, Europe's dominant classes faced formidable imperial structures and merchant networks blocking any expansion of the boundaries of the Atlantic-centered world-economy created in the long sixteenth century. By the mid-nineteenth century, however, vast new areas were incorporated into the capitalist world-economy, most notably the Indian subcontinent, the Ottoman Empire, the Russian Empire, and parts of western Africa and eastern Asia.

This process was propelled, as is well known, by the productive innovations and new international division of labor associated with the British Industrial Revolution and the creation of mature capitalist political and ideological forms propagated through the American and especially French revolutions. Riding the tide of innovation and war, Britain would become the hegemonic world power by the mid-nineteenth century. In direct contrast to their actions in the preceding century, British policymakers promoted abolition, free trade, and decolonization in the Americas. Defeated rival France was forced to bury its ambitions in the Americas and Europe, as did the Netherlands in Southeast Asia, while the Spanish and Portuguese empires collapsed. By 1850 the European world-economy under British hegemony had burst its previous boundaries, reorganized the uses of land, labor, and capital, and was bidding to become a planetary social system. At the same time new national identities were emerging as the people affected by this process began to collectively organize to regain control over their material lives. A new world, unthinkable a century earlier, had emerged.

What this conventional and linear account of the rise of the West underplays, however, are wider relationships that linked world empires and world-economies and that had a formative and often ignored impact on the construction of a capitalist world-economy in this period. Among the most central of these networks was the formation of an international monetary system based on silver and its worldwide production and exchange (Chaudhuri 1997). Europe's domination of silver flows allowed it to "plug directly into the huge Asian economy and transform the intersecting regional trade networks into global networks" (Robertson 2003: 88). While silver provided financial liquidity to fuel the wheels of commerce that linked the trading states, the material integration of the presumably "self-contained parts of the world" was also aided by the invention and continued development of the "roundship," warfare by sea and land, and the discovery of the steam engine (Chaudhuri 1997: 296). More general and growing world-scale interconnections also served to propel systemic transitions in this period, particularly migration, conquest, and commerce. Complementing these arguments are studies that demonstrate world-economic integration during the "Asian Age," when China was a dominant empire (e.g., Frank 1998; Menzies 2003).

While centered upon very different locations and powers, all these sources chart a common story: the growing integration of Asia, Africa, Europe, and the Americas. Even for the European-centered arguments of Chaudhuri and Robertson, European development was unequivocally dependent on expansive trade networks. As Robertson says, "[i]nternal reforms [in Europe] could never have generated similar wealth" (2003: 88). Europe would not have been able to position itself at the center of world trade and finance without the continual demand for spices, the deposits of silver from the Americas, and imperial China's demand for silver. Everywhere social and economic change quickened as commodity production for world-linked markets accelerated. Under such conditions, as Robertson stresses, "nothing stayed the same: not the societies providing the much-needed raw materials, not the traders and societies now excluded from the new trading deals, and certainly not those communities that once provided goods for exchange at different points along the trade chain. Everything was forever changed" (2003: 88).

Most centrally, warfare and conquest in Europe irrevocably turned outward toward commercial and naval rivalry. Thus Spain, after freeing itself from Muslim control in the late fifteenth century, exterminated the indigenous population in the Caribbean by trying to grow sugar cane while plundering Mexico and Peru for gold and silver. Farther afield the Portuguese gained control of the spice trade in the Indian Ocean by occupying Goa in India, while the Dutch, before replacing the Portuguese in Southeast Asia, controlled the flow of Japanese silver. England, being a latecomer in the Americas, benefited from the flows of bullion as English pirates, often in partnership with the state, seized Spanish and Portuguese ships laden with silver.

Tracking the flow of silver reveals relationships among world regions, which directly altered global and local sociopolitical relations. The first and most important route "ran directly across the Pacific from Acapulco on the west coast of modern Mexico to the Philippine Islands," which were colonized by Spain between the 1560s and 1570s (Atwell 1997: 145). A second route ran to China, shipping first from Mexico and Panama to Seville, then through Portugal, and onward around the cape of Good Hope to Goa, Malacca, Macao, and then China (Atwell 1997: 147–48). In the third, smaller, route, silver shipped to Seville was transported to Amsterdam and London, where the British and Dutch East India companies carried it to Southeast Asia to purchase pepper, spices, and Chinese silk and porcelain. In summary, the bullion trade and the rise of an international monetary standard not only opened up the vibrant Asian regional economy to Europe but also radically transformed European societies and systematically deepened the links between the Americas, Europe, the Mediterranean, and Asia.

The three routes of the silver system also reveal the unequal relationships among trading states, including both imperial rivalry among European states and the hierarchy of trade relations between the metropole and its colonies abroad. Taken together these relationships transformed the pattern of capitalist development and European expansion. Thus the English-Dutch rivalry in the early 1600s led to the Dutch monopoly of the Spice Islands in the Indonesian archipelago, while England gained a stronger merchant navy as well as New Amsterdam in North America. This made possible in turn the Dutch and British East India companies' ability to exploit these areas, leading to ecological disasters in Southeast Asia (Robertson 2003: 95–96). Similar ecological destruction occurred in the Americas wherever mining for silver took place, resulting in the near extermination of entire indigenous populations. Accordingly, not only were relations between states reorganized but also social relations at particular sites of production. These examples illustrate the necessity of exploring beyond the traditional accounts of the birth of capitalism and rivalry among modern nation-states in northwestern Europe. They suggest a much broader canvas of both transformation and the forces behind it, pushing us beyond the boundaries of the states and capitals enclosed within the European world-economy.

Core Transformative Movements

Whether within or outside the boundaries of Europe, however, few chart any role for anticapitalist, much less antisystemic, movements in these grand transitions. The major exception for this period is, of course, the French Revolution. In the classic social interpretation, the French Revolution marked the turning point in the birth of capitalism, signaling all at once the vindication of the Enlightenment, the overthrow of the feudal order by a revolutionary, secular bourgeoisie, the entrance of popular masses onto the world stage, and the creation of the rule of the modern nation-state and its citizens. As subsequent scholarly debates over the political impact and interpretation of the French Revolution reveal, however, there were far fewer radical changes in the relations among dominant and subordinate classes than had long been accepted.[1] The case is even weaker for the American "Revolution," where radical social change was much less in evidence.

Approached from a world perspective, however, a strong case can be made for the revolution's wider impact outside France itself. Two legacies in particular have been put forward. One, the French Revolution has been widely hailed for the origins and diffusion of an optimistic, scientific liberalism that accepted and promoted continual social change. Second, and more important for our topic here, many argue that the French Revolution marked the first instance of a mass movement that demanded the rule of the nation and civil rights, as opposed to royal rule and absolutist rights. As Wallerstein (1989: 111) argues, the revolution gave "rise to the first significant antisystemic (that is, anticapitalist) movement in the history of the modern world-system, that of the French 'popular masses'. As such, it was of course a failure, but as such it has been the spiritual basis of all subsequent antisystemic movements."

There was, of course, much antisystemic activity to buttress these interpretations. Popular forces did, as exemplified by the sans-culottes and the Babouvistes, contest the legitimacy of private property and capital accumulation, sought to destroy hierarchical class structures, and supported egalitarian and communitarian visions of the future. Early rebellions and uprisings that culminated in the storming of the Bastille were led, for example, by poor women and men from Paris's working class neighborhoods. It was, however, only between 1793 and 1794 that lower classes, most notably the indigent workers of Paris along with the unemployed and property-less, became empowered politically under the title of the "sans-culottes." By late 1793 the Jacobin leadership included two sans-culottes representatives on the twelve-member Committee of Public Safety, and the sans-culottes began to "terrorize" the bourgeois order by confiscating foods and appropriating goods as their "right" for an equal distribution of wealth, destroying the property and possessions of the rich, attacking small and big merchants as "thieves," and calling for the guillotine for all of them—not only for the aristocracy and the clergy (Soboul 1972: 14–25). These militants called for nothing less than the creation of a true "fraternity" through economic egalitarianism. These clearly were anticapitalist and antisystemic actions. By 1794 fierce repression turned against the sans-culottes, while the 1795 Babeuf conspiracy—which aimed to abolish private property, limit wealth and money, curtail trade and commerce, and establish a one-class society—was brutally crushed.

As these famous examples attest, the French Revolution generated new modes of political action based on popular demands. These were aimed at taking over the state in order to radically transform the economic, social, and political order. While these movements failed, they provided inspiration and models for later movements across Europe—as rebellions in 1848 would reveal. Yet the tracing out of these influences and legacies often shortchanges the meaning of the French Revolution by limiting discussion to the diffusion of French national patterns and ideologies to other, later, national cases (see Klaits and Haltzel 1994); rarely is the French Revolution considered part of a worldwide social upheaval. This is most conspicuous in the writings of national(ist) historians who, even during the outpouring of writing surrounding the 1989 bicentennial of the French Revolution, largely restricted themselves to the celebration of French national events and the influence of France upon other areas of the world.

For students of the world-system, the French Revolution has largely been treated as part of a long competitive struggle for hegemony among European states—with the revolution following, in Wallerstein's terms, "in the wake of and as a result of France's sense of impending defeat" in the struggle with Britain (Wallerstein 1989: 94). As this suggests, the revolution is seen as an event that developed in the context of economic crises and competition and war among European states.[2] While this marks an advance upon earlier treatments that unearthed only "external, international" determinants of the revolution (Skocpol 1979), the French Revolution remains an inter-/state-centered event, rather than a world-centered event. We need to push beyond these Eurocentric boundaries and locate the revolution as part of the volatile world of which it was but one part.

Toward World Revolutions

To "de-privilege" the role that the French Revolution occupies in social movement discourse and theory—but not to undermine its world-historical importance—and to begin to move toward a conception of "world revolutions," we start by asking: looking across the capitalist world-economy and even beyond, what major clusters of social resistance served to shape the startling transitions between the mid-eighteenth and mid-nineteenth centuries?

We clearly cannot detail here the long list of even major episodes of unrest and resistance. We select instead key clusters, from key world zones, that illustrate major forms of resistance to the capitalist world-economy and its territorial expansion. We are particularly concerned to include areas and forms of resistance that have escaped those who have focused only upon key European states. When one looks at this long century, the major countermovements related to emerging processes of the world-economy include:

- revolts against plantation slavery in the Americas;
- "nationalist" and secessionist movements from within colonial and imperial systems, crossing from the Balkans to the Americas;
- movements reaching across Asia and the Middle East to the Americas against inclusion or incorporation into the world-economy, including attempts to delink or escape into alternative social worlds; and
- civilizational movements, most often termed *religious* or *cultural* movements, that resisted European and capitalist cultures and ranged across the Middle East, Africa, Asia, and the Americas.

From this short and incomplete typology we first examine the movements—most notably slave revolts and increasingly "white" settler demands for decolonization—that shook the foundations of capitalist development in the Americas during the eighteenth century and ushered in not only new forms of labor and a new international division of labor but also a new hegemon and a reconfigured interstate system. Second, we examine resistance associated with the expansion of the world-economy to the (Middle) East, most notably within previously existing world empires, particularly in and surrounding the Ottoman Empire. Finally, we move toward Asia and chart how movements in the Indonesian archipelago served to delimit the boundaries and shape the form of the expanding European world-economy. The sequence of our study is not meant to privilege any one set or region of "transformative" movements over another. Indeed, the diverse "transformative" movements in the Americas, Ottoman Empire, and Asia during this epoch were not unrelated: they were all responding to the threat of European capitalist expansion that radically restructured everyday life.

The Revolutionary Wave in the Americas

Resistance to capitalist expansion across the Americas can be traced as far back as the fifteenth century. By the eighteenth century many indigenous peoples who had resisted colonization and enslavement had been killed, while still millions of others died from disease and harsh labor. Nonetheless, repeated waves of rebellion had driven dominant classes to resort to fierce repression, reform, or a combination of the two (as in response to the indigenous uprising of 1553 in Colombia). In turn, as European settlements and plantation economies became more firmly established in the Americas, the aims and nature of indigenous rebellions began to be transformed toward activities that we refer to here as anticapitalist.

Nowhere was this more evident than in the United States, where the expansion of European settlement and plantation agriculture triggered new forms of resistance by indigenous peoples. The American Revolution, from which a new non-English or "American" identity emerged, only accelerated this process. The creation of the new republic led to the policy of "Indian removal," which dispossessed, relocated, and attempted to confine the indigenous populations to marginal locations. In response to relentless settler expansion, autonomous Native American villages, as among the Cherokee and Creek in the Southwest, became increasingly linked into confederations from the eighteenth century onward. Wars with the Creek in 1813–1814 and Andrew Jackson's campaign against the Seminole in 1817–1818 advanced the idea of removing all Native Americans to land that was west of the Mississippi. In 1830 removal became the law of the Republic and was pushed forward between 1820 and 1840. In these two decades, three-quarters of the 125,000 Native Americans living east of the Mississippi were "removed," with the loss of one-fourth to one-third of all southern Native American lives (Wolf 1982: 284).

These wars illustrated the widespread logic of maroonage as a communal survival strategy among indigenous and enslaved peoples, which existed all across American and Caribbean colonial spaces. Thus some of the Creek, who had been fighting for their land against Spanish, English, French, and American settlers, established a community in the swamps and forests and waged a series of guerrilla attacks against intruders. A steady rise in the number of runaway slaves also invigorated collective acts of resistance among diverse maroon communities. The elimination of any radical elements as the American Revolution proceeded and the entrenchment of merchant and planter power cemented these patterns for the rest of the nineteenth century.

Besides maroonage, revolts by peoples whose lands were occupied in the Americas combined very similar forces, often to more explosive effect. This was especially evident in Spain's confrontation with American struggles for independence. Increased taxes, state monopolies, the dramatic decline of agricultural prices, and the violent expropriation of labor and land (especially for large landholdings and mining operations) generated successive outbreaks of resistance by indigenous populations of which the Pugachev uprising of 1773–1775 and the Tupac Amaru rebellion of 1780 were among the most notable.

The Tupac Amaru rebellion in particular illustrates the formation and limits of revolt based on the social hierarchies constructed under colonialism in the Americas. Propelled by indigenous peoples, the rebellion was unable to secure the support of the Creoles who controlled the economic and social life of indigenous peoples and were secure within the social and racial privileges of conquered Peru. Rebellions elsewhere in Spanish America, such as the Communero Rebellion in Nueva Granada (1781–1783), also reflected these divisions. Across the continent a pattern emerged whereby Creoles assumed the leadership of independence movements, with the result that the commitment of indigenous peoples and "non-white" Creoles to the settler movements fell away after 1780. While Creole elites were inspired by settler decolonization in British North America, indigenous elements looked for inspiration to uprisings by Native and African peoples.

The most radical challenges to colonial rule and slavery would emerge, however, not from within the declining Spanish colonial system but from the heart of the French empire in the Americas. Indeed, the fate of the Spanish empire would to a surprising degree turn upon developments in French-ruled Haiti, where a revolution would propel the end of not just slavery but of both the Spanish and French American empires. Indeed, among all the revolutions and rebellions during our epoch, the Haitian Revolution of 1789–1804 stands front and center for hastening and clarifying both settler decolonization and popular resistance to the new capitalist world forged in the Americas. Notwithstanding earlier revolts and large maroon communities, most famously the Palmares community in Brazil, the violent birth of the first black republic was the most successful slave rebellion in the history of the capitalist world-economy. Haiti brought together antislavery activities, antiracist movements, and anticolonization movements—and forced the issue of freedom into the heart of even the French Revolution.

A wave of rebellions had moved across the Atlantic slave complex in the decades before the Haitian Revolution, advancing from the 1730s onward to a peak in the 1760 Tacky's revolt and including conspiracies and revolts in North America, the French and British Caribbean, South America, and even Atlantic western Africa. As the Haitian Revolution developed, it clearly drew upon these previous rebellions, advancing and merging maroonage traditions with the aims and actions of conspirators living on plantations, many of whom often became "short-term maroons for the purpose of organizing" (Fick 1997: 240). In towns parallel relationships emerged between maroonage and free blacks, whose large numbers reflected Haiti's dominant role in the Caribbean economy. The preceding Makandal rebellion (1757–1758) exhibited these internal connections and prefigured "the possibility of forging out of maroonage a center of organized black resistance" against the white ruling class (Fick 1997: 240; James 1989: 20–21).

Rebellion moved toward revolution as an organized black guerrilla army of men, women, and children was forged from black slaves as well as mulatto and "free" black elements (Fick 1997: 242–46). Shifting coalitions among these groups would, eventually, not only lead to the abolition of slavery but also prevent the installation of any new plantation labor regime after independence in 1804. In this instance victorious slaves would permit no return to plantation life, not even when proposed by independent Haiti's black presidents who desperately sought to revive large-scale, export-oriented, commercial agriculture. By comparison to the American or French revolutions, the revolution achieved by Haiti's slaves fully deserved its name, bringing social freedom through the absolute destruction of old ruling classes, the termination of dominant modes of labor exploitation and their racial foundations, and a redistribution of property and land.

In achieving this, the revolution had a direct impact on slaves in other colonies, the fate of existing colonial empires, and the rise of British hegemony. Most immediately affected was the French empire. In the last half of the eighteenth century Haiti had been the jewel of the French empire and the largest and most profitable center of plantation production in all of the Caribbean. Saint-Domingue (Haiti) had produced half the coffee and sugar consumed in Europe, and accounted for fully two-fifths of all of France's overseas trade (Geggus 1991: 402). From these realities flowed the British and United States' support for France's desperate struggle to reclaim Haiti—leading to the last, spectacular loss of almost the whole of Napoleon's 60,000-man expeditionary force sent to reconquer and reimpose slavery on Haiti. France's defeat in Haiti led directly to its abandonment of its imperial ambitions in the Americas, the strengthening of the white republics (most notably the United States through the Louisiana Purchase), and a critical weakening of France's position in its struggle with Great Britain.

Yet Haiti posed new problems as well for Great Britain, which like France and Spain faced increasingly unruly settlers, unruly Creoles, and rebellious slaves. When Britain, for example, in 1795 organized blacks in West India regiments in order to check white settlers' ambitions and police unruly slaves across the British West Indies, it was shortly repaid with a mutiny of black soldiers in Dominica who questioned their legal status as slaves (Geggus 1997: 6). In a similar fashion, as planters fled Haiti their attendant slaves brought with them Haitian revolutionary ideas and activities, facilitating revolts in Curaçao, Venezuela, and, especially, Louisiana (LaChance 2001). Elsewhere rumors of Haitian assistance propelled revolt, from Denmark Vesey's prediction to his followers that help would arrive to support the capture of Charleston to Aponte's use of portraits of Haitian leaders to build a following in Havana. From rumors of freedom to strategies of revolt, Haiti had electrified circuits of resistance all across the Caribbean and indeed the Americas. Revolutionary flows moved in other directions as well, as in the influx to Haiti of revolutionary supporters from France, Germany, and Poland and in the Haitian Revolution's impact on Europe, where abolitionists were forced to push toward real support for freeing slaves, most notably in the case of the French Revolution itself (Fick 1997).

It was moreover not only slaves and abolitionists that connected ideologies of freedom and revolt across the Caribbean, the Americas, and Europe. Central here were those who had been impressed into the massive carrying trade that the transoceanic world-economy demanded: the sailors of the Atlantic and Caribbean oceans. By the seventeenth century the massive transoceanic trades had led to ships' crews being recruited, as Braudel tells us, "from among the wretched classes of Europe and the world. Dutch ships, which were victorious over all the seas in the seventeenth century, were no exception to the rule. The same was true of the amazing American sailors, 'Englishmen of the second kind' ... who went off to conquer the seas at the end of the eighteenth century in tiny ships ... from Philadelphia or New York to China" (Braudel 1981: 425).

This "motley crew" increasingly linked revolts, as Linebaugh and Rediker account for our epoch. Thus "Revolution in America and St. Domingue opened the way for other movements, as the motley crew carried its news and experience to Europe and Latin America" across "divides of continents, empire, class, and race" (Linebaugh and Rediker 2000: 301). In this respect the ship became "both an engine of capitalism ... and a setting of resistance, a place to which and in which the ideas and practices of revolutionaries ... re-formed, circulated, and persisted" (Linebaugh and Rediker 2000: 144–45).

Seamen struggled for themselves as well, defending customary rights and protesting impressment, confinement, and discipline. Beginning in British North America in the 1740s, "impressment riots" took place against both the British and the U.S. navies. Seamen's resistance ranged from attacks on naval and maritime properties to the destruction of the very machines of empires, namely, ships and shipyards. More critical for us here was the role sailors played in linking different forms of resistance in widely disparate locations, connecting maroon and banditry communities, urban and rural slave communities, dockers' communities, and the pirate and seamen communities. Sailors served to bridge the diversified acts of resistance from the sea to the hinterland, from ocean to ocean. As Julius Scott (1986) has demonstrated, "a common wind" carried news of slave revolts, revolutions, and freedom to come.

The dissemination of revolt from the Caribbean and particularly Haiti inaugurated a counterrevolutionary response that spread well beyond the embargo placed upon Haiti by the U.S. and European powers. This even slowed the pace of settler decolonization, as fears spread of revolts that might link slaves, Creoles, and mulattoes. Everywhere tighter controls were placed upon free blacks, while Creole fears of slave revolts led many to reaffirm their loyalty to European colonial powers and monarchs. Even when Britain cut Spanish maritime links with its American colonies, many white settlers remained loyal, fearing slave revolts and British abolitionists. This did not stop resistance, as revolts in Argentina, Chile, Mexico, and Caracas took place due to economic polarization and rising discontent among less-privileged classes. The 1810 Mexican version of the Tupac Amaru revolt proved particularly radical as it was supported first by indigenous peoples and then mestizos. Predictably the major obstacle to decolonization often arose from white Creole fears, as shown in the Cuzco rebellion in Peru (1814–1815). The fear of slave revolts was also well founded. Reflecting the imposition of a "second slavery" in the wake of Haitian independence (Tomich 1988, 1997), revolts moved from Louisiana and Cuba (1811, 1812) to Puerto Rico and Santo Domingo (1812) among others.

Decolonization movements coupled with indigenous and black revolts would bring about the end of the Spanish empire, paralleling the forced retreat of France and the rise of the new U.S. Republic. A new map of the Americas emerged, with local white elites more dominant than ever before, despite the real advances achieved by the struggles of rebellious slaves, sailors, and indigenous peoples across the hemisphere. Britain's victory over European rivals owed no small part to the opportunities provided by these American struggles and would open up new landscapes of revolt by spurring a vast expansion of the reach of the capitalist world-economy beyond the unruly Atlantic world.

Imperial Resistance and Nationalist Revolts in Europe

Adding force to American developments in shaping the eighteenth-century world-economy were revolts all across Europe. Here the effects of the

French Revolution were more direct, following the course and outcome of the Napoleonic Wars that transformed the landscape of Europe and especially its relations with northern Africa, the Middle East, and the Balkans. While the French Revolution had few direct repercussions in the Balkans, Napoleon's conquests reorganized the states within Europe and destabilized the political structure of the region, which "demonstrated the vulnerability of the states that had previously seemed overwhelming" (Tilly 1993: 93). Most importantly, these events ratified the principle of nationality as a basis of independence movements. The French Revolution in this respect introduced new possibilities in the use of political power and transformed the basis of legitimacy for rulers. As the Declaration of the Rights of Man and of the Citizen stated, "The principle of sovereignty resides essentially in the Nation; no body of man, no individual can exercise that authority that does not emanate expressly from it" (Kedourie 1993: 5).

Older empires were particularly vulnerable to these influences. The Ottoman, the Austrian, and the Spanish empires all suffered from separatist movements inspired by the secular ideals of liberty, equality, and fraternity. As these ideas spread they created unrest in traditional empires that led to the formation of new states, as in the cases of Greece (1831), Belgium (1830), and even Haiti (1804) as discussed earlier. Founded upon the principle of nationality, these new independence movements were quite different from the rebellions of the previous century. As Tilly notes, the "acceleration of independence movements from 1803 onward marked a dramatic change from the eighteenth century politics of provincial rebellion" (1993: 93). Even where movements drew their inspiration from different sources—as would be the case between many nationalist and religious movements—they clearly were variant expressions of the same processes of European territorial and market expansion, the disintegration of empires, and the reintegration of the European interstate system by existing and newly formed nation-states.

The early nineteenth-century transformation of the Ottoman Empire offers the most striking example of these processes at work. Within the space of but a few decades this massive, multiethnic empire was transformed into a series of nation-states in the Balkans and the Middle East. This transformation can be conceived of as a change of collective identity among the major religious groups, caused by changes in the traditional social structure and the religious communal systems (*millets*) established by the Ottoman government in the fourteenth and fifteenth centuries. The nations that emerged in the Balkans and the Middle East in the nineteenth and twentieth centuries were created as a result of "the socioeconomic and religious cultural conditions that had been created and shaped by forces" that undermined the Ottoman Empire (Karpat 1973: i).

Debates by scholars over the meaning and character of nationalism indicate the difficulties in defining and classifying revolts in this area and period.[3] This makes it especially critical to specify the key temporal, geographic, religious, and ethnic characteristics that served as bases from which movements were spawned. As we will see, external influences, such as the diffusion of European ideas and intervention by European powers in the internal affairs of the empire, were no less important.

Focusing initially on the transformation of the Ottoman system and the development of "nationalist revolts," we must track the formation of national identities and the subsequent emergence of independent nation-states from the Ottoman Empire. This requires us to examine the prevalence of ethnic, communal, and religious identities, and the reorganization of the European world-economy.[4] These factors contributed in two different ways to a national awakening: first, by facilitating the consolidation of various ethnic cultures at the grassroots level, which served as a foundation for formulating a national identity, and second, by opening the way for new leaders and intellectuals who played leading roles in national uprisings.[5]

Karpat identifies the disintegration of the medieval socioeconomic (social estates) and religious-communal organizations (*millets*) of the Ottoman Empire and their restructuration into nations under the leadership of new economic, cultural, and political elites after the seventeenth century as factors that generated increasing resentment toward the state (Karpat 1973: ii). This situation was exacerbated by the inability of the sultan, who was viewed as the defender of the peasantry, to curb the pressure on and exploitation of the *millet* by the corrupted military-administrative establishment. Within the army, the *sipahi* lost its importance. In addition, changes in the distribution of land and the ownership system, demographic shifts, and rapid commercial and industrial developments contributed to these communities' resentment toward the state.

These changes mutually influenced one another. Pressure from the constantly expanding economy of Western Europe eventually undermined the *timar* land system. The influx of New World bullion began to affect the empire by debasing the value of Ottoman *akca*. The resulting price inflation disorganized the old economic system, including the land regime, which undermined the living standards of government officials who in turn increased their pressure on the peasantry. Consequently, the *timar* land system was abandoned and was replaced with the more onerous *chiflik* system. The oppressiveness of the *chiflik* system, alongside the disorder and brigandage that arose from the deterioration of central authority, led to widespread discontent and even depopulation in the countryside. Accordingly, the peasantry in the Balkans was forced out of its isolation and political apathy.

Demographic changes underwrote the scale of this transformation. The social disintegration of the medieval estate system in the sixteenth century had been preceded and accompanied by a sharp growth in population. At the same time that population increased in size, unemployment rose because rigid land regulations did not permit changes in ownership and cultivation methods. Meanwhile migration from the eastern provinces of the empire to the Balkan regions during the fifteenth and sixteenth centuries produced new population centers that became regional markets for the rural populations. The formation of cities broke the rural isolation of the Balkan villages and contributed to their political and social mobilization. At the same time a new group of elites emerged in the cities, responding to new opportunities of increasing connections with the rural populations.

The period of Ottoman decline in the Balkan lands was also characterized by the rapid development of commerce and industry. This was mainly a result of the rapid integration of the empire into the expanding world-economy beginning in the eighteenth century. For Egypt and Levant, the process gained momentum during the first quarter of the nineteenth century, whereas the volume of trade in Anatolia only began to increase by the 1830s (Keyder and Islamoglu 1987). Between 1820 and 1853, this integration proceeded primarily through the expansion of foreign trade (Pamuk 1987: 11), which involved a rise in the volume of trade and changes in the pattern of trade toward the new hegemon, Great Britain. The rise of the *chiflik* system facilitated this by fostering the widespread cultivation and export of new colonial products such as cotton and maize.

These rapid economic changes were accompanied by a rise in importance of the class of merchants, ship owners, and mariners who would form the "new middle class" (Karpat 1973) in the Balkan lands and serve to network revolts and revolutions. Karpat identifies merchants' freedom from direct government control, possession of financial resources, and thus knowledge of the outside world as factors that might have led them to play important roles in the political developments of the eighteenth and nineteenth centuries (1973: 31). Accordingly, those better off and well-educated Christian merchant groups, many of whose sons studied in the West, had established relations with the outside world at the same time as they developed a sense of common interest with their kin in the rural areas of the empire. Merchants and mariners were also quick to absorb revolutionary doctrines while abroad, and usually spread their new ideas with zeal and enthusiasm among their discontented countrymen (Stavrianos 2000: 211). Serbian merchants in southern Hungary, Bulgarian merchants in southern Russia, and Greek merchants in central and eastern Europe would thus play important roles during the nineteenth century in aiding their undeveloped brothers under Ottoman rule to win their independence. The Habsburg Serbs, especially, contributed to the liberation of their fellow Serbs across the Danube (Stavrianos 2000: 138).

Yet merchants' and mariners' influence was not limited to adopting and spreading revolutionary ideas. Christian intellectuals, as Karpat points out, also "provided information about the historical roots of their past, which became the basis for an interpretation of the national history in accordance with the ideas of Enlightenment and nationhood" (Karpat 1973: 60). Hence, these diasporic communities "contributed greatly to the intellectual awakening of their fellows by bestowing upon their native towns and villages with lavish gifts of books, equipment and money. Frequently, they financed the education of young men of their race in foreign universities. Also they made possible the publication of books and newspapers in their native languages" (Stavrianos 2000: 146). Moreover, there was a new type of nonreligious education, which was no longer primarily religious, but instead was profoundly influenced by the Enlightenment in Western Europe (Stavrianos 2000: 146). Those students who studied abroad returned with a firsthand knowledge of the new body of thinking. The works of Voltaire, Rousseau, Locke, Descartes, Leibnitz, and others were being translated, usually into Greek first and then into other Balkan languages (Stavrianos 2000: 146).

The Greeks took the lead in transforming the knowledge system primarily because they had more contacts geographically and commercially with the West. The Greek diasporic communities were also more prevalent and in a better position to provide funds for education. Despite their dominance in the Orthodox Church schools, the Greeks were thus the first to break the clerical control of education and to establish secular schools (Stavrianos 2000: 147). These schools were of great importance for the national movements of the nineteenth century because they provided one of the major links among different movements. Romanian, Bulgarian, and Serbian students attended these Greek schools, which spread the ideas of the Enlightenment and the French Revolution. The Bulgarian students who were educated in the newly formed Greek schools, for instance, returned to their homeland and opened "Greco-Slav" schools. These schools contributed greatly to the national awakening of Bulgarians (Stavrianos 2000: 147).

Besides the class of merchants, ship owners, and mariners, the rise of a new military class played an important part in changing the structure of the Ottoman Empire in the nineteenth century. The decision in the Balkans to recruit considerable numbers from among local populations created a new class open to new horizons with military skills. A considerable number of Serbians who served in the Austrian armies, and veterans—for instance, a local hero, Karageorge—played an important role in the 1804 Serbian uprising. Greeks who served under the French and the Russians similarly provided much leadership in the Greek War of Independence (Stavrianos 2000: 213).

Alongside the active part played by these various groups in challenging and altering the organization of the Ottoman Empire, the ideals associated with the French Revolution also began to spread through the Ottoman territories through the "systematic propaganda directed from Paris with the aim of undermining Ottoman authority" (Stavrianos 2000:

211). The propaganda campaign was particularly intense during the years of Franco-Turkish hostility. This was not, however, simply a one-way flow from Paris, for certain sections of the Balkan people were very receptive to the aims and ideology of the French Revolution, and they began to express such ideals in their own ways. Nonetheless, the actual uprisings in Paris remained decisive. As Stavrianos tells us,

> Masonic lounges and other secret organizations were established in the principal towns. Newspapers were founded dedicated to the spreading of revolutionary principles and to the overthrow of Turkish domination. The revolutionary ideology may not have been transferred intact from West to East, and the concepts of liberty, equality and fraternity may have been but barely comprehended. Yet, the uprisings in Paris and the exploits of Napoleon made the subject Balkan peoples more restless, more independent and more determined to win their freedom. (Stavrianos 2000: 211)

More generally evident was the rise of nationalism throughout Europe and its direct application by the example of the French Revolution (Kedourie 1993). Yet this influence of the French Revolution was neither homogeneous nor universal. In the Balkans, French influence varied from one region to another. It was quite marked in the Adriatic lands, but only because that was where French rule prevailed the longest. Indeed, the creation of the Illyrian Provinces by the French stimulated a few decades later a Yugoslav national movement (Stavrianos 2000). One reason for this situation was that the French pushed the cultural as well as the economic development of the provinces, building schools, subsidizing the publication of grammar books and dictionaries, and encouraging the organization of a national theatre. In other places, such as Greece, the national awakening was more directly stimulated by the excitement of the French Revolution and Napoleon.

Rivalries between the various states (or powers) during this period also contributed greatly to the process of national awakening among the Balkan populations. While the French Revolution and Napoleon's invasion changed the social and cultural boundaries of Europe, the emergence of Russia as a great power that assumed the role of protector of Christians, following the Treaty of Kucuk Kaynarca in 1774, "injected an ideological ingredient into the situation" (Karpat 1973: 54). Russia looked upon the Greeks as potential political allies in her expansion southward into the Balkans and, hence, at some stages supported the Greek independence movement. Among the major uprisings against Ottoman rule in the Balkans, the Greek War of Independence stands out as the first "nationalist" movement, which later became the "essential preliminary condition" for the evolution and/or the source of inspiration for other Balkan nationalist movements (Hobsbawm 1962: 140).

In this particular case, one can easily identify the factors that we have discussed in the preceding pages: the leadership of the movement was mainly from the Greek diaspora (Stavrianos 2000: 280), it was nourished by Western political ideas, and it was initially supported by Russia and then by other European powers. First, the role of the Greek diaspora was significant in terms of providing the most effective medium of communication among the Balkan peoples and among diverse nationalist movements. It provided a web of diasporas that covered the whole peninsula and extended beyond the Ottoman borders into central Europe, Italy, and Russia. Second, ethnic and religious identities drew upon Greece's classical heritage and the Greek Orthodox Church, which were significant factors in the creation of a Greek nationalist movement. Moreover, the triumphant end of their battle for independence led to international public support for the national and constitutional goals of the Greek struggle against an autocracy.

Yet, not all Balkan populations were as successful as the Greeks, one of the wealthiest and most powerful groups in the empire. Thus, although many Bulgarians joined the Philike Hetairia and fought in the Greek War of Independence or with the Serbs under Karageorge, they did not make their bid for independence until the 1830s. Slavs, who had been as divided in cultural and political matters as the Greeks, also began struggling for independence although their divisions would prevent a cohesive national uprising. Serbs in Hungary who took advantage of the new commercial opportunities, and emerged as a new class of merchants, had the same dynamic effect upon Serbian society as the Greek merchants had in the Greek world. The first Serbian books and newspapers came from the wealthy and progressive Serbian communities in Karlowitz, Buda, and Vienna, reflecting a Serbian intellectual and literary renaissance (Stavrianos 2000: 241). When the Serbs of the Belgrade rose in revolt in 1804, they received vital assistance from their brothers in other parts of the Balkans. Accordingly, it was the comparatively backward Turkish-ruled Serbs who first gained autonomy and who developed the nucleus of the Yugoslav state. However, the Serbian insurrection of 1804 began as a fundamentally different movement from the Greek War of Independence. Its aim was to restore the old order of peace and security in the region, rather than fighting with or separating from the Ottoman Empire (Stavrianos 2000: 246). Yet what started as a revolt to maintain order (or the status quo) became a full-fledged war for independence, due to the decision of some of the Serbian leaders to cooperate with the Russian tsar who offered his assistance.

Nor was the Russian Empire free of crisis: its ruler experienced a similar situation of social unrest as the Balkans under Ottoman rule. Catherine II's accession to the throne in 1762 has been considered a turning point for the Russian Empire, for it was she who transformed Russia's government and reorganized Russia's internal space (Wallerstein 1989: 186). This reorganization occurred through oppression and a massive displacement of the Russian peasantry. A combination of labor coercion, deteriorating economic conditions, and terrible working conditions, in addition to the massive discontent that had already begun in the mid-eighteenth century, provoked the people toward rebellion. In the mid-eighteenth century unrest erupted in the Urals, largely caused by the sudden worsening of peasant conditions by the redefinition of seignorial rights, and rising food prices (Wallerstein 1989: 163; Portal 1950). However, except for the Polish uprising, these were rural revolts fundamentally different from the rebellions in the Balkans that demanded secession. Since the defeat of Polish revolutionaries under the leadership of Kosciuszko in 1793, Polish rebels had been watching their Russian rulers closely for signs of vulnerability. The first nineteenth-century Polish rebellion, the "November Insurrection," took place in 1830 when Nicholas I decided to send the Polish army to suppress the revolutions of 1830 in Belgium and France. However, after fighting for six months with the Russian forces, the Polish revolutionary forces were defeated.

The discussion thus far reveals one clear cluster of movements formed by the Serbian Uprising (1804), popular unrest in Moldova and Wallachia (1806–1848), the independence movement in Greece (1821–1831), the Bulgarian revolt (1834), and the Polish uprising (1830–1831). Although these movements differed from one another because of their particular historical location, a broader set of processes underpinned them all: the deterioration of economic and social conditions, great power rivalry, the rise of new elites who acted as important agents in the various movements, and, in various ways, the influence of the French Revolution. The strategies adopted by these movements and their ultimate targets are evidence that the movements were responding to a similar set of processes despite their local conditions. Almost all of these movements aimed at achieving independence or ending foreign rule. They were organized in Masonic societies, benefited from the connections provided by the diasporic communities, and were influenced by the ideas of the French Revolution that had spread all around the continent through various agents such as the students, merchants, mariners, and army service men.

These nationalist uprisings would, by fighting against empires, change the political and ideological map of the European continent. Constitutional theories, nationalist sentiments, democratic credos, and economic doctrines had long been in existence, but none of them were fully developed in the eighteenth century. By 1830, however, they all came vigorously into play. At the same time, political parties, classes, and social groups, far removed from earlier conceptions of nobles, guildsmen, and peasants, had emerged as actors in this new world of national passions (Ford 1989: 344–45). Hence, the Europe of the 1830s was fundamentally different from the Europe of the 1780s. The uprisings of the 1830s were clearly affected by the early revolutionary wave that swept the European continent.

Indeed, Hobsbawm (1962) refers to these uprisings as the "second wave of revolutions" that marked the definitive defeat of aristocratic power by the bourgeoisie and propelled a radical innovation in politics, which can be observed through the emergence of working classes. The prominence of memories, legends, and historical references inspired by the great Revolution was itself one of the elements that distinguished the new crisis in 1830 not only in France but also in England, Belgium, and Italy from earlier social unrest. In France, the unrest exploded following the decisions by Charles X to dissolve the Chamber of Deputies in the spring of 1830 and to promulgate the July Ordinances, which imposed further censorship and provided for the revision of the electoral law. Within a matter of hours after the ordinances were promulgated, barricades were up in the streets of Paris (Ford 1989: 337). By October, Paris was under rebel control and a majority of the Chamber of Deputies proclaimed a new king of France, Louis Philippe of the House of Bourbon-Orleans. Thus, an entire line of the monarchy had come crashing down (Ford 1989: 338). The other notable instance of the restoration's collapse in Western Europe occurred in Belgium. Although the repressive measures adopted by the king went back to 1827, the events culminated with the French uprising of 1830 and the newly formed provisional government in Brussels declared its formal separation from the Dutch, amid threats of intervention by Russia and Prussia (Ford 1989: 338). Hence, a new entity was created as a result of the revolutions of 1830.

The beginnings of "nationalist" movements that solidified the cultural identity of various ethnic populations contributed to the demise of the Ottoman Empire and the creation of autonomous states in the nineteenth century. The "religious" movements that occurred at the same time were equally important in producing these two outcomes. Religious uprisings did indeed occur in the Ottoman Empire in the nineteenth century. However, they were not totally dissimilar or disconnected from the religious movements that were also occurring elsewhere. We now turn our attention toward the second cluster of movements and, geographically, to the Middle East and northern Africa.

Movement in the Middle East and Northern Africa

As we argued above, diverse nationalist and religious movements were often expressions of the parallel processes of European capitalist expansion, the disintegration of empires, and the reintegration of the interstate system. The fact that the two clusters of movements are not similar requires us, however, to identify their differences. The organizational structure, key actors, and aims of the religious uprisings emerged out of different local circumstances and contributed to the demise of the empire in their own, different ways. Two "subclusters" existed: the "sectarian" uprisings and the "revivalist" movements, each with different strategies and different relationships to core European states. While the sectarian uprisings benefited from the European presence in the region, the revivalist movements rebelled against the penetration of foreign powers. We first turn, however, to Egypt, an important site of war and discontent in northern Africa that provides an illuminating movement example.

Historically, Egypt was a province of the Ottoman Empire that played an important role as both the "granary" and the key node in trade between Europe and Asia (Wallerstein and Kasaba 1980). Egypt thus became a valuable target for Napoleon in his attempt to capture a viable route to the Far East. Napoleon's invasion in 1798 dismantled the social and political order of the country by destroying the Ottoman administration and simultaneously introducing Western ideas and techniques. Mohammed Ali, after being appointed the governor of Egypt, not only adopted these new ideas and techniques but also embarked on a program of Westernization and industrialization including military, administrative, and economic reforms. Cotton was introduced as an export crop that led a large number of peasants to lose all decision-making power over their land (Richards 1987). These measures weakened the protective organization of the village and forced large numbers of peasants to abandon their land. The peasants responded to these dislocations by "rebelling, fleeing from the land and by mutilating themselves" (Richards 1987: 218). In addition to disrupting the livelihood of the Egyptian peasants, Mohammed Ali also invaded Ottoman provinces such as Syria and Mount Lebanon in 1831, disrupting the social, political, and economic order of the region. Although Mohammed Ali did not succeed in creating an independent state and was defeated by the British, this offensive had long-lasting implications in the region for it led to the awakening of subject populations—first as a reaction to the Egyptian invader, and then in conflicts among themselves.

The incorporation of and uprisings within less-developed and more isolated regions, such as Mount Lebanon and Palestine, followed a different path from those in Egypt or Syria. The arrival of Europeans in these inner regions in the mid-nineteenth century heralded the beginning of unrest among the local inhabitants. This "gentle crusade," as Makdisi puts it (2000: 17), of British, French, and American missionaries, travelers, artists, poets, and exiled revolutionaries "laid the foundations of a Maronite perception and (to a lesser extent) Druze perception that France and England were the loci of a benevolent modernity, and that they, as Maronites or Druzes, were entitled to it" (2000: 16). Thus, together with the Ottomans and Europeans, Maronite and Druze elites struggled to define an equitable relationship of the Maronite and Druze communities to a modernizing Ottoman state.

Despite his defeat, Mohammed Ali's invasion of Syria and Mount Lebanon, which lasted until the 1840s, precipitated a series of uprisings that culminated in a revolt by the Druze and Maronite groups. Taking advantage of these revolts, the Ottomans and British defeated Moham- mad Ali's forces and restored order in the region. Following this event, the Druze elites, returning from an exile imposed by the Egyptians, began to reclaim their former properties from the Christian peasants, thus intensifying preexisting tension between the two groups. These tensions led to the first major sectarian clashes between Druze and Maronite groups in Mount Lebanon in 1841. Aware of the weakness of the Ottoman center, these groups tried to align themselves behind one or another of the Great Powers; thus, the English supported the Druzes and the French maintained close relations with the Maronites.

These alliances also served the interests of the European powers, which needed local communities to justify their involvement in the Otto- man Empire. In addition, these groups invoked their rights promised by the *Tanzimat* reforms—the Druzes demanded restoration of their previous rights, while the Maronites saw the *Tanzimat* as a rupture from Druze control and, accordingly, demanded the equality and protection guaran- teed to them by the *Tanzimat* (Makdisi 2000: 63). Taking advantage of the both external and internal conditions—particularly the internal *Tanzimat* reforms by which the sultan promised "equality and freedom" (Karpat 1973: 86)—the Druzes and Maronites, as Ottoman historians chart (e.g., Makdisi 2000), created a culture of sectarianism in the region. In an at- tempt to bring a peaceful solution to the sectarian clashes in 1842, the British and Ottomans decided on a plan that envisaged the partition of the region along religious lines. However, a crisis over communal representa- tion unfolded in Mount Lebanon after the partition and reached its peak in a popular revolt in the predominantly Maronite district of Kisrawan in 1858. This revolt later spread to the mixed districts, precipitating the Druze-Maronite war of 1860, which not only signified the collapse of the old order but also sowed the seeds of future conflict among the different religious groups in the region.

Finally, we turn to the twenty-four or twenty-six "revivalist" move- ments that occurred in the nineteenth-century Ottoman Empire. While the nationalist movements and local religious groups in Mount Lebanon benefited from political relations with Europe, the revivalist movements, similar to those occurring in the Indonesian archipelago as we shall see later, emerged in response to the vast structural transformation that was caused by European capitalist expansion, European occupation of the Muslim lands, and the reforms that the state carried out to remedy these growing problems. As a result of the latter, those who were in- volved in revivalist movements viewed their government as "corrupt" and "illegitimate." They advocated for a return to the basic foundations of Islam—the Koran and Sunna—while criticizing the Muslim government's absolutism and despotism. More importantly, these movements were tar- geted primarily against the Russian, Dutch, French, English, and Italian occupation of central Asia and the Caucasus, the East Indies, northern Africa, and Egypt (Karpat 2001: 21).

For the purposes of this chapter, we cannot discuss these movements at length. Detailed studies are necessary that examine these movements from the perspective of transformative movements. But following Karpat we have to make one point clear: major movements such as Wahhabism, the Nakshbandia-Muraddiyya movement, or the Sanusiyya movement should not be confused with common accounts of contemporary fundamentalist movements. While the latter can involve a rejection of European civilization, the revivalist movements under scrutiny here were by contrast grassroots movements that mobilized the people around economic and social dislocations caused by European and Russian expansionism that "brought the Muslim society's problems into the open" (Karpat 2001: 46). As a result, the solutions offered by the revivalists differed from those of the nationalist or fundamentalist movements. The revivalist movements sought to morally regenerate and revive Islamic society from the inside and, hence, offered ways to adapt to the new conditions. The leadership came from the lower urban, upper agrarian, and tribal segments of the middle classes as well as from some of the old religious elites.

Impact on Europe: Toward 1848

These nationalist and religious movements during the early nineteenth century not only brought about tremendous, unanticipated social changes in the Ottoman Empire, Middle East, India, and northern Africa, but also significantly impacted Europe. Alongside the remarkable acceleration of social change around the world since 1830, the modern capitalist economy seemed to absorb larger quantities of goods and encouraged revolutionary methods of production (Hobsbawm 1962: 357). The increased rate of production and technological innovation not only further encouraged European territorial expansion in pursuit of new markets but also coincided with the formation of a working class within Europe. Hence, this period witnessed the emergence and strengthening of a new social actor, which would for the first time play a significant role in the revolutions of 1848. Increasingly, impoverished peoples and the laboring poor would stand against the old regimes and demand a new state and society.

The Chartists were among the first of these new movements to attempt to seize state power. Although they failed in their attempt, they emerged as the model of the revolutionary working-class party, particularly as celebrated by Marx and Engels in the *Communist Manifesto*.[6] Chartism, for Engels, was "essentially a social movement" that had clarified the issues facing the English working class, revealing that the proletariat must either give up its fight against the power of competition, and fall back into its former servitude, or utterly destroy the competitive capitalist system.

This judgment rested on a complex history. After the end of the Napoleonic Wars in 1815, the movement, known as the Radical party, was the strongest in Birmingham and Manchester. Although for some time they allied themselves with the liberal middle classes to break the power of oligarchy that dominated the unreformed House of Commons, this alliance did not last long. By 1843, when the disagreements between the two groups surfaced during a national convention held at Birmingham, Chartism became a "purely working-class movement." Yet at the same time it was not sharply differentiated from the Radical movement supported by the lower middle classes. These two groups combined their annual national conventions and, subsequently, accepted the points of the People's Charter as their objective. However, by the 1840s the attention of the middle classes was diverted to repealing the Corn Laws, while working classes realized that they would gain little from the repeal of the Corn Laws. It was, however, only after an uprising by workers that middle classes realized that they could collaborate with and still dominate workers. During the convention, discussions concerning the word "charter" broke the alliance, and hence, the movement attained its "purely" working-class character as Engels recounted (1968: 260–66).

The revolutionary year of 1848 demonstrated the Chartist's real character. As Post (1999: 65–76) details, the Chartist Association was far from a disciplined party and its ideology was a rather diffuse radicalism that mainly appealed to a labor culture that was being superseded. By the 1840s, with regular work forming around the mills, factory-employed spinners and weavers began to replace the peasants and artisans. The Chartists failed to apprehend this transition from an artisanal to a mass working class and, therefore, could not develop an effective strategy or organization to address these changed conditions.

At the same time revolutionary movements in France continued to spread quickly to the neighboring countries and regions. Thus social unrest in the Habsburg territories inspired revolutionary movements in the provinces of Moldavia and Wallachia, as well as Transylvania. What happened in Moldavia and other Romanian lands in 1848 can be seen as a repetition in miniature of the 1848 revolutions in other parts of Europe. In March 1848 the Society of Romanian Students in Paris sent a delegation to the French provisional government, inspiring the revival of the Romanian nationalist movement in Moldavia and Wallachia in 1848. The provinces were united under a single government in 1849.

By the beginning of the nineteenth century the Balkan world, like Europe and the wider world-economy, was thoroughly transformed. The inability of the sultan to curb the military, political, and economic pressure on and exploitation of the peasantry by the administrative establishment on the one hand and, on the other hand, the diffusion of the European concepts of "nation," "political rights," and "equality" created a fertile environment for the emergence of revolts organized by vastly different populations such as the Greeks, Serbs, Bulgarians, and, later, Arabs in the Middle East.

In short, as our study of the various movements in this part of the world indicates, the demise of the Ottoman Empire was related to, as well as accompanied by, the emergence of "new" nationally defined identities or groups of people within and beyond the boundaries of the empire. The nascent national identities were not merely by-products of religious or ethnic affiliations or purely local developments: they materialized from the pressure of and were shaped in response to European political and economic expansion. The weakening of the power of the sultan, which provided the opportunity for various groups of people from different social positions to directly challenge the sultan's control of the empire, was but one example of a wider world process.

Asia and the Indonesian Archipelago: Colonization, Proselytization, and Resistance

Similar processes can be observed in Asia, where new identities and states were formed through a long process of European intrusion, settlement, and commercial and military contest. Once a region that consisted of a diversity of peoples, Asia increasingly became a place defined by nationality and the boundaries of nation-states.

Yet discussions of the capitalist world in the eighteenth century have rarely encompassed Asia. The reasons advanced are quite direct: Asia is usually argued to be "external" to the European world-economy's division of labor, linked at best to Europe by luxury, not essential, trades, such as spices to be consumed by European elites as opposed to the mass consumption and industrial products of the Caribbean (see, for example, Wallerstein 1989: 177–85; Stavrianos 1981: 141–68). As our opening pages discussing the growing integration of the world in this period have already suggested, this ignores more substantive relationships established between Europe, the Americas, and Asia. As recent writings by world-historians on Indian Ocean world-economies argue more concretely (Frank 1998; Abu-Lughod 1989), traditional accounts very seriously underestimate the historic strengths of Asian economies and their political and religious responses to European attempts to dominate the area.

Accounts of Portuguese expansion into eastern Africa and southern Asia during the sixteenth century are, for example, largely constructed around the seizure of strategic ports such as Goa in 1510, Hormuz in 1515, and Malacca in 1519, and the building of trading ports. On the one hand, the great wealth generated by displacing the previous Muslim trade network underwrote Portuguese power in Europe. On the other hand, Portuguese power was actually quite limited by the strength of Asian states: the Portuguese never would establish any significant control over

Asian land and labor. Nor did Portuguese attempts in eastern Africa fare any better (Isaacman 1972). Accounts of Dutch expansion and replacement of the Portuguese follow similar lines. As Wolf summarizes, "In spite of Dutch successes against the Portuguese, their victory in the East proved hollow. The [Dutch East India] Company made profits but at heavy costs, the chief of these being the cost of war" (1982: 239). Britain, trading in the shadow of the Dutch empire, fared even worse in its initial forays into southern Asia, having to remain content with accepting the sovereignty of local rulers.

What such accounts fail to develop is how the interplay of European capitalist states and regional Asian powers in the eighteenth and early nineteenth centuries, by disrupting commercial and social life in Asia, would both enrich and shape rival European powers as well as transform the region and its powers. From this process would emerge a series of major challenges to European domination. As both Dutch and regional Muslim states declined in the eighteenth century, for example, the British East India Company was able to become the dominant power in southern Asia, considerably strengthening its bid for world hegemony. Central here was the breakup of the Mughal Empire, beset by rebellions particularly by Marathi-speaking Hindu populations. The rise of the Maratha Confederacy after the 1647 rebellion prefigured this process. Based in Calcutta, British support for a local rebellion led to the defeat of the Mughal provincial governor's troops at Plassey in 1757—leading to the wholesale plunder of the Bengali state. From this point onward, the East India Company sought to take over the whole of the Indian peninsula, slowly but steadily seizing political control, diverting tribute payments into its hands, and reallocating and reorganizing the use of land and labor.

The rise of British power in the subcontinent was neither inevitable nor uncontested. Missing in this narrative is a rolling series of revolts and wars after midcentury by successor states to the Mughal Empire, challenging the British as they moved forward from bases in Mumbai, Chennai, and Calcutta. Hyderabad, Mysore, and, especially, the Maratha federation that controlled roughly 75 percent of the subcontinent by the second quarter of the eighteenth century (Cooper 2003: 8) all threatened British power.

Indeed, Britain was often evenly matched both on the field and off, as local, modernizing rulers, who at times could match or even surpass British military strategy and equipment (Cooper 2003), sought interstate alliances with regional and European powers. Both Haidar Ali, who rose to full power in Mysore in 1760–1761, and his son Tippu Sultan, who succeeded him in 1782, sought as did other rulers to use competing European powers to advance the modernization and defense of their regimes. Particular attention was paid by both Haidar Ali and Tippu to building alliances with Britain's rival France and the Ottoman Empire, with Tippu attempting to solicit troops from both France and the Ottoman Empire through the 1780s (Habib 1999: xxxvii). When the final British invasion took place in 1799, France was, however, in the midst of its own revolution, and could offer no assistance to "Citizen Tippu," as he had been proclaimed by the local Jacobin Club in Srirangapatna (Habib, 1999: xl). Two generations of state formation, replete with new diplomatic relations with Europe as well as the reshaping of local political and social relations, could not save Tippu, who fell in the final British onslaught.

The fate of Mysore reveals a common pattern of British confrontation with incipient, modern states, and not the traditional religious powers of so many conventional histories of the subcontinent. Nevertheless, regional states' internal divisions, their inability to coordinate resistance among themselves when not engaged in direct conflict among themselves, and Britain's adeptness at exploiting both international opportunities and the regional military market led to successive British victories over Hyderabad in 1789, Mysore as noted above in 1799, and the Maratha federation in 1803 and 1816–1818 (Cooper 2003). These outcomes, taking place during the period of the Caribbean and European revolutions, would directly support Britain's rivalry with France as well as shape the contours of local resistance in succeeding generations.

Moving farther east to the Indonesian archipelago provides an even clearer and earlier case of the world processes at work. On the one hand, the Indonesian archipelago—which beginning in the sixteenth century included the Malay Peninsula; Sumatra; Java; part of Borneo; the Maluku Islands (or Spice Islands/Spiceries); and hundreds of smaller islands—would long play an invaluable role for Spanish, Portuguese, Dutch, and British commerce. On the other hand, competition among European powers would trigger intense local reactions that would shape the future role of the area in the world-economy.

To comprehend why this archipelago was so contentious, it is necessary to appreciate the centrality of this area not only for the Europeans, but also for the Chinese and Japanese empires. The archipelago's seasonal currents and geographical location, spread across the Pacific and Indian oceans and the South China Sea, made it the ideal place for trade to the east as well as to the west of the archipelago.[7] The Indonesian archipelago, for example, had always carried China's trade to the west where the land routes could not reach. While the archipelago had seen much conflict, it became much more violent and complicated when Europeans began to colonize, monopolize, and proselytize across the region. By dominating the main commercial route and monopolizing the supply of spices in the Indonesian archipelago, the different European powers were able not only to carry spices back to their home countries and to sell them in European markets but also to establish direct trade relations with China for the first time. These developments were linked to those in the Americas, for while the Indonesian archipelago provided the trade route to China, European colonization in the Americas provided the Europeans with the silver to support trade with China. Indeed, the growth of the "modern" money economy in China was made possible by the influx of silver into the empire through the Chinese-Spanish trade at Manila, the Chinese-Dutch trade at Nagasaki, the presence of the East India companies at Canton, and the arrival of American merchants in 1784. As the copper-silver exchange rate shifted, a debasement of the copper coinage that was used in everyday transactions took place, engendering a fiscal crisis of the imperial regime at all levels and rising social discontent.

In China these processes led directly to what historians have called the Opium War of 1840–1842, as imperial crisis and anti-opium campaigns were mixed with protests by commoners and peasant uprisings. As a result of its defeat, the empire became increasingly subordinated to Western powers, seriously weakening its regional geopolitical and geocultural power. Resentment at the corruption of the imperial regime and at Western political domination propelled further incidents of banditry, riots, and unrest, building upon the already serious pressure of increased populations, flood, famine, and poverty. Resistance against the Ching dynasty was readily transformed into a rejection of state corruption and Western political interference. The expulsion of the British by the Cantonese militia in 1841 was but one major example at the end of our period; as the next chapter charts, these confluences would explode in the Nien and Taiping rebellions.

Clashes between the expanding European capitalist world-economy and Asian polities long preceded these well-known events of the last half of the nineteenth century. Among the most enduring and notable of these clashes took place in the Indonesian archipelago, where competition for spice routes, strategic positions, and proselytization occurred with violent force. For the missionaries who traveled with merchant fleets, the islands were filled with potential converts. Indeed, conversion was readily seen as a necessary part of the process of pacifying the sultans and peoples who refused to restrict their sale of spices to one specific European power and resisted European occupation.

As Europeans entered the region in force, countermovements based on civilizational and religious networks thus pushed forward—most notably those involving Christianity and Islamization (Reid 1993: 152–54; Laffan 2003). Conversions to Christianity or Islam reflected the profound disruption and reorganization of the region due to the rapid commercialization of the region by Chinese, Muslim, and European merchants in the sixteenth century. When the Portuguese arrived the area was already the center of a diverse, thriving set of trading communities: this was not an area of simple, rural peasants (Scott 1986; Adas 1981). Nor were the peoples of the islands all connected by the same religious faith, Islam, which underpins present-day scholars' conceptions of "revivalist" or religious movements. The peoples of the islands had instead been religiously and ethnically diverse, having been transformed through successive interactions with foreigners who came themselves from different parts of the world. Peoples' "everyday existence" had thus historically extended well beyond the boundaries of the islands and their rural interiors. From these relations and histories we can begin to discern the source of resistance against European intrusion.

When the Portuguese captured Malacca in 1511, for example, they found "merchants and sailors from all the lands between Arabia and China, whether Moors, Jews, or heathens" (Lach 1994: 513). Directly across from Malacca, on the opposite side of the strait, is Sumatra, which the Portuguese sought to control. Because of its strategic location across the strait, its vassalage status vis-à-vis Malacca and its Malay cultural base were firmly established prior to any intrusion from outside the region. However, despite the Malay cultural base and language that Sumatra shared with Malacca in the sixteenth century, Sumatra was more closely related by geography, ethnography, and language to Java and Borneo (Lach 1994: 572). Well before Christianity appeared, "merchants and priests from south India and emissaries from Han China appear to have touched upon southern Sumatra, western Java, and eastern Borneo" (Lach 1994: 572).

Through these early contacts with India and China, Hindu culture and religion were introduced and became influential in the archipelago. Indeed, the center of political power in Java by the end of the thirteenth century was the Buddhist state of Majapahit, whose rulers were determined not only "to establish imperial rule over the rest of Indonesia," but also "to stand off the growing power of Islam" (Lach 1994: 572). As the Moors from Persia, Arabia, Gujarat, Hindustan, and Bengal began to trade, Islam gradually also began to assert itself in the region. When Majapahit's power declined after 1389, Islam was able to spread more rapidly throughout the archipelago as Muslim merchants traded without restraint, which opened the door for converting many non-Muslim merchants to Islam.

Still, the entire archipelago was not Islamic prior to the permanent settlement of the Portuguese and the Spaniards in the region. As Anthony Reid (1993) notes, the Islamization and Christianization were both part of a shared process of intense disruption to the social order within the broader Southeast Asia region (Reid 1993: 152; Laffan 2003). This disruptive process consisted of (1) the rapid commercialization of the region in the sixteenth century by Chinese, Muslim, and European merchants (see also Lach 1994: 573); (2) direct contact with Europe and the Middle East in the late sixteenth century, which facilitated increased trade, the travel of Arab scholars, and the dispatch of Southeast Asian priests to Europe; and (3) political crusades carried on by the Spaniards and Portuguese against the Muslim traders.

As a result of attacks by the Spaniards and Portuguese, "the Muslims of Southeast Asia, particularly those involved in the spice trade, tended to regroup around explicitly Islamic centers prepared to counterattack" (Reid 1993: 164). The rise of Aceh in the Indonesian archipelago was precisely an outcome of this process of commercial, religious, and political contestation (see also Lach 1994: 578). The formation of Aceh in northern Sumatra was significant, as the Portuguese "drove all the more Islamic, commercial, or simply patriotic elements to support Sultan Ali Mughayat Syah in his drive to unite the north Sumatran coast during the 1520s into a new and explicitly anti-Portuguese kingdom" (Reid 1993: 164).

Portuguese intrusion into Java triggered a similar response, with the leaders of the Muslim state of Japra fearing that Europeans would destroy free passage in the archipelago and send a fleet against Malacca in 1513. Javanese merchants in turn would be expelled from Malacca, an unprecedented event. After establishing a permanent settlement in Malacca, the Portuguese rapidly continued their expansion south and east. In response to the aggressive expansion of the Portuguese toward Sumatra, "[t]he refugee sultan of Malacca himself helped to spread word of the Portuguese conquest to distant China by sending an emissary there to request support from his suzerain" (Lach 1994: 571). Other groups of people in the strait also spread to surrounding islands an alarm about the immediate threat that the Portuguese posed to the general interest of the people in the archipelago.[8] The defeat of the Javanese fleet by the Portuguese in 1538 occasioned a wave of conversion to Christianity in the strategic and spice-laden western part of the Indonesian archipelago (or the Maluku). Another subsequent Muslim defeat in 1569 solidified the Portuguese position in central and southern Maluku.

The Portuguese would dominate Amboina until the Dutch captured it from them. The Dutch also quickly destroyed the English settlement in Amboina in 1623. They became the mercantile power in this part of the archipelago by the seventeenth century. The first Dutch fleets were sent to the Indonesian archipelago for spices in 1594 and did not return to the Netherlands until 1597. A surge of commercial companies for trading in the East Indies immediately followed this expedition, causing higher spice prices in Asia and lower prices in Europe (Boxer 1965: 23) and leading to the formation in 1602 of one monopolistic corporation, the United Netherlands Chartered East India Company (VOC). The VOC was given not only a twenty-one-year monopoly of Dutch trade and navigation east of the Cape of Good Hope and west of the Straits of Magellan, but also powers usually reserved for sovereign states including the right "to conclude treaties of peace and alliance, to wage defensive war, and to build fortresses and strongholds in that region" (Boxer 1965: 24). With these powers, the VOC attacked Portuguese colonial possessions throughout the tropics. By 1604 the VOC succeeded in expelling the Portuguese from Amboina and capturing the island, subsequently forcing the *Orang Kayas* (headmen—literally "rich men") to sell their cloves only to the Dutch company (Masselman 1963: 164).

The Banda Islands, however, suffered a violent fate when they stymied the VOC's objective to completely monopolize the spice trade in the Maluku: direct control of these particular islands was necessary because the local merchants consistently refused to adhere to their (forced) contractual agreements with the VOC to sell their spices exclusively to the Dutch. In January 1621, Jan Pieterszn Coen, the governor-general of the VOC, arrived on the coast of the island of Banda and ordered the massacre of reportedly 15,000 Bandanese people as their punishment for trading with Dutch rivals. Coen shortly "remove[d] all the original inhabitants from the islands and repopulate[d] them with settlers from elsewhere that would be fully loyal to the VOC" (Boxer 1965: 100). Many Bandanese people were subsequently shipped to Djakarta (or Jakarta/ Batavia) as slaves.

Although violent campaigns of territorial conquest such as the one in Banda were costly affairs in both money and men, the directors of the VOC, and especially their subordinates in the East, were not at all hesitant to use force to firmly safeguard their cherished possessions in the Maluku. Thus, to enforce the VOC's spice monopoly in this area, the Dutch captured the remaining Portuguese forts and made them Dutch naval and military bases (Boxer 1965: 188). Dutch territorial possessions further expanded when they "felt the need of a 'general rendezvous' where their homeward- and outward-bound fleets could load and unload their cargoes, and where goods from the interport trade of Asia could be collected, stored or transshipped" (Boxer 1965: 188–89). In 1684 the VOC fully occupied Bantam, bringing to an end the century-long struggle for the company's complete control of the Moluccan spice crop (Boxer 1965: 99).

In a parallel fashion the local commander sought to conquer the city of Djakarta by force, despite opposition from both the sultan of Bantam and the VOC board of directors (Masselman 1963: 390–91; Boxer 1965: 189–94). Following this attack, Djakarta was baptized with the new name Batavia, and Chinese were kidnapped by the company to help populate the city.[9] Although the VOC established its command center in Batavia after the attack, the empire of Mataram in the interior of East Java remained a force to contend with. In 1677 the Dutch Governor-General Maetsuyker intervened in Mataram's succession dispute and, with the help of Speelman and Van Goens, restored the deposed susuhunan's heir. A new wave of succession disputes ensued, ending with the collapse of the Mataram empire in 1755. In its place, two new states, Surakarta and Jogjakarta, emerged. "By this time," Boxer writes, "the Company had extended its hegemony over the whole island and reduced all the Javanese sultanates to the position of client or vassal states" (Boxer 1965: 194). Unlike the Portuguese, the Dutch effectively subordinated and alienated the most powerful sultanates who at one point had controlled the Strait of Malacca. They also, unlike the Portuguese, directly governed local populations, transforming land, labor, and taxing practices.

As British power began to prevail over the Dutch in the late eighteenth century, new opportunities arose for anti-European resistance. The debilitated power of the sultans in key areas added to these opportunities, leading segments of the population to rally around new leaders who channeled popular discontent with the European domination. In the Moluccas Thomas Matulesi (better known as Pattimura)—a noncommissioned officer from the British Moluccan corps—was chosen as the commander of a large group of discontented Moluccans in 1817. The Moluccans' discontent was related to the shifting of power between the Dutch and the British, with the British finally asserting power over the Moluccas in 1817. The Dutch had lost the East Indies to the British during Napoleon's rule over the Netherlands, but in 1813 the British returned to the Dutch their possessions in the East Indies. However, in 1817, the British reasserted their power over the Moluccas. Each shift in power brought with it changes that reflected the interest (or concern) of the ruling power. In this particular instance, the Moluccans' appointment of Pattimura as their commander was triggered by rumor that the Moluccan Protestant Institution was again to be changed. With this as their pretext, the Moluccans took over Fort Duurstede on Saparua Island. Pattimura and his followers received support from other islanders because the people had become weary of Dutch occupation and did not want to see a return to Dutch rule. Pattimura and his followers were captured and hanged in Fort Victoria on 16 December 1817.

The occupation of Fort Duurstede in 1817 by Pattimura and his followers illustrated how a movement to preserve a religious institution could became an anti-Dutch movement in the Strait of Malacca. Indeed, militant as well as reformist Islam in Sumatra posed a major challenge to European rule during the early nineteenth century. Because the Portuguese were controlling the main spice route in the Indonesian archipelago and forcing Arab and Indian merchants to use the Indian Ocean as an alternative trade route, direct contact between Muslims from Arabia and Southeast Asia had long deepened Islamic influences in Sumatra. The increased number of Islamic scholars (or the *ulama*) from Arabia and returned pilgrims from Mecca (the *hadjis*) since the seventeenth century had already heightened awareness of Islam. By the late eighteenth century, the authority of the *ulamas* as well as the *hadjis* in Islamic societies unequivocally expanded.

Thus the *padri* of Minangkabau, which lies to the west of Sumatra, was formed out of the call of three *hadjis* to purge their society of non-Islamic elements. Inspired by Wahhabism (a Western term given to the strict form of Islam practiced in Hijaz, or what is today Saudi Arabia), which they encountered while in Mecca, the *padri* leaders urged the reform of Minangkabau Islamic society along puritanical lines. The traditional system of matrilineal inheritance and consumption of alcohol and opium were challenged by strict Islamic laws and practices, while followers were required to adhere to a strict dress code of white robes and turbans (hence, their name, *"padri"*). More importantly, for the *padris*, the Europeans were to be purged. Local chiefs who inherited their lands and titles through the female line naturally became alarmed by the reformers and feared that a religious government would displace them. Armed conflicts consequently emerged between the two groups, followed by the secular (or customary law, *adat*) leaders' turn to the Dutch in Java for assistance. Dutch intervention antagonized feudal nobles, who then decided to join the *padris*. Between 1821 and 1838 the Padri War eventually led to the pacification of Minangkabau and subsequent Dutch control over western Sumatra.

The significance of the Padri War, however, is not only that it represented an anti-Dutch struggle but that it also challenged the conception that resistance invoking Islam or "revivalist" movements are necessarily "traditional." In the instance of the Padri War, the *padri's* notion of reform demanded the elimination of indigenous secular institutions. A strict interpretation of Islamic laws supplanted local secular laws, but the Islamic laws subsequently became a force to unify the people of Sumatra and Java in the early nineteenth century. Thus, Islam gained prominence in a way that it never did when the religion first appeared in the archipelago. It was at this point that Islam, because of its anti-European position, progressively turned into an inspiration for various groups of people, from different social positions, to collectively express their discontent with Dutch rule.

The case of the Java War of 1825–1830 illustrates these processes on a larger scale. By this time Mataram had suffered severe political decline as the Dutch, exploiting rivalries and internal divisions among local kingdoms, annexed one outer province after another. Still, indigenous forms of taxing and tribute remained as the Dutch exploited land and labor through tribute systems. Prince Pangeran Diponegoro's rebellion, or the Java War of 1825–1830, thus took place against a long history of the transformation of local and regional economic and political life, with the lives and fate of both farmers and local elites increasingly intertwined with foreign forces stretching into Europe. The cost of the war for all sides was high: the Dutch and their allies suffered the loss of over 15,000 men, as many as 200,000 Javanese were killed, and over two million people were directly affected by the war (Adas 1979: 11).

Similar to the *padris* in western Sumatra, the followers of Prince Diponegoro in Jogjakarta were also mostly Islamic, but they combined Islam with a messianic belief in the coming of a Just Ruler who would restore the harmony of the kingdom. Even though they were preoccupied with the Padri War, the Dutch moved against Prince Diponegoro in

Jogjakarta, which was formerly part of the Mataram empire that ruled central and eastern Java. While the Java War has often been explained by reference to the disappointed ambitions of Prince Diponegoro, who had been passed over for the succession to the throne of Jogjakarta, the causes were reflected in the transformation of local kingdoms, land, and labor as commercialization and foreign intrusion had advanced in preceding decades. The rebellion drew upon multiple sources, including the aristocratic landholders of Jogjakarta who were resentful because the contracts for the lease of their lands to Europeans were cancelled by the governor-general; Islamic leaders who faced proselytization and competitive merchants; and an increasingly impoverished, discontented agrarian population who were awaiting the coming of a Just Ruler. Drought in 1821, 1822, and 1824, as well as the outbreak of cholera and flood in 1823, exacerbated these problems.

Through the use of guerrilla strategies and with support from various groups in Jogjakarta, rebels were able to persistently challenge Dutch authority for five years, with Diponegoro occupying a pivotal position that defined the strength and character of the Java War of 1825–1830 (see Adas 1979: 93–99). His education and disposition bridged both Islamic and mystical elements. Through his education, he was acquainted with the teachings of the traditional Islamic schools (*pesantren*) in the rural village where he lived as a child with his grandmother. He also claimed to have experienced a vision in which the Goddess of the Southern Ocean promised that he was a future king. Thus, a combination of his royal status as the senior prince of the Jogjakarta kingdom, religious insight, and rural dwelling with his grandmother placed Diponegoro in a unique position to mobilize aristocratic elites as well as the rice-producing agrarian population. Diponegoro's knowledge of Islam and Javanese mysticism also held considerable popular appeal. Using the Dutch decision to build a road across a piece of his property that contained a sacred tomb as his pretext, Diponegoro united discontented groups against the Dutch in 1825.

The revolt spread quickly across central and east Java, almost causing Dutch colonial rule to collapse. The Dutch, however, returned with a force that was not anticipated by the Javanese guerilla fighters. When the Dutch adopted the "fortress system"—a strategy of posting smaller units of mobile troops in forts scattered through the contested territory—they were able to successfully suppress the insurgency. The Java War officially came to an end when the Dutch treacherously seized Diponegoro during truce negotiations and exiled him to Celebes.

While the end of this war represented the demise of the old aristocratic order in Java for the Javanese, the Dutch viewed the outcome of the Java War as the end of a new colonial order that the British Governor-General Raffles tried to establish over the East Indies when Britain took over the possessions of the VOC in 1811. When the Dutch returned to Java between 1816 and 1820 and sought to overturn many of the reforms introduced by the British, the aftermath of the Java War provided the Dutch with the opportunity to reorganize Javanese society. Van den Bosch, who took over the government from Du Bus de Gisignes on 16 January 1830, implemented the cultivation system and the refeudalization of the government.

Under the cultivation system all estates on Java were declared properties of the Dutch colonial government. Every farmer was required to use one-fifth of his land for the cultivation of products like indigo, sugar, and coffee. In addition, the government had the rights over the labor of the Javanese farmers. Cooperation of the local Javanese leadership was crucial to ensure the success of the cultivation system, which led to the refeudalization of the government (Fasseur 1992: 238), including the promotion of the regents, who received part of their salary in land, were given control over their own militia (*barisan*), and had their positions made inheritable. More importantly, they were rewarded with "culture percentages," which were fees derived from the production of sugar, coffee, or indigo. While the regents were provided with incentives for ensuring the success of the cultivation system, the farmers or laborers actually were exploited more intensely.

The enforcement of the cultivation system would provide the impetus for resistances against the Dutch in the latter half of the nineteenth century. Beginning in the 1830s, cultivation of indigo, sugar, and coffee intensified. Plantations were expanded while more factories were built to support this new economic interest. This process of economic transformation, however, did not proceed without challenges from the local populations. For instance, indigo gardens that already existed in the Preanger regencies were extended and eighteen factories were soon set up in this area, but the effort to introduce the indigo culture in the residence of Cheribon was frustrated by the local population.

The production of sugar generated a different set of problems (Knight 2000). The sugar industry's demand for labor was insatiable. Work on the sugarcane fields, from the cutting of the canes to the transport of the canes to the sugar mills, was very labor intensive, with forced labor used to build sugar mills. Preparing rice fields for the planting of sugarcane also demanded labor. All these demands drew many Javanese into the cultivation system. The diversion of land and labor toward the cultivation of sugar consequently hampered the production of rice, which increasingly affected the supply of rice that the people on the island and other islands in the archipelago consumed. In response to the expansion of sugar production, the residents of Besoeki set afire sugarcane fields. The Pasoeroean Javanese protested in front of the house of the resident. To calm the protestors, the resident actually promised that they would not have to produce sugarcane for an entire year. Lastly, coffee production was brought under the Department of Cultures in 1832.

While the production of indigo lagged and sugar increased only slowly, coffee production rose from the 288,000 pikol (or picul, about 133 lbs.) in 1830 to 360,000 pikol in 1833. By the end of the nineteenth century, Java would be ranked as the world's second largest producer and exporter of cane sugar in the world, surpassed only by Cuba. Europeans began to replace the Chinese entrepreneurs and skilled Chinese laborers who had been in this industry for centuries, which created new tensions between the Europeans and the Chinese (Knight 2000: xvi). These developments turned Java into a major asset for the Netherlands. As Cornelis Fasseur indicates, "[d]uring the period 1850–59, about 90 percent of Indies profits came from the profits on the sale of commodities produced by the Cultivation System" (1992: 151). These profits led the government to ignore residents' "complaints about increasing shortage of suitable land [for cultivating coffee] and a threatened exhaustion of coffee plantations" (Fasseur 1992: 154).

Across Java, the plight of the people varied according to the type of cultivation imposed upon the area. For instance, the regent of Demak remained untouched by the cultivation system until government tobacco cultivation was introduced in 1843. As soon as tobacco cultivation came in, however, the people were impoverished as rice production was neglected in favor of tobacco cultivation. Even though rice was still available in the neighboring regent of Semarang, the people of Demak had no money to purchase rice, leading to high mortality rates and a massive flight of people from the area.

In short, the cultivation system was a disaster for local peoples, setting the stage for the social rebellions of the late nineteenth century and even the twentieth century. Because the cultivation system produced the prototypical, nineteenth-century "peasant," subsequent social rebellions have often been recorded as traditional peasant revolts. Yet, as we have seen, at the core of peasant revolts stands a persistently powerful, anti-European and anticapitalist thrust that began as early as the seventeenth century. Through this long-term, collective resistance against European intruders, national identities flourished among the peoples of the Indonesian archipelago. In this respect the various movements and wars we examined here not only shaped the boundaries and character of local and foreign rulers but also provided the seeds for future nationalist movements in this part of the world. By reducing early movements in this region to peasant revolts, the broader impact that they have had on the region and the larger world-economy has long been obscured.

Conclusion

As we noted at the beginning of this chapter, the lack of world-historical studies of global movements prior to the twentieth century works strongly against what we have attempted here: to recover key clusters of movements that have expressed common and connected life experiences through resistance to the expanding capitalist world-economy. As we have argued, examining the European capitalist world-economy and its engagement with other social worlds in the seventeenth and eighteenth centuries reveals a remarkable range of movements, movements directed against fundamental processes of world accumulation and increasing European political aggression. Of particular note there were transoceanic clusters surrounding 1790 that brought down the old imperial orders and slavery, and those around 1830 that largely responded to the opportunities afforded by rising discontent amidst the transition to Britain's hegemony. As we have seen, revolts in these periods existed in the Americas, Europe, and Asia.

These movements did not simply exist: their struggles served to force the shape and expansion of this new, expanding world-economy that would emerge by the mid-nineteenth century. Successful campaigns to end slavery in the Americas would, for example, bring freedom for millions of slaves—and yet serve in turn to trigger a second phase of slave production and the emergence on the horizon of coerced coolie, tenant, and sharecropping labor as the century developed. The demise of old colonial empires in the Americas and Asia was also in large part a product of localized yet often connected struggles as we have seen time and again. This served to propel and shape the rise of British hegemony in turn—which by the mid-nineteenth century would become the target of new movements worldwide.

More startling in the telling was the rise of attempts to defend the possibility of social life outside the clutches of capitalism. Maroonage and flight provided one model here and could be seen all along the periphery of the world-economy. Perhaps more unusual was the emergence, as we have seen in both the Americas and Asia, of new communities and states whose construction arose directly from the struggle against capitalist invaders. These were often moments of innovation, pursuing what would be called in the last half of the twentieth century tactics of "delinking" from the capitalist world-economy and more recently "subsistence" or "decommodification" anticapitalist strategies (e.g., Bennholdt-Thomsen et al. 2001).

Each of our accounts also reveals a startling transnational and transoceanic connection among local movements, something that is often held to be possible only in today's age of globalization, after long centuries of statist and nationalist movements. Contrary to these accounts and expectations, in every instance we have seen the movement of not only ideas but also strategies, tactics, and actors across long distances. Seamen, merchants, and diasporic communities were, in one way or another, central to the emergence, sustenance, and success of movements from the Caribbean and the Americas as a whole, through Europe, the Balkans, and the Middle East, to the far reaches of Asia.

Few of these movements achieved their aims. In alliance with other anticolonial and anti-incorporation activity, they did, however, substantially shape the evolution of the reach and structure of the mid-nineteenth century interstate system, as we have seen. In this they would provide, yet again, a systemic feature that the new movements of 1848 would tackle: the necessity of organized and institutionalized movement activity directed from within and against existing states. In this both the achievements and shortcomings of the world movements of the preceding century were revealed.

Notes

1. There is a vast, classic literature here on the events, class composition, and implications of the revolution, as illustrated by the works of Pierre Chaunu, François Furet, Georges Lefebvre, George Rudé, Albert Soboul, and Alexis de Tocqueville among many others. The bicentennial of the revolution in 1989 also generated new assessments and debates; see, among others, Kaplan 1995; Best 1988; Hobsbawm 1990; and the special issue of *Social Research* (56, 1, Spr. 1989).

2. See, for example, Silver and Slater (1999: 160), who argue that "on the one hand, the balance of class forces was transformed in the course of the long economic expansion.... On the other hand, the expansion itself began to sputter.... With the breakdown of intra-elite unity and the alienation of the 'middle classes,' the space was opened for revolts from below by the excluded and exploited."

3. There has been an extensive debate among the students of Ottoman history on the emergence and evolution of nationalism in the Balkans and the Middle East. A customary approach, exemplified by R. W. Seton-Watson (1917) and Hans Kohn (1929), argues that the process of national awakening among non-Muslims differed to a large extent from that of the Muslim peoples of the empire. A later school places the Muslim and non-Muslim subjects in one general framework and argues that the "rise of nationalism and nationalities in the Ottoman state was actually the consequence of social and economic transformation" (Karpat 1973: iii). This latter approach also differentiated the nationality problem in the Ottoman state from Western Europe's notion of nationalism. It maintained that the former was a special form of nationalism because of its background and especially because of the conditions from which it evolved (Karpat 1973: 3).

4. Ethnic groups were organized into *millets* or religious communities, such as Orthodox, Armenian, and Muslim. In addition, since between the fifteenth and seventeenth centuries, the Ottoman system categorized the rural masses according to their ethnic characteristics, which became their chief cultural trait and which eventually formed the basis of their national-cultural identity.

5. The Ottoman conquest and the rule of the Balkans contributed to the development of local communities and new leaders by liquidating the old dynasties and leaders. The loss of political and cultural leaders, as Karpat points out, especially among the Slavs and the southern Greeks in the Balkans, "had the effect of consolidating the ethnic culture at the grassroots level" (1973: 15). In the following decades, the primates who acted as representatives of their communities and the local clergy played important leadership roles in mobilizing the masses during national struggles.

6. Indeed, Engels dates back the origins of Chartism to the 1780s, when a democratic party developed simultaneously with the growth of the proletariat. With respect to its possible links with the French Revolution, he argued that the latter fostered this democratic movement, particularly in London. Moreover, the revolution served as an example to the Chartists who recalled the "days of the French Revolution when the making of pikes became a popular hobby" (1968: 260). See also Post (1999: 69).

7. As Masselman (1963: 194) explains,

> The periodic monsoons dictated the flow of this early [China] trade, as they would for centuries to come. From about April to September the prevailing winds in the Indian Ocean and the China Sea blew from the southwest, thus facilitating voyages from west to east and north to China and Japan. During this same period, winds in the Java and Banda seas, being located south of the equator, blew from the southeast, thus favoring a passage from east to west. A look at the map will show that these three routes converged in the Strait of Malacca. In the early stage, when vessels were small, the Isthmus of Kra was a favored transfer point, the goods being carried overland. In due course, however, it proved cheaper to sail around the Malay Peninsula, thus enhancing the importance of the Strait of Malacca as the artery through which all east-west trade must flow.

8. As Lach (1994: 571) tells us, "Gujarati and Javanese traders, who had opposed Albuquerque [the Portuguese captain who captured Malacca], let it be known in other parts that the new power in southeast Asia was a religious, commercial, and political threat to entrenched interests."

9. The growth of the Chinese community and the strengthening of its economic base in Batavia became a threat to the company. The rumor of a possible Chinese rebellion against the Dutch in 1740 set off a massacre that killed most of the Chinese community at Batavia.

*

Chapter 2

Reformers and Revolutionaries: The Rise of Antisystemic Movements and the Paradox of Power, 1848–1917

Caleb M. Bush

> Nothing and nobody can detain the triumphal march of the revolutionary movement. Does the bourgeoisie want peace? Then let it become the working class! Is peace what the authorities want? Then let them take off their coats and take up the pickax and cudgel, the plough and the hoe! Because as long as there is inequality, as long as some work so that others consume ... there will be no peace.
>
> *Ricardo Flores Magón, quoted in Hodges 1995: 191*

Flores, a leading intellectual of the 1910 Mexican Revolution with ties to anarchism in the Americas and Europe, wrote such scathing indictments of class inequalities from exile in places like St. Louis, Missouri. In Flores, the connections linking antisystemic activities and the revolutionary fervor of 1848–1917 are made apparent. Inspiration came from many sources as movement ideals and movements themselves traveled with increasing pace and frequency over the period 1848–1917. Without question, opening from the "World Revolution" of 1848, the seventy years to 1917 overflow with antisystemic activity. The years 1848 and 1917, coming at the beginning and end of this period, are, of course, highly significant in and of themselves—perhaps *least* of all for the sheer volume of scholarship produced concerning each.[1] The details of the movements and struggles between these dates—the challenges leveled at historical capitalism by Flores and a legion of other antisystemic actors—make this period crucial to understanding the larger history of antisystemic movements and the capitalist system they opposed and shaped. The world after 1917 would not be the same, and movements drove many of the major changes home.

Much antisystemic activity took on easily identifiable and sustained organizational form in this period, realizing possibilities introduced by revolution in 1789.[2] Of seemingly little consequence, antisystemic activity increasingly gained names and titles that included words like *party, congress, association, brotherhood,* etc. at this time; such organizational form (and sometimes even the names) has proven rather robust historically. One cannot help but acknowledge the period's "central antisystemic force" (Arrighi 1990) in the rise of the modern labor movement from 1848 to 1917. Yet, labor and an often closely related socialism are only part of an overall challenge here. The resistance and revolt brought to bear against imperial expansion in places like India or Jamaica, the challenges posed by anarchism throughout Europe and the Americas, and the wave of revolutions that close the period (excluding even Russia) provide a more complete picture. These many movements served to challenge and shape an emerging capitalism at this time, in many ways consolidating aspects of the world-economy even as they hoped to alter or even over-throw capitalism. As such, movements from 1848 to 1917 *reflected as well as structured* the operations of the capitalist world-economy. As radical political parties and massive labor movements grew in power throughout the world-system, some even attaining control of the state by 1917, their efforts paradoxically served to strengthen state structures and to rou-tinize struggle. While an unquestionable "success," these developments also pulled antisystemic resistance within safer bounds for the ongoing operations of historical capitalism.

Making sense of the challenges pushed forward during this period presents a complex task. This argument works through several steps to emphasize key themes for the period. Relying heavily on the weight of the historical record, the argument breaks into three shorter periods, roughly twenty to twenty-five years in length, 1848–1873, 1873–1896, and 1896–1917.[3] For each period I discuss important movements, their impact in terms of world-economic change, and links between movements. As will be seen, the notion of a singular "movement" or "event" often disappears under close consideration. From as early as the 1848 Revolu-tion, activity happening in one locale was mirrored in and/or linked to numerous other locations both in space and time. In a certain sense for 1848–1917, a movement anywhere is seen to exist in a "cluster" of varying shapes and sizes. The idea of a "cluster" captures the linkages between movements in terms of their objectives, antagonists, ideologies, shared leaderships, overlapping memberships, etc. Anarchist struggles or resistance to colonialism in Africa, for example, are best understood as clusters of antisystemic activity across time/space. Potent temporal examples, the Paris Commune or Haymarket, lie at the center of vast clusters of antisystemic struggle that have looked to Paris or the first May Day as inspiration and cause célèbre ever since.

Moving forward, the relatively quiet years immediately following 1848 were marked by open challenges to imperial expansion and control on the edges of "empire" as well as the (re)emergence of worker and socialist agitation in Europe and North America. Critical here, from roughly 1873 to 1896, working-class struggles, socialist movements, and anarchist efforts targeting capitalism as well as nationalist struggles targeting imperialism made great (and often first) strides. These depression years of 1873–1896 heralded the beginning of an era of imperialism and great power rivalry that would forever change the globe—a change contested *but also unwittingly aided* in no small part by movements. By the middle of the overall period, antisystemic activity took on differing, yet related, guises as they became real, organized movements. As Wallerstein argues,

> The great expansion of the organized working-class movements of Europe from 1870 to 1914 took place at the same time as, and within the context of, the last great imperial territorial expansion of Europe in modern history. Therefore, at the very moment the socialist movements were seeking to find their way as antisystemic movements emphasizing anticapitalism, there emerged nationalist movements in the periphery, seeking to find their way as antisystemic movements emphasizing antiimperialism. (1990: 22)

In the sections to come I pull context to the forefront, indicating the numerous ways in which important movements impacted the system they opposed and vice versa.[4] A central aim is exposing the forgotten background behind the expansion of historical capitalism. Antisystemic movements as historical actors contested the very terms of "progress," fundamentally shaping the capitalist world-economy they inherited.

The revolutions after the turn of the twentieth century, including but in no way limited to Russia in 1905 and 1917, represent one major outcome of the struggles building from 1848 onward. Beginning the period under serious repression, by 1917 movements—through competing and often contradictory strategies of reform, revolution, and all that falls in between—were vying for control of the state, even gaining state power. These developments constituted the most significant turn for movements and movement strategy. In many ways, part of the aftermath of 1848 is a reaffirmation of state power,[5] certainly the state's monopoly of violence (see Tilly 1990; also Lane 1979), against domestic unrest.[6] This can be easily recognized in World War I, which closes the period; in 1914, total war emerged between competing states and on the world stage. The increasing import of state structures (and, in turn, the ongoing consolidation of the interstate system) is reinforced by the fact that movements began increasingly to look to the state, holding accountable those who wield power and eventually seeing the attainment of state power as a viable option. This antisystemic strategy would result in deepening states and the interstate system as well as fundamentally altering movement strategy for a considerable time to come.[7]

With increasingly consolidated state structures in place, many movements throughout the core of the capitalist world looked increasingly toward reformist measures by 1917. Nascent anti-imperial struggles as well as struggles over states elsewhere in the world looked more toward revolt for outright change. Resistance thereby shaped the very *possibilities* of capitalism (as well as future struggles) while, in a seemingly contradictory fashion, serving to consolidate this "evolving capitalism" (McMichael 1987). Antisystemic movements as organized, collective efforts with sustaining memberships emerged fully in the years 1848–1917 to play a central role in the historical processes of the time.

1848–1873: A Little Revolt in a Time of (Relative?) Quiet

The rapid spread of unrest in Europe around 1848 presents a good initial example of the relationship and ties that form between antisystemic struggles. The year 1848 provides a first example of an antisystemic cluster. That 1848 is considered a "World Revolution" at all connotes this fact. Breuilly confirms that

> in four weeks the political situation in France, Germany, Italy and the Hapsburg Empire had been transformed. There was a republic in France; the Hapsburg Empire no longer controlled Hungary or northern Italy and was barely master in Vienna; the King of Prussia had been humiliated by crowd action in his capital; most of the smaller German and Italian states had promised new constitutions and appointed new ministers. Freedom of publication, assembly, association and speech had generally been achieved. (2000: 112)

Spurring these sudden changes, news of the February events in France quickly spread, and the fall of Louis Philippe undoubtedly had something of a "demonstration effect" for those unhappy with old orders throughout Europe. No small feat, 1848 in France, Wallerstein conveys, "marked the first time that a proletarian-based political group made a serious attempt to achieve power and legitimize worker's power" (1990: 16)—setting an early precedent here for movement activity. There is little doubt that such struggles were aware of each other, often through a network of free presses and organizational centers that sprang up around the 1848 opening. News of 1848 in Europe also quickly reached the United States where American Fourierists, for example, "immediately hailed [the Revolution] and followed its progress" (Guarneri 1991). These same Fourierists held mass meetings of support, made public speeches proclaiming the Revolution, and even traveled to France to see the Revolution and participate in person—clear indications of the ties that linked struggles around 1848 throughout the world in a common cluster.

Amid its world revolutionary implications, 1848 was also the year of the Seneca Falls Women's Rights Convention, identified today as the beginning of the women right's movement and a moment that "led to a transformation of consciousness and a movement of empowerment" (Lerner 1998, 35; see also DuBois 1999; Marilley 1996; Offen 1999). That Seneca Falls occurred in the same year as the "World Revolution" is no coincidence. Indeed, 1848 also welcomed a "radical international feminist movement" that flourished for roughly a decade (Anderson 1998; D'Itri 1999). Interestingly, the leadership of this international movement had connections to earlier antisystemic struggles. Parisian feminists came from a background of active participation in Saint-Simonian and Fourierist socialism (Anderson 1998), while in the United States, several participants of the convention were veterans of the Fourierist movement and/or had previously worked in antislavery struggles. Many of these early feminists or their children remained active in struggles throughout the period. These linkages seen with Seneca Falls—between Europe and the United States; between past (Saint-Simon, Fourier, socialism, antislavery), contemporary (1848 Revolution), and future struggles (in terms of leadership and as a historical centerpiece for women's rights movements)—provide an interesting instance of antisystemic activity visible as a movement cluster (see figure 2.1).

The year 1848 ended almost as quickly as it began. In the face of such hopeful signs of change, counterrevolution and repression quickly followed. Yet, in its aftermath alone the "antisystemicity" of 1848 had tremendous impact. The struggles of 1848 helped to lay a foundation for the formal, organized, and sustained movements to come. In the German Federation and France, for example, the 1848 revolutionary period marked a decisive turn in the road to an independent labor movement (Judt 1986; Kocka 1986), as indicated by numerous strikes and the formation of the General Workers' Brotherhood in Germany. Wallerstein (1991) argues that antisystemic movements made their forceful appearance after 1848, and in many ways, the actions of 1848 revolutionaries made that possible.

Figure 2.1: Stylized Movement Cluster: Seneca Falls

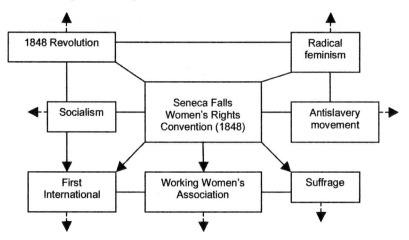

Note: Arrows convey movements arising later in time. Dashed arrows imply open ties to other movements.

As suggested previously, a marked increase in state power stands out as a clear consequence of the state's response to antisystemic struggles during 1848. This had a dramatic impact, whereby "the repression of revolutionary radicalism and the toughening of the existing state with bureaucratic and populist measures placed massive obstacles in the path of revolution" (Breuilly 2000: 128). As it were, systemic forces *gained* from the very struggles against the system—not in the least by placing revolution in unfavorable light as an unobtainable solution. In France, the imperial reaction also made unions illegal (changed only in 1884), resulting in a twenty-year gap in labor action (Judt 1986; Magraw 1989). Socialism, of course, did not disappear, although such activity became increasing difficult for some time. Yet, movements pushed the state here, resulting in, however unforeseen, the consolidation of power in increasingly centralized structures. This then marked the state as a necessary and attainable end (especially as the vote was increasingly extended),[8] a strategy of many movements for decades, if not forever. What stands out is a fundamental paradox of antisystemic activity—systemic structures, in this case the power of the state, *hardened* or made stronger by a seeming *softening* of that very power through the extension of the vote and other "benefits" to the laboring classes. It would seem that the closer state power approaches the core of movement objectives, the more tenuous any movement's antisystemic ambition becomes.

Indeed, the world-economic hegemon of the time, Great Britain, stands out as a model for other European regimes post-1848. In Great Britain, a well-coordinated and repressive state response was quick to quash agitation, taking to the streets to crush the Chartist-led mobilizations of 1848. There can be little doubt that the nature of British hegemony placed the state in a position of strength vis-à-vis such popular resistance, a situation not true in many places in Europe in 1848. Afterward and for some time, the "great mass movements ... like Chartism ... were dead. Socialism had disappeared from the country of its birth" (Hobsbawm 1969: 126). For Silver and Slater (1999), following the defeat of revolutionary possibilities after 1848, the high point of British hegemony and a concomitant systemwide expansion corresponded to a relatively low point in working-class activity. The apogee of British hegemony came at a time of closely connected repression in the core of the world-economy.

Repression did not last, however, and a sustained, organized form of antisystemic activity began to emerge by the close of this opening period. Following the relative quiet of the years after 1848 (a "long decade" of quiescence) and the reassertion of state power, the 1860s began to see the emergence and/or consolidation of some of the most significant antisystemic movements in history. Over roughly a decade, from the 1864 formation of the International Workingmen's Association (the First International or IWA), the 1860s foreshadowed the absolute surge in organized antisystemic activity and unrest that closed out the nineteenth century (1873–1896).

With the First International and the heralded Paris Commune in 1871, antisystemic forces again took center stage in critical attacks on the capitalist system. By 1870, the First International, Lause confides, "had united some of the most radically-minded militants of different industrial nations" (1993: 64)—providing a common forum and umbrella for followers of Fourier, Proudhon, Bakunin, Marx (Grebing 1985). The Paris Commune also brought together different strands of political opinion as well, with Blanquists, Proudhonists, and IWA Marxists among the Communards. As labor began increasingly to organize around this time, the IWA also provided an overarching ideology and ally for such struggles (while in the process also dividing the movement in many ways). The Paris Commune, a significant event if perhaps a "last hurrah" for revolutionary utopianism in Europe, was celebrated nationally and transnationally (Haupt 1986). Nationally, communes formed elsewhere in France in 1871—in Saint Étienne and Marseilles, for example. In late 1871, the transnational impact of the commune was seen in "the most public achievement of the IWA in the United States, a New York City demonstration of tens of thousands commemorating the Paris Commune" (Lause 1993). Such an event demonstrated the significance of *both* major antisystemic concerns at this time. In fact, the commune, despite its eventually violent overthrow and the severe repression that followed (five years of martial law and the First International outlawed), "became an idea, a profession of faith and a confirmation of a historical future"

(Haupt 1986: 28).[9] The commune was exceptional for the emergence of the working class as revolutionaries, while 1871 would not be the last time barricades went up in Paris.

Key industrial locations in the world-economy also began to see significant antisystemic formations at this time. The organizations that played a significant role in future struggles began to take shape after the quiet following 1848. Germany, for example, saw significant organizational activity. This is reflected in the formation of the German General Workers' Association in 1863 as well as the later formation of the Social Democratic Workers' Party and General Union of German Workers in 1869 (which split the labor movement).

The United States, meanwhile, entering, fighting, or emerging from Civil War for all of the 1860s, also saw workers begin to unite in movements against the exploitation and oppression of industrial capitalism. The years following the war began the consolidation of labor organizations, trade unions, and other radical associations in the United States—in which socialists, amongst others, played a substantial role (Shefter 1986; Kimmeldorf and Stepan-Norris 1992). In 1866, the National Labor Union (NLU) was launched in Baltimore to become the country's first major labor federation. The Working Women's Association formed in 1868, a "pioneering attempt" to link the sexual division of labor and class relations (DuBois 1999). By 1869, the NLU openly debated affiliation to the First International, an early radical internationalism on the part of U.S. labor.[10] That same year the Knights of Labor emerged with the stated purpose of abolishing the wage system in favor of producer cooperatives (Kimmeldorf and Stepan-Norris 1992). Here again, important pockets of resistance began to solidify into a concerted effort at radical change.

The discussion so far says little about activity outside the confines of Europe and the United States. In fact, an interesting cluster of such activity can be pointed to on the edges of empire in these relatively quiet years (see table 2.1); these efforts hang together in taking a nascent imperialism (often brought by British hegemony) and the often associated changes in land tenure and labor organization as targets for unrest. For example, British colonial India gave rise to the Indian Revolt of 1857 (Masselos 1985), an event hailed as the "First National War of Independence" (Chaudhuri 1957) or as a "primary resistance movement" (Stokes 1978). What began as a mutiny of Indian soldiers against British authority swelled into a larger peasant revolt against British presence and the land changes the British imposed—an event offering tantalizing early evidence of anti-imperialist struggle. This revolt, even though brutally suppressed by British forces, was still followed by India's Indigo Revolt or Blue Mutiny of 1859. Both events together marked imperial India as an important node of early resistance to British hegemony.

Elsewhere in the British Empire, Jamaica witnessed a long period of unrest that challenged the colonial status quo (Campbell 1987). Over 1863

Table 2.1: Early Anti-Imperial Movement Cluster: 1848–1873

Movement	Date	Location	Antagonist
Maori Wars	1845–1847	New Zealand	British
	1860–1866		
1857 revolt	1857	India	British
Blue Mutiny	1859	India	British
Morant Bay Rebellion	1865	Jamaica	British
Taiping/Nien rebellions	1850–1864	China	Dynastic rule allied with colonial powers
1868 rebellion/ Ten Years War	1868–1878	Cuba	Spanish and slavery
Indian Wars	1860–1890	United States	United States

and 1864, strikes erupted on the sugar estates protesting coercive labor policies in a "free" Jamaica. This and other unrest led up to the Morant Bay Rebellion in 1865 (see Holt 1992; Mintz 1974)—a direct expression of the grievances felt by the impoverished in colonial Jamaica. The revolt, led by Paul Bogle, presented a forceful "resistant response" to the British imposition of a plantation economy and colonialism in Jamaica. Here again, as in India and elsewhere at this time, movements with a strong agrarian base sought to resist changes to the land base imposed by imperial powers. Yet, this "war of the races" in the eyes of British interests (Holt 1992) was again viciously crushed, leading to more direct Crown Colony rule.[11]

The period 1848–1873 was also the time of China's Taiping Rebellion, an "antidynastic rebellion" (Feuerwerker 1975) with significant import in the history of China and movements there (see especially Yu-wen 1973). Stretching from 1850 to 1864, the Taiping Rebellion represented more than just rebellion, "for it was a revolutionary protest against many of the basic features of traditional Chinese society and government" (Gregory 1969: ix). Indeed, when combined with the Nien and other "lesser" rebellions (see Chiang 1954; Feuerwerker 1975), the Taiping Rebellion made China a particularly interesting locus of activity at this time.

Taking place upon the heels of the Opium Wars, a time when the "West" aggressively pursued empire in Asia, Taiping revealed as well the overlap of domestic and international factors in resistance. Britain, for instance, as well as France and the United States, all had serious designs on gaining a foothold in China.[12] To that end, Britain, for example, first courted Taiping, then maintained neutrality, only to eventually intervene in the conflict on the side of the Chinese state. Foreign troops (British and French) then played a small but important role in defending Shanghai from the Taiping Rebellion in 1860 and 1862 while also helping to regain cities captured.[13] For the British, intervention was a calculated move, an issue of "commercial advantage" and a "future market" for British goods (Gregory 1969). Jian confirms that "what the Taipings failed to recognize was the expedient character of the [initial] western neutrality, offshoot of an overall policy directed almost exclusively by the desire to protect and expand commercial privileges" (1973: 443). Thereby, the Taipings ended up in a struggle with the markings of an anti-imperialist campaign, where powers such as Great Britain entered civil war with the express interest of maintaining conditions most suitable for commercial expansion.

The year 1848 remains important outside the confines of Europe for other reasons as well—most notably the second abolition of slavery in the French empire. Under intense pressure from uprisings in Guadeloupe, Martinique, and elsewhere, the French were forced to abolish slavery. In the Danish Caribbean, similar pressures forced the governor to abolish slavery as well. Again, antisystemic forces act as motive agents in the course of world history. Later, in 1868 separatist rebellion also broke out in Cuba, initiating the Ten Years War on the island. Interestingly, this rebellion also took as its challenge colonial rule *and* the slave system in Cuba (Schmidt-Nowara 1998).[14] It also followed one month behind the September Revolution in metropole Spain, raising interesting suggestions of links across the Atlantic. Certainly, the collapse of the Spanish crown presented a political opportunity on the island.

Yet, at this historical juncture, the power of the state and an attendant empire to repress any and all uprisings remained tantamount. The Paris Commune, the most significant singular event near the crux of this opening stage, 1848–1873, was brutally repressed—thereby making most revolutionary activity simply impossible throughout Europe, including even the First International (Joll 1979). Following the revolutions of 1848, the expansion of the world-economy and British hegemony also meant the absolute repression of popular uprisings like Taiping, the 1857 revolt in India (Silver and Slater 1999), and Morant Bay in Jamaica. Consider as well the ongoing suppression of Native American resistance to westward expansion in the United States—a constant feature of these years leading into the early twentieth century. Indeed, the Indian Wars raged across the western United States from roughly 1860 to 1890, when the last bands of Chiricahua Apaches were captured and placed on reservation lands (see, especially, Brown 1970). However, this small cluster of early struggles points out the difficulty of empire, placing a burden on imperial bureaucracies and armies, or even *aims*, through such resistance. Clearly, such antisystemic efforts arose in challenge and response to the many conditions of empire, ongoing or newly imposed, testing the limits of capital early in this important time. Changes to land and labor introduced under imperialism were contested.

Striking Back at the Empire:
Antisystemic Movements at Century's End

The close of the nineteenth century, 1873–1896, is crucial to understanding the nature of movement activity and the limits of capitalism for the overall period (and even beyond 1917). Give or take a few years, the closing decades of the nineteenth century are targeted as the beginning or key period for any number of resistance efforts.[15] In Africa, for instance, following the partition by European powers, "resistance flared up almost everywhere in the late 1890s" (Lewis 1987: 69). Ongoing systemic interests certainly faced increasing pressure. As early as 1873, the region of Africa that would become Tanganyika experienced an explosive slave revolt that Glassman describes as "a conscious social movement, sparked by the efforts of the planter class to impose a new labor regime" (1995: 109). Indeed, the flight peaked at a moment of rapid plantation development in the region. Recalling earlier events in the 1857 and Indigo revolts, Great Britain in 1885 confronted concerted pressure with the formation of the Indian National Congress, the tentative beginnings of an organized nationalist movement (Masselos 1985).[16] The 1891 Tobacco Rebellion in Iran presented an early instance of mass resistance to state and allied foreign interests, in this case British and even Russian imperial involvement (Foran 1993). The year 1896 brought revolution in the Philippines against Spain, a "national struggle" that in 1899 became the United States–Philippines War (Schirmer and Shalom 1987). Anti-imperialism as well as a more general anticapitalism thus continued to drive a remarkable plethora of movements throughout the world-economy, placing a movement stamp on what transpired.

Anti-Imperialist Struggle and the Partition of Africa

Frank and Fuentes comment that "there seems to have been significant bunching or clustering of social movements" (1990: 144) at different points in history—with the 1890s and 1900s their relevant examples. Mirroring the history of labor/socialist struggles, the second half of the nineteenth century was also marked by a rise of peasant movements and revolts (Amin 1990a). As the capitalist rivals of the period turned their attention to the acquisition of empire and monopoly (the Berlin Conference of 1884–1885), these revolts would often acquire anticolonial, anticapitalist, and/or nationalist overtones.

When the "robber statesmen" of Europe (Rodney 1970) met for the Berlin Conference of 1884–1885, an entire continent came under the gaze of expansionist monopoly capitalism. The partition really consolidated a long-standing European intervention in Africa, introducing a period of direct and near-total colonization that immediately met with widespread resistance to the changes forcibly introduced. Lewis conveys the scope of this challenge. "In 1896, the Italians suffered the greatest of all nineteenth century European humiliations in Ethiopia. That same year and for much of the next, the Shona and Ndebele people of the Rhodesias erupted against British rule" (Lewis 1987: 72). Quite simply, resistance was found in all parts of the continent, and major eruptions—as significant as the Italian defeat or the Shona-Ndebele *chimurenga*, one of the "great dramas" of Rhodesian history (Ranger 1967)—were often concurrent events. Major moments such as these are easily identifiable acts of resistance with clear antisystemic implications.[17] Much as Great Britain had faced earlier in places like India and Jamaica, the pursuit of empire in Africa was highly contested. In the face of massive land grabs and new labor regimes, resistance again played an important role in shaping the process of change. The early years of the outright colonial era in Africa were thus filled with collective acts of anti-imperial resistance (see table 2.2).

Keeping in mind Cooper's assertion that "politics in a colony should not be reduced to anticolonial politics or to nationalism" (1994: 1519), the two decades or so before the century's end were a tumultuous time in Africa. They presented an immediate peak in such antisystemic activity as imperialist ambition stretched the capitalist powers. Africans were quick to resist (further) colonial incursion into the continent while also challenging concomitant efforts to impose new labor regimes and to enforce direct taxation through head and hut taxes. For example, in Central Africa what would be known as the Swahili War started in 1892. Lewis again relates, "The Swahili War in Central Africa was more than a Belgian nightmare. It also signaled to the British, French, Germans, and Italians that their own dreams of empire could be dashed by the volatile

Table 2.2: Select Resistance to European Partition of Africa, 1873–1898

Antisystemic Activity	Date	Location	Antagonist
Slave revolt	1873	Tanganyika	British labor regime
Ture-led rebellion	1882	West Africa	French/British
Battle of Dogali	1887	Ethiopia	Italians
Resistance to occupation	1888	Tanganyika	Germans
Swahili war	1892	Central Africa	Belgians
Ekumeku rebellion	1893	West Africa	British
Ndebele war	1893	Southern Africa	British
Ethiopian war	1896	Ethiopia	Italians
Shona-Ndebele *chimurenga*	1896	Rhodesia	British
Hut Tax rebellion	1898	Sierra Leone	British
Asante rebellion	1898	Gold Coast	British

reactions of the continent" (1987: 72). These challenges came at a time of increased great power rivalry when doubts of a fading British hegemony grew frequent and were formalized in the competitive struggle for empire. South Africa's Boer War around the turn of the century demonstrated this fact most clearly, as Great Britain deployed "scorched-earth" military might against an Afrikaner challenge to British intervention in the region (a precursor to the horrible tactics that emerged fully with World War I). Ultimately, the larger resistance seen throughout Africa was part of a process of "expansion, domination, and partition which had its roots in monopoly capital" (Rodney 1970: 105). Anti-imperial resistance worked its way into the story of empire, shaping the very process of expansion from its beginnings in Africa and elsewhere. Resistance was a near universal to the incursion of European empire in Africa.

Labor and Socialism at Century's End

Within a decade or so of 1873, a wide number of powerful labor/socialist movements, even parties, emerged in locations throughout the world-economy. Socialism was already a driving force behind much labor activity, and this only intensified—making the late nineteenth century (and the early twentieth) something of a heyday for radical, antisystemic labor. While factionalism helped to end the First International—a notable sort of negative internationalism that accompanies *any* positive ties and links[18]—in 1889 the Second International was formed, bringing together important antisystemic movements, most now organized as *nationally* based organizations. The "serious, national working-class parties and serious national trade-union federations" (Wallerstein 1990: 18) behind the new International enjoyed greater unity of purpose as aims and ideals began to coalesce. The organizations within the Second International were now sustained organizational efforts geared toward the realization of radical change *within* the confines of particular states. This distinction, in stark contrast to the First International, marks the particular movement trajectory realized herein—movements became named, nationally based organizations with large, sustaining memberships and hierarchical organizational structures.

Multiple locales tell a similar tale. After 1880 in France, Judt confirms, "Socialism was the organizational channel for many workers" (1986: 104). In the United States, "syndicalists and socialists were widespread and highly influential within major unions from the late nineteenth century until World War I" (Kimmeldorf and Stepan-Norris 1992: 498). American socialist Eugene Debs's American Railway Union was born in 1893, while socialists had a major voice in the Knights of Labor after 1890. Remarkably, many of these struggles were nonexistent or in their infancy at the beginning of the 1870s; over the course of the decades leading up to

World War I, labor would explode to become arguably *the* antisystemic movement of this time (Arrighi 1990).

The period 1873–1896 is truly remarkable for the level of union formation. Starting in 1888 until 1918, British trade unionism grew faster than at any other time in its history—from 750,000 members in 1888 to 6.5 million in 1918 (Davis 1993; Hobsbawm 1987). This rise of "new unionism" in England from the 1880s and 1890s was accompanied by "the growth of socialism, the foundation of the Labour Party [in 1900 as the Labour Representation Committee], the conversion of the working class from liberalism, and the demand for social reform" (Jones 1983: 181). Germany, meanwhile, in the late nineteenth century produced the largest, best-organized workers' movement in the world (Nolan 1986), and by 1914, had the world's largest socialist party (Geary 1989). In the United States, the American Federation of Labor (AFL), eventual foil to Debs's union and outlook and without question one of the most important labor organizations then and today, was founded in 1886.[19] The formation of the AFL stands as "a symbol of the resurgence of trade unionism across America" (Weir 1997). In France, the important anarcho-syndicalist Confédération Générale du Travail (CGT) got its start in 1895. Without doubt, the emergence of these sustained organizations with massive membership rolls, many still around in one way or another even today, marked a major shift in the trajectory and modalities of antisystemic movements. At this time, movement became movements—sustained, organized efforts bringing many people together to realize often-radical social change.

This late nineteenth century rise of labor as an antisystemic force was mirrored in a variety of additional locations. The 1890s saw the rise of a "new trade unionism" in Australia. Korzeniewicz describes the 1880s and 1890s in Argentina as a "transition period," where "after the late 1880s strikes, labor organizations, and formal contracts became regular features of capital-labor relations" (1989: 90). The year 1883 marked the beginning of the period that laid the base for Peru's modern labor movement (Blanchard 1982). Finally, significant labor struggles also occurred in colonial India during the 1890s. Basu (1998) provides detail on the militant protests of mill workers against the imposition of extended work hours and increased workloads in the mills around Calcutta. This collective action by Indian workers shows the increasing assertiveness (with serious nationalist overtones) of labor against colonial capital and authority (see also Chakrabarty 1981; Sarkar 1984).

Basu makes the connection between labor struggles and nationalist efforts quite clear as laborers pushed a new agenda on nationalist leaders (a situation that would become familiar in the decolonization struggles throughout Africa after World War II). A similar situation arose elsewhere at this time as nationalism appeared in 1890s Brazil when Brazilian Jacobins "united sectors of the urban, middle and working classes, and soldiers to fight the traditionally dominant latifundários for control of the government" (Topik 1978: 101). Hope for a republican revolution and an admitted ideological debt to the French Jacobins made the struggle of Brazil's Jacobins another of the many interesting movements and moments that took place in the two decades or so at century's end. This, taken together with the end of Brazilian slavery in 1888 helped in part "through massive flights from plantations in the 1880s" (Childs 1998: 728; see also Conrad 1972), unquestionably another form of labor resistance, made turn-of-the-century Brazil another world-economic locus of antisystemic activity.

Once organized into formal movements, a major weapon wielded by labor became the strike, and strikes occurred in waves from 1873 to 1896. Accompanying the sheer growth in unions, the frequency and scale of labor strikes by these movements reached unprecedented levels from the mid-1870s on (see table 2.3).[20] Of particular note, these surges or waves were most often led by the newly emerging labor organizations mentioned previously.

Alongside these more general waves, some of the most significant, symbolic moments of resistance also happened following 1873. In the United States, while labor struggled entering this middle phase, it quickly took world stage in a series of events over the following years. The year 1877 brought the Great Railway Strike, part of a larger burst of activity and "the first great collision between American capital and labor" (Meltzer 1967). This strike and the violent Pittsburgh strike of the same year would also draw considerable international attention, catching the eye of Kropotkin, for one, as an indicator of revolutionary potential in the United States (Cahm 1989).

Along these lines, 1886 brought Haymarket, perhaps the most famous, single antisystemic struggle and an event that inspired action then and since.[21] Haymarket, importantly, was part of a larger struggle, as the Federation of Organized Trades and Labor (founded in 1881 and later the American Federation of Labor) had called May 1—the first May

Table 2.3: Strike Waves under Industrialization, 1873–1896

Location	Strike Wave Years (heightened unrest)
France	1893 (1879–1880)
Germany	1888–1889 (1883–1889)
Great Britain	1888–1892 (1889 Dock Strike)
Sweden	1890–1891
United States	1886–1887, 1894 (1880s)

Sources: Edwards 1981; Shefter 1986; Magraw 1989; Shorter and Tilly 1974; Phillips 1989; Hobsbawm 1987; Nolan 1986; Ahn 1996.

Day—as the deadline for the implementation of eight-hour legislation. In the trial and execution of four of the eight Haymarket "anarchists" that followed the violent confrontation, this event took on a magnitude that electrified antisystemic struggle around the world. Anarchists in Spain, for example, enduring a period of severe repression, attached revolutionary significance to Haymarket, May Day, even the eight-hour struggle (Esenwein 1989). Several years later, the strike against Pullman in 1894, "one of the most important labor disputes at the end of the nineteenth century" (Edwards 1981: 122), again demonstrated the marked divide splitting a confrontational labor force and capital. A significant factor uniting these strikes and others like 1892's Homestead was the sheer, highly repressive violence wrought against laborers by capital, even a "benevolent" Pullman, and an allied state, escalating the confrontation between them and workers at this critical time.

The years 1873–1896 thus represent a relative peak of some of the most significant antisystemic activity in history—this time in the emergence of massive, sustained labor/socialist struggles primarily (but not exclusively) in the core. Described as the "Great Upheaval" for the scope of the challenge to the power structures of the time (Weir 1997),[22] the struggles of labor/socialist movements peaked here alongside the emerging resistance efforts of those coming under imperial advance. Imperialism and capitalism were intimately related here, and this transitional period provided opportunity for existing movements to strengthen and new movements to rise.

Anarchism at Century's End: Antisystemic Internationalism

Alongside the movements already discussed, and at times indiscernible from them, anarchism presents a particularly interesting example of the clustering of antisystemic activity during the heart of this periodization. Associated with some of the most important names of the nineteenth century—Proudhoun, Bakunin, and Kropotkin—anarchism was a product of their thought and times (Joll 1979) and emerged as a serious political force in the late 1860s and early 1870s.[23] Anarchism played a prominent role behind antisystemic movements all over the Americas and Europe across the whole 1848–1917 period, particularly in the critical decades of the 1880s and 1890s. The famous split between Bakunin and Marx, representing a schism of theory and practice between anarchism and socialism in general, helped precipitate the end of the First International (Joll 1979; see also Hunter 1969; Thomas 1980) and divided proponents of each everywhere. Anarchists traveled, too, bringing their ideas and methods with them and making such emigration a vector for the spread of anarchism. The cluster nature of anarchism is visible in the ties (complementary and competitive) between its founders and other important antisystemic figures, as well as in the migration that brought anarchism to disparate areas of the world-system as this time.

In Europe, Italy and Spain are most often noted for the prominence of anarchism and anarchists. These two countries, starting around the early 1870s, saw anarchists most active in fomenting revolution. It was in these two countries that the anarchist credo "propaganda by deed" was put into (often violent) action.[24] In Spain, especially from the September Revolution of 1868, anarchism remained a revolutionary force for decades (Esenwein 1989). For example, in a time of widespread insurrection around the 1873 abdication of the Spanish king, anarchists in Andalusia initiated militant strikes (Cahm 1989; Esenwein 1989; Hunter 1969)—contributing to several years of revolutionary turmoil in the country. Anarchists also helped form the Federación Regional Española in 1870 and its successor the Federación de Trabajadores de la Región Española in 1881, both attached to the International (Esenwein 1989). At the same time, circa 1873, Italy was marked by a massive series of strikes, and the Italian state "appeared on the brink of collapse" (Levy 1999). Here again, the International emerged, led by Italian anarchists who assumed leadership of numerous unions and were active in the Socialist Party. Overlapping the next movement phase, 1896–1917, "the influence of the great anarchist Errico Malatesta in the crisis of 1898 and the Red Week of 1914 best illustrates how the anarchists were at the epicenter of protest waves that unsettled Italy until the Great War" (Levy 1999: 11).

As suggested earlier, anarchists traveled and so did the movement, clustering struggles throughout the world-system. Such migration—back and forth across Europe, the Atlantic, and elsewhere—reflected much larger, mass migrations that served to link peoples around the world at this time on a level never before seen. Spain, at the center of another exemplary movement "cluster" as illustrated in figure 2.2, was targeted early by Bakunin's followers in the International, who crossed into Spain after the September Revolution and were immediately influential (Esenwein 1989).

Under the waves of repression that followed, many Spanish anarchists then emigrated (by choice or force) to places like Mexico, adding impetus to the anarchist movement there (Hart 1978; Wolf 1969). Mexican anarchists, combining foreign and indigenous sources, then went on to play an important role in the Mexican Revolution, with the anarchist Ricardo Flores Magón widely considered the "intellectual author" of the revolution (Hodges 1995).

Elsewhere in Latin America, "in Argentina, Chile, and Brazil, Spanish and Italian workers introduced anarcho-syndicalism into the early trade unions" (Urrutia 1969: 55). The Italian anarchist Pietro Gori added serious support to the anarchist movement in Argentina, where in 1896 these same anarchists played a major role in organizing railroad workers (Thompson 1984). Additionally, anarchist thought played a role in the rise of "revolutionary terrorism" in Bengal, India, at the turn of the century, where militant nationalists had direct ties to European anarchists (Heehs 1994). Finally, Dirlik demonstrates the many ways in which "anarchism was to play a central part in articulating an emerging social radicalism in the Chinese Revolution" (1991: 10). Through the World Society, established in Paris in 1906, and the Society for the Study of Socialism, started in Tokyo in 1907, Chinese and European anarchists began a dialogue, bringing anarchist thought to bear on the revolution.

In the United States, anarchists from Europe were also prominent and influential. For example, the French radical Victor Drury, "a committed anarchist," helped mold the vision of the Knights of Labor (Weir 1997). In 1882, Johann Most also brought anarchist thought to the United States (Hunter 1969). Emigration played such a role that "during these years [1880s–1890s] the anarchist movement in the United States was almost entirely a foreign one; and it was in German, Russian, Italian or Yiddish that the famous agitators made their speeches" (Joll 1979: 123). A prominent example, anarchism played a crucial role in linking movements into diffuse clusters at the end of the nineteenth century (see figure 2.2), helping to make 1873–1896 a critical juncture for antisystemic activity. In fact, anarchism's tale of emigration by choice and by force reflects a much larger history of the movement of peoples seen in the world at this time. Immigration pushed the working class all over the world, and the movement of radicalism directly parallels this larger movement of people. Such a mass movement of people, as it has accelerated in scale and/or pace over time, makes it again impossible to think of movements like anarchism in terms of historical singularities. Certainly, at this time

Figure 2.2: Stylized Movement Cluster: Spanish Anarchism, circa 1868

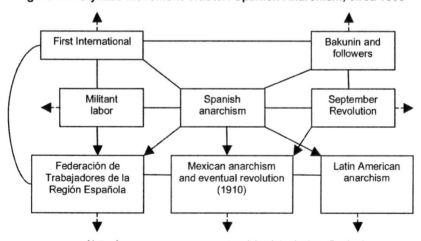

Note: Arrows convey movements arising later in time. Dashed arrows imply open ties to other movements.

unlike any other before, antisystemic struggle became organized into sustained movements with millions of people from all over the world coming together bent on social change.

Antisystemic Movements Approaching 1917: Revolution

The years 1896–1917 present a period, culminating in the Russian Revolution, in which the movement trends of previous decades came to fruition. Historic connections are readily made between the Mexican Revolution, for example, and the prior decades of nationalism, agrarian movements, and anarchist influence in Mexico (Garza 1979; Hart 1978; Mallon 1995).[25] Most notably, the years 1896–1917 were a tumultuous period of revolution, something numerous movements had long advocated and finally began to attempt and to achieve. With China's Boxer Rebellion in 1900, revolution in Russia in 1905, Iran in 1906, the Ottoman Empire in 1908, Mexico in 1910, Russia again in 1917, even the beginnings of revolution again in China in 1911, the close of 1848–1917 brings a key cluster of revolt, pulling antisystemic movements into contests for and even control of the state. For instance, the Boxer Rebellion, rooted in decades of resistance to increased Western influence, "shook the world" when the "anti-Christian, anti-missionary, and anti-foreign" Boxers openly challenged a widening imperial presence in China at the turn of the century (Preston 1999, 2000a, 2000b). The Boxers' attack on foreign presence and exploitation opened a tumultuous period at the beginning of the twentieth century. This chain of revolutions "marked a new stage in the history of the developing world and brought several competing ideologies—nationalism, democracy, religion, and socialism—into open confrontation" (Afary 1994: 21). These revolutions on the "periphery" of the capitalist world-economy (Foran 1991, 1993, 1993a), as well as constitutionalist struggles (Sohrabi 1995), won important concessions and helped overthrow dictatorial regimes—marking movement accomplishments and indicators of their growth over the course of 1848–1917.

Nearly bookending this critical juncture, Russia in 1905 and 1917 carried symbolic and inspirational weight for movements around the world. In Russia, the 1905 revolution had an especially

> strong impact on Iran, the Ottoman Empire, and China, as well as on the "Extremists" of the budding Indian nationalist movement. It created an effervescent atmosphere, in which the overthrow of autocracy or of an imperial overlord came into the realm of possibility.... By stimulating the struggle against foreign intervention and control, tolerated by decadent autocratic regimes, it helped pave the way for the rise and intensification of nationalism and anti-colonialism in Asia. (Spector 1962: 111–12)

Yet again, the import of antisystemic action as a world-scale cluster is notable. Revolution in Russia became a motivating example for a variety of movements, "a hallowed model of how revolutions were made and guided toward a successful conclusion" (Wolf 1969: 98). Driven by antisystemic forces, these many revolutions toppled old regimes, won significant concessions, and brought new movements to power.

Here, only a few brief comments on Russia of 1905–1917 are in order. Aided by humiliating defeat to Japan, the remarkable events in Russia that led to revolutions in 1905 and later in 1917 point to the nature of antisystemic activity at the close of the period. Both revolutions had roots in the same regime crisis and the same "intellectual tradition" (Perrie 2000), most notably in this case, competing variants of Marxist thought applied to the Russian context. In both revolutions as well, workers played a crucial role. Tilly perhaps best identifies the sum of factors at work:

> The war and revolution of 1904–6 marked the limits of Russian imperial expansion, exposed the vulnerability of the czarist state, established workers as major political actors, introduced the Soviet as a form of revolutionary government, publicized the general strike as an effective means of popular anti-state action, identified Bolsheviks, Mensheviks and Social Revolutionaries as credible challengers to the existing power. (1993: 216)

The year 1917 realized many of the conditions set forth in 1905, while the Revolution, in tandem with others at the time, highlighted the emergent antisystemic movements' ability to affect social change. Lenin "advocated civil war as a means to the establishment of socialism ... [and] justified the use of revolutionary terror against his opponents" (Perrie 2000: 166), one particular means to an end exemplified in Russia.

Russia of 1905 also had connections to the revolutions in the Ottoman Empire and Iran, pulling these struggles immediately together (see also Sohrabi 1995). In both cases, the victory of Japan over Russia in 1905 gave emerging revolutionary groups hope, serving as inspiration and model for their own causes (Foran 1991, 1993). The defeat, coupled with Russia's own revolution, made change appear possible through open confrontation. First, in Iran a broad-based alliance of class interests openly challenged the king and, through a series of often-violent demonstrations, eventually forced concessions and won a national assembly in 1906.[26] Despite a conservative backlash in a few short years (aided by czarist Russia's intervention in 1911), the revolution's consequences cannot go without note. After the revolution, "political life assumed a level of freedom unseen until then in the Middle East, with a proliferation of parties, clubs, newspapers, and popular expressions of resistance to the state and foreign capital in Iran" (Foran 1991: 795). Meanwhile, the 1908 Young Turk Revolution in the Ottoman Empire, while more of a "revolution from above," had similar consequences for the Ottomans. While the organizers of the important Committee of Union and Progress quickly consolidated their hold on the country, the revolution took a radical turn during World War I, eventually resulting in Ataturk's war of national liberation (Foran 1993). In *both* instances, these early revolutions mounted serious challenges to the old order.

The Mexican Revolution, a significant event in its own right (see especially Womack 1968; also Goldfrank 1979; Wolf 1969), brings the anarchist struggles of the previous period into further consideration. In 1900, the first general strike was staged in Mexico, marking the beginnings of modern syndicalism (Hart 1978), while the anarchist *Partido Liberal Mexicano* (PLM) was founded by Flores in 1905 (from exile in St. Louis, Missouri). The PLM almost immediately called for armed struggle against Porforio Diaz. Shortly after the start of the Revolution, the PLM's program of 1911 "called for a war to the death against private property, political authority, and the established church" (Hodges 1995: 11). Flores and the PLM worked closely with Emiliano Zapata in the south, and provided a radical current to the overall complexity of the revolutionary situation. At the beginning of the twentieth century, rural unrest and political instability combined with critical movements like anarchism to begin a revolutionary process that eventually overthrew Diaz and won a new constitution.

The Mexican Revolution again demonstrates the interesting, transnational overlap or clustering of aims found in movement activity. In the Sonora region of Mexico in 1910 and 1911, Gonzales writes, "Copper miners helped put workers' grievances against capital on the national revolutionary agenda, pressured local Maderista leaders to take up arms against Victoriano Huerta, and supported the Constitutionalists' nationalist campaign against the privileged position of foreign interests" (1996: 505). The miners' struggle was first launched at Cananea in 1907 against a U.S. mining multinational (predating the revolution), yet the grievances quickly merged with larger revolutionary aims.[27] Defending the U.S. mining operation, armed Americans, a group of Arizona Rangers, entered Mexico to suppress the strike. On the side of the miners, the Industrial Workers of the World (IWW or the Wobblies) sent representatives to Sonora. These allied sides present the starkest picture of systemic forces and antisystemic resistance as they emerged and consolidated over the course of the years 1848–1917.

Interlude: Labor and . . .

Mention of the Industrial Workers of the World merits a brief sidebar to highlight the ongoing resistance posed by aspects of organized labor and socialism during this final phase of the period 1848–1917. Indeed, the Wobblies were a prominent part of this final phase, founded in 1905 with the express aim of organizing the unorganized into "one big union" (Joll 1979; see also Dubofsky 1988). Bringing together anarchists, socialists, and other labor leaders, the IWW looked to build a "revolutionary industrial unionism" and abolish the system (Conlin 1969)[28]—notably, as a calculated objection to the strategies of the reformist AFL. As indicated by the Mexican case, the IWW, particularly "Big Bill" Heywood, was actively involved in transnational labor struggles that placed the IWW within often overlapping clusters of movement activity.

Elsewhere, radical labor movements continued to appear where they previously had not been or had been seriously repressed. In 1911, Spanish workers organized into the Confederación Nacional de Trabajo, continuing the anarchist tradition of previous decades (although in a syndicalist guise) (Joll 1979). In Costa Rica, the Marxist Confederación General de Trabajadores formed in 1913, and a new "working class insurgency began to initiate changes in existing state structures and class relations" (Hytrek 1999: 45). Shortly thereafter in 1914, a nascent Bolivian labor movement had its first significant Marxist group, the Centro Obrero de Estudios Sociales (Lora 1977). Interestingly, many of Bolivia's early labor leaders were returned emigrants from countries like Chile and Argentina, where they were influenced by the Marxist and anarchist labor struggles discussed earlier—thereby echoing again the thread provided by migration for radical connections between movement locales.

Certainly, strike activity remained important during the close of the period, often led by the emerging movements discussed here.[29] France's anarcho-syndicalist CGT staged a major general strike in 1906. Peru's historic first general strike, hailed as "a tremendous success" (Blanchard 1982), came in 1911. In the United States, the Lawrence Strike, what Meltzer (1991) calls an "industrial revolt" led in large part by the IWW, took place in 1912. In 1907, Argentina saw its first national strike where again anarchists were among the participating activists (Thompson 1984). Adelman (1993), studying port workers, in fact, describes 1910 as a turning point for Argentine labor struggles; the strikes that came in 1911–1912 initiated a new pattern of class struggle in which workers openly challenged employers and pushed a socialist agenda.

Anticolonial, Nationalist, Pan-African Movements Approaching the Russian Revolution

As if revolution and ongoing labor militancy were not enough, the early twentieth century also saw the continued clustering of anticolonial/ imperialist resistance in Africa. The tremendous Maji Maji Rebellion began in 1905 in Tanganyika to protest forced labor, taxation, general oppression and ultimately aimed to expel the Germans from the region (Boahen

1987; Iliffe 1979; Sunseri 1995). In southern Africa, 1904 and 1906 saw the Herero Revolt of South West Africa and the Bambata Rebellion of South Africa, respectively. Meanwhile, from 1907 to 1912, brothers Kabongo and Kasongo Nyembo led an armed resistance against the wage labor demands of the territorial administration of the Belgian Congo (Higginson 1989). In 1915 there was the Chilembwe uprising in Nyasaland, a struggle led by an American-educated African to protest poor treatment and wage policies on coffee plantations in the region (James 1969). On a somewhat different note, but important as well, the African National Congress (ANC) of South Africa had its start in 1912, ushering in an era of anticolonial nationalism in that country that would last the rest of the twentieth century.[30]

These years are significant for another, related reason—the rise of Pan-Africanism in the pantheon of (institutionalized) antisystemic movements as the first Pan-African Congress was held in London in 1900. Organized by H. Sylvester Williams, this first of many such congresses in the twentieth century "grew out of the response of Africans to their oppression and served as a coordinating point for the different struggles which were going on among blacks" (Campbell 1987: 51). Looking at the perceived source of this oppression, a Pan-Africanist leader such as W.E.B. Du Bois is described as being "anti-capitalist long before he was socialist" (Moses 1978: 130). The rise of Pan-Africanism and a continued resistance to the impositions of colonialism (labor demands, coercion, taxation, etc.) contribute to make the close of the period 1848–1917 a significant time.

And Reform: Trajectories, Outcomes, and Modalities in Movement Activity, 1848–1917

The Russian Revolution in 1917, while obviously to some extent an arbitrary breaking point for this discussion, does represent a culmination for movement activity of this time (and really since); with the revolution, antisystemic forces gained *state* power, ushering in a new era for such struggle. The weapons of resistance developed in the previous decades, such as organized labor and its mass industrial strikes, radical political organizations and considered intellectual traditions, and violent revolts, were serious factors in this revolutionary period (Tilly 1993; Wolf 1969). Where states were perhaps weaker and more open to radical overthrow, antisystemic struggle had accomplished what movements circa 1848 could not—sustained control of the state through revolutionary means. The impressive cluster of revolutions that closed the period 1848–1917—China, Russia, Iran, the Ottoman Empire, Mexico—occurred on the margins of the world-system. Yet, they demonstrated the revolutionary potential of antisystemic activity in the periphery and perhaps, as powerful industrialists and their political allies feared, in much of the core as well.

While beginning the period under serious repression or even non-existent repression, many antisystemic movements by 1917 took center stage in states and in an increasingly consolidated (and modern) interstate system—wittingly and unwittingly contributing to that very consolidation. Looking to the future, Soviet Russia then provided an ongoing alternative vision and resources, even an example in the Revolution, for other movements seeking power. As Perrie concludes, the October Revolution "was to cast as long a shadow over the history of the twentieth century as the French Revolution had over the nineteenth" (2000: 168). Elsewhere, movements were now seen as real threats, often forcing a reticent recognition by powerful states and their leaders who chose reform over the revolutionary possibilities that seemed more real than ever before.

In 1848, it is difficult, if not impossible, to talk of antisystemic struggles as *movements* in the conventional sense. By the close of 1917, it is simply impossible to talk of real movements or even revolutions in isolation from each other. The many antisystemic struggles, as they became organized and sustained efforts to realize change, began to accumulate and coalesce around common causes. Linkages and connections between movements become easier to note and impossible to ignore over the course of the years 1848–1917. The complexity of the movement "clusters" I have suggested here increases over time. By the time one considers the cluster around Spanish anarchism, for example (figure 2.2), the linkages become almost overwhelming. More so than ever before, movement actors exemplified by (but not limited to) important anarchist figures like Pietro Gori, Victor Drury, and Johann Most began moving all around the world, taking their radical, antisystemic ideas with them. Mass migration pushed millions of people beyond these leaders around the world, linking laborers, radical nationalists, and others. Major international organizations like the Second International brought together disparate national organizations where they cooperated and sometimes competed with each other. In fact, the many labor, socialist, anarchist, and other organizations that composed the Second International did not even exist before the 1848–1917 period. Once impossible and now common, such movement linkages increasingly troubled the centers of capitalism from 1848 to 1917.

In another sense, the Russian Revolution, alongside other revolutions and rebellions at the beginning of the twentieth century, represents one particular strategy of overthrowing the system (violently if and when necessary). Reform, work within the system, represents another tactic readily apparent in movements throughout the world-economy alongside (and often directly counter to) the revolutionary impulse. Avoiding a crass dualism (neither are absolutes) that oversimplifies a greater complexity,[31] some important observations need to be made.

Leading up to World War I and the Russian Revolution of 1917, movements for the first time became parties in numerous places throughout the world-system, often choosing reformism as a viable option to advance their ends. Where they did not become parties, movement activity was often normalized and routinized as a regular feature of the ongoing operations of capitalism.[32] Unions, for example, outlawed or simply impossible in many locations throughout the world-economy at the beginning of the period, by the end rose throughout the world-economy, gaining massive memberships and important political-economic roles. This denotes as well the creation of massive, formal, and sustained organizations—of a wide variety of political persuasions[33]—that became an irrevocable part of the social, economic, and political landscape of the centers of capitalism and outward from there during the late nineteenth century forward. Organizations became a major (but not the only) vehicle by which people sought collectively to impact change, by contesting state power and challenging capital's many demands. This routinized participation in the processes of the state served as a control over unrest from this time forward. By 1917, this more reformist, participatory trajectory grew quite common across core regions of the world.

Examples of political parties and political participation as a movement strategy certainly abound: in 1901, the Socialist Party of America formed, and its leader, unionist Eugene Debs, ran for president five times in the opening decades of the twentieth century. More notable still, Great Britain's Labour Representation Committee, renamed the Labour Party in 1906, was almost immediately a major force in British politics (Jones 1983) and has had obvious "success" since. Germany's Social Democratic Party, formed in 1875, was the largest party in Germany by 1914 (Geary 1989). Australia's own Labour Party won its first majority in Parliament in 1910 and held it until World War II (Bosch 1997).

This move to a "reformist parliamentary socialism" (Davis 1993), in Great Britain and Australia (or some variety of it elsewhere), raises serious questions, I believe, about the antisystemic nature of the movements (as parties) after such reformist choices were made. I also believe this marks the earliest beginnings of the "trajectory of decline" visible in labor/socialism's radical potential in many locales. By the time of World War I, for example, many labor movements endorsed and aided the war effort, thereby aligning with the state (if not already *in* state power).[34] World War I at the close of this period was perhaps most notable for dampening the rising tide of unrest as movements came under the thrall of the state. In a Europe at war in 1914, class struggle dropped to levels not seen in many years; by 1917, the same situation existed in the United States as it entered the war. Eugene Debs captured the essence of the war's impact and scope, in words that ring true even today: "Wars throughout history have been waged for conquest and plunder ... And that is war in a nutshell. The master class has always declared the wars, the subject class has always fought the battles" (quoted in Zinn 1995: 358). The fervor of patriotism was difficult for a number of important antisystemic movements here. The IWW, for example, was decimated by a suppressive state during World War I and never recovered. During the war, the Second International and anarchism faced difficult challenges, so that by 1917 these global movements had also collapsed.

Without question, total war meant a changing social and political landscape on a *global* scale at the close of the period 1848–1917. As many antisystemic movements were defeated and compromised at home, the war mobilization effort throughout the empires of Europe changed the consciousness of a generation of Africans and Asians. Almost paradoxically, these colonial subjects, aiding in the war effort of the imperial powers, later provided the first foundations for the anticolonial/nationalist movements of the next period.[35] As one antisystemic trajectory diminished, another one grew.

Perhaps most interesting, the very conditions for even being able to work from within the state or wanting to do so (attaining the vote, holding the state accountable, seeing the state as a goal, etc.) were put into motion by the very activities of the antisystemic movements; this includes the failures of revolutionary possibilities in 1848 (where full enfranchisement was a hesitant initial outcome) as well as the later Paris Commune. The Boxer Rebellion even precipitated reforms that provided the basis for the modern Chinese state (Preston 2000a) while also serving as an earlier ideal for later revolution in China (Cohen 1997). Joll remarks on this change, first put in motion by the movements, where "by the end of the century the legal and constitutional machinery for obtaining social reform was more efficient than it had been at any time since the industrial revolution" (1979: 126). Taylor also confirms that "opening up the future to political contest led to new tools of resistance" (1997: 7). Critically, movement activity had changed the state, forcing open the doors to the halls of power in ways quite impossible in 1848. In return, the nature of state power changed as well, *broadening* to include more voices at the same time the possibilities for truly radical change *narrowed*.

In locations throughout the world-economy where movements and their members gained a regularized political role (a stake in the system, so to speak), many saw these new options as one road to social change. Almost paradoxically, the movements' many challenges pushed the political and economic formations that emerged and in turn later eroded much antisystemic potential. Where such options were not available, "in those countries where laborers found themselves most frustrated by the parliamentarianism of social democracy at the end of the nineteenth century [throughout Latin America, the Iberian Peninsula, Italy]" (Hart 1978: 10), anarchism and more broadly revolution stood out as prominent options. Reform versus revolution, while too simple and risky a dichotomy (prone to making anarchism or revolution, for example, a "less-evolved" form of social protest), does, however, capture something of the essence of movement activity as it progressed across the period 1848–1917. In both cases, a shift toward the state and the movements behind it made states *the* sight of contestation and antisystemic activity, regardless of the means used. Antisystemic movements increasingly took on state-based organizational identities by the close of the period in question—recognizable in the diversity of the national organizations within the Second International. Movements had institutional names, many still recognizable today (see table 2.4).

Here again, by the end of the overall period, the movements realized the possibilities and limits set forth before them and by them. An increasingly consolidated, modern interstate system resulted, pushed, and developed in no uncertain terms by the movements themselves. In this sense, the world in 1917 was markedly different from the world in 1848. The rise of imperial capitalism occurred across the period 1848–1917, tempered by rising anti-imperial and nationalist struggles in Africa, Asia, and elsewhere. The cluster of anti-imperial resistance in Africa after partition kept European colonial ambitions in check; in Ethiopia, resistance denied such ambition altogether. At every turn, antisystemic movements, old and new, challenged the spread of capitalism. Anti-imperialist struggles in India and throughout the sprawling empire also demonstrated cracks in the edifice of British hegemony unimaginable in 1848.

Yet, alongside this ascent of movements into political power, best epitomized by labor movements and socialism in much of the industrialized core, another strand of movement activity was also beginning to emerge. Certain advantaged movements gained political power, through reform or revolution, and began a rise to an apogee of influence realized by the mid-twentieth century at the very same time that anti-imperial and/or nationalist resistance also began its road toward prominence (reached again after World War II). Later, these very same "movements

Table 2.4: Select Organizations Formed 1848–1917, Recognizable in Name

Movement	Year of Origin
Trades Union Congress (Great Britain)	1868
Indian National Congress (India)	1885
American Federation of Labor (United States)	1886
Unión General de Trabajadores (Spain)	1888
Labour Party (Australia)	1891
Confédération Générale du Travail (France)	1895
Labour Party (Great Britain)	1900
African National Congress (South Africa)	1912

turned parties" often confronted antisystemic movements pushing for the end of imperialism around the globe. Often, this anti-imperial resistance came in the form of spontaneous uprisings quite unlike the sustained movements emerging. This places importance on an attention to such activity as well, often harder to glean from history but no less crucial to any understanding (Cooper 1994; Phimister and Van Onselen 1997).

Conclusion

Many differing strands of resistance, an increasingly ensconced and reformist labor and socialism in much of the industrialized core, and an early anti-imperialism/nationalism in much of the colonized world were part of the same process (Wallerstein 1990), resisting and shaping the different forms of labor and broader social control that an expanding capitalism and its attendant capitalist class hoped to assert. There is no doubt that movements at this critical historical juncture, even within the more trying years of economic downturn before the end of the nineteenth century, placed significant, new burdens and alternate agendas upon the forces of capitalism. Labor struggles, coming together into unions and resisting oppressive working conditions, forever changed the landscape of the capitalist world-economy. Anarchism directly challenged state and capital, often meeting state violence in kind. Revolution, seen throughout the world at the opening of the twentieth century, overthrew autocratic regimes and brought antisystemic movements to power. Anti-imperial efforts made the process of imperial expansion difficult from the very beginning, testing the will of the imperialists in their efforts to extract wealth and implement a variety of capitalist labor regimes in colonies new and old. In short, capitalism and imperialism were intimately connected in the years assessed here (Rodney 1970, 1972; Williams 1944), and the variety of antisystemic struggles at this time reflect as well as ensure this fact.

By the end of the period discussed here, it is possible to speak of important movement "clusters" rather easily. The examples highlighted here include a diverse array of struggles around women's rights (Seneca Falls) and in 1848 across much of the "core," anti-imperialism in colonial locales as far apart as India and Jamaica, as well as the critical conjuncture of "peripheral" revolutions that opened the twentieth century. Linked by increasing migration, anarchists challenged capital in Europe, the Americas, and elsewhere beginning in the critical middle decades of 1848–1917. Exemplified by Haymarket (and a host of other major antisystemic actions), the apogee period of the "Great Upheaval" just prior to the turn of the nineteenth century also linked labor/socialist struggles in North America and around the world. The Paris Commune near the opening of the period here exposed the revolutionary potential of laborers for a host of other radical movements then and ever since. This idea, that movements cannot be understood in isolation, stands in stark contrast to much literature on social movements (see Skocpol 1979 and especially Ragin 1987). Looking through the prism of world history, antisystemic activity became antisystemic movements at this time, intricately linked through the increasingly rapid spread of ideas, leaders, and laborers, and pushed by the omnipresent growth of historical capitalism. These increasingly dense "clusters" played a critical role in shaping the world-economy and the interstate system at this time.

In an apparent paradox, the rise of working-class movements, whose labor drove the factories of the metropole, played no small role in the ability of relatively young European states to pursue imperial expansion.[36] Indeed, labor power fueled the advances that in turn went into steamships and improved European firepower—two technological factors that aided European expansion (Headrick 1979). Likewise, this imperial expansion helped fuel this particular era of capitalist accumulation. Often in response to movement challenges, new modes of labor control and systems of domination sprang up throughout the capitalist world. In turn, anti-imperial/proto-nationalist movements clearly pushed the limits of the capitalist system from the other direction—visible around the world at this time. More to the point (and more eloquently) "'evolving capitalism' is an empirical process rooted in a developing nexus between state structures, capitalists, and subordinate classes … the category 'world market' is a profoundly historical category embedded in states and class relations but not analytically excluded by—or secondary to—them" (McMichael 1987: 224). The antisystemic struggles of 1848–1917 elucidate this dynamic dialectic, resisting an "evolving capitalism" while ultimately shaping the very outlines of a selfsame capitalism. The paradox of power captured many movements from 1848 to 1917, and such a paradox shapes movement activity even still.

Notes

1. Frame (1995), for example, has compiled an absolutely daunting bibliography of works in English (only!) concerning the Russian Revolution. See as well, Breuilly 2000; Perrie 2000; Price 1996; Tilly 1993; Tilly, Tilly, and Tilly 1975; Trotsky 1959; Wolf 1969.

2. Wallerstein (1991) explains antisystemic movements as the third and final post-1789 "institutional innovation," one that fully emerges after 1848 (see also Taylor 1997). Arrighi, Hopkins, and Wallerstein (1989) in turn target "late-nineteenth and early-twentieth century Europe" for the emergence of historically powerful antisystemic movements that shape their very understanding.

3. Prior work, in different ways, has treated the notion of surges or waves in antisystemic activity and the underlying causes for such escalation. In many ways, these accounts lend further support for the stylized division of 1848–1917 into three

shorter periods. Arrighi (1990), assessing 150 years of labor/socialist activity, anchors his argument in three periods based on Kondratieff waves. Of particular interest, his first period begins in 1848 and ends in 1896, overlapping nicely with the period of concern here. For Arrighi, the modern labor movement ascends to the apogee of its power during the B-phase Great Depression years (1873–1896). A complementary argument can be found in recent work by Silver and Slater (1999) and Taylor (1997), both of whom pay particular attention to hegemony, notably the beginning of the decline of British hegemony around 1873, as an explanatory factor in antisystemic activity (see also Hopkins 1990).

4. A central question remains: what is antisystemic for this time? Clearly, movements that (1) challenge capital's absolute control of labor and the conditions of work, (2) question capitalism as the very mode for organizing society, as well as (3) challenge the spread and maintenance of power.

5. Skocpol and Trimberger here suggest that "all revolutions during the evolution of world capitalism have given rise to more bureaucratized and centralized states" (1978: 132; see also Skocpol 1979). The year 1848 seems to fit such a prescription— which also nicely places struggle at the center of such world-economic processes. This, of course, also fits nicely with Skocpol's attentiveness to the state's import in revolutionary processes.

6. Marx's *Eighteenth Brumaire of Louis Bonaparte* (1984 [1852]), for example, brings this point to vivid life as the French proletariat is crushed in the name of state and society.

7. Following 1968, for example, the "new social movement" strategy of not targeting state power as an objective presents a turn away from the trajectory movements laid out over the course of 1848–1917. It is notable that such a change comes fifty years or more after the movements discussed herein. Likewise, this "new" strategy does not make sense without reference to the struggles that emerged over the period 1848–1917.

8. The Reform Act of 1867 in Great Britain, for example, created an electoral system in which working-class votes had tremendous impact. With the vote and a seeming stake in the political system, the working class had new options placed in front of them during this time.

9. As Haupt also points out, the Paris Commune would also work as an example for competing political theories, most notably in the debates between Bakunin and Marx in the First International (Haupt 1986).

10. Such internationalism is evident in a familiar refrain from the NLU's leader, William Sylvis: "An international alliance 'would destroy the power of the capitalists to supplant workingmen struggling for their rights in one portion of the world by the importation of help from another'" (quoted in Meltzer 1967: 80).

11. Interestingly, in the suppression that followed the rebellion, Haitians were deported from Jamaica, direct evidence of the ideological weight of the Haitian Revolution from an earlier time.

12. Teng (1971) provides an interesting and detailed account of such states' relations to Taiping as well as imperial China.

13. Here, Wilson (1976 [1868]) provides an early account of the "Ever Victorious Army" led by the British C. G. Gordon in China.

14. Schmidt-Nowara (1998) also provides detail on the inner workings of the development of the radical antislavery movement in Spain.

15. Assessing antisystemic movements, Arrighi, Hopkins, and Wallerstein (1989) point to roughly this period, 1873–1896, as the starting point of numerous, powerful antisystemic movements. Hobsbawm agrees, "The era of the Great Depression was

also the era of the emergence of mass socialist (that is, mainly Marxist) working-class parties all over Europe, organized in a Marxist International" (1969: 129).

16. The antisystemic character of the Indian National Congress at this time is highly debatable, as it was more collaborationist in these early years. Yet, it is important to note the organization's emergence, as by the early 1900s, the Indian National Congress would shift toward a more confrontational stance against the British (Palat, 7 March 2004, personal communication).

17. Here, while paying attention to these most obvious features of antisystemic struggle, I also want to point out the nature of the total situation in Africa. As Cooper contends, "[C]olonial conquests and heavy-handed interventions into African life were vigorously challenged, guerrilla warfare within decentralized politics was as important as the fielding of armies by African states, women as well as men engaged in acts of resistance, and individual action ... complemented collective action" (1994: 154). Behind the story of big events and moments of antisystemic resistance, there are all sorts of less visible actions of protest.

18. Besides the division among the leadership and their followers, notable differences emerged along the lines of strategies and goals to fracture the First International. On the reality of the Paris Commune, for instance, many leaders of the British labor movement "recoiled in horror and were the first to turn tail, thereby precipitating the downfall of the international" (Davis 1993: 87).

19. Debs's union would quickly "bump heads" with the moderate American Federation of Labor. Indeed, Debs and the AFL's Samuel Gompers embody the competing strains of unionism here and after. As Debs himself once said, "The issue is socialism versus capitalism. I am for socialism because I am for humanity" (quoted in Meltzer 1967: 166).

20. One could stand to gain from the work of the World Labor Unrest research working group (Silver, Arrighi, and Dubofsky 1995), but their data do not reach back enough into this time period to be useful.

21. See Wischmann (1987), for a nice account of the Haymarket events and subsequent trial.

22. Weir also importantly points out the divisions that marked the movements of the time of the Great Upheaval. In this case, the Knights of Labor, the largest labor organization of the time, and the United Labor Party of Henry George both "attained their zenith" around 1886 but were also at odds with each other throughout the same time.

23. For an impressive source covering anarchist thought specifically, see Nursey-Bray's annotated bibliography (1992).

24. In Kropotkin's words, "A single deed makes more propaganda in a few days than a thousand pamphlets. The government defends itself, it rages piteously; but by this it only causes further deeds to be committed by one or more persons, and drives the insurgents to heroism. One deed brings forth another; opponents join the mutiny; the government splits into factions; harshness intensifies the conflict; concessions come too late; the revolution breaks out" (quoted in Hunter 1969: 52).

25. This, of course, says nothing about the Mexican Revolution's importance to movements that have come since, most visible in today's Zapatistas but also for any number of radical movements in Mexico and elsewhere.

26. As my treatment here is by necessity brief, for a more complete history of the revolution in Iran, see Kamali (1997); Foran (1991, 1993, 1993a); Martin (1989). Foran (1993) and Martin (1989) also provide details on the 1908 revolution in the Ottoman Empire

27. Nugent (1998) provides an often compelling collection on the extent of U.S.

intervention in Mexico and its many consequences, including precipitating unrest and revolt around this time. This also serves to historicize U.S. economic imperialism from an early period, providing background for the ongoing dependency represented in labor migration and the North American Free Trade Agreement.

28. It should be noted that Conlin (1969) also links the formation of the IWW to a more general syndicalist movement in labor affecting much of Europe, Australia, South Africa, and Latin America. The nature of a cluster becomes apparent.

29. Labor unrest could also certainly be found in places where organized labor movements were still years, if not decades, away from existence. For example, in southern Africa under increasingly difficult labor conditions (mine compounds, force labor, etc.), "deliberate wastefulness, the destruction of mine property and equipment, and loafing or idling all became increasingly common in the years before 1914 … Desertions, too, grew in number after the turn of the century" (Phimister and van Onselen 1997: 5). In 1905 Guyana, as well, strikes among port workers and on the sugar estates spread into generalized riot against the state. In a familiar refrain to this point, "the cumulative effect of this mass rebellion against conditions so demonstrated the effective power of the workers that the capitalists and the State—then two facets of one class—crushed them with every severity of the law" (Chase 1964: 20). However, such repression did not prevent strikes in 1906 and thereafter nor the formation of the first Guyanese unions in 1919.

30. On the ANC, Campbell describes it as "one of the first organizations to emphasize the liberation of Africa as part of its political mobilization" (1994: 291).

31. Movement strategy resembles perhaps a scale rather than a polarized dichotomy.

32. This can be seen in the nationally based, well-organized parties that came to form the Second International.

33. To the point, in the discussion of the overall period, I have pointedly focused on movements of a more "radical" bent. The discussion of the period 1896–1917, for example, provides a number of instances of more radical movements and their activity to balance the weight of the overall discussion of reform. Reform or revolution quite intentionally presents the stark poles of this overall scale.

34. This is, of course, not true across the board as more radical elements of labor and socialist struggle took a more critical stance toward war and armed aggression by the state in general. For example, in 1907 the Second International passed a resolution condemning colonialism and another one in 1910 calling for workers to oppose war (Davis 1993)—something many labor organizations ultimately did not do.

35. For this discussion of World War I, I am grateful for the many useful and insightful comments of the participants of the WAM workshop held on 7 March 2004—especially Michael West, Ravi Palat, and Richard Lee.

36. Labor power being the crucial factor behind the very process of capital accumulation (Marx 1976 [1867]).

*

Chapter 3

Empires Crumble, Movements Fall: Antisystemic Struggle, 1917–1968

Caleb M. Bush and Rochelle Morris

At what point does an antisystemic movement stop being antisystemic? The period in question, 1917–1968, offers an illuminating look at this question. Following World War II, a large number of antisystemic movements, from radical labor and socialism to nationalist struggles in much of the colonized world, realized the ambition of attaining state power. This development forever altered the course of the modern world-system and the movements that challenge the operations of capitalism. Movements, coordinated and sustained efforts that bring large numbers of people together to challenge and confront authorities and/or elites (very often states) (Tarrow 1998), stop being (antisystemic) movements when they enter the halls of power. Unlike any other period in the past 300 years or more, 1917–1968 demonstrates the danger to oppositional movements that pursue *acquiring state power* as a primary goal.

Over the course of 1917–1968, a period of fifty-one years, the world was completely transformed. Hobsbawm (1994) notes that "an age of Catastrophe from 1914 to the aftermath of World War II was followed by some twenty-five or thirty years of extraordinary economic growth and social transformation, which probably changed human society more profoundly than any other period of comparable brevity."[1] In fact, this epoch covers roughly one Kondratieff wave, entering the economic downturn associated with the Great Depression by the end of World War I followed by an era of unprecedented expansion after World War II. With the world mired in economic instability, the struggle for hegemony would not be resolved until the end of World War II. Then, with Europe decimated from war and Japan temporarily out of the picture, the United States ushered in an era of great economic expansion that concretized its hegemonic position.

Without doubt, economically, politically, and socially, the world looked remarkably different in 1968 than it did in 1917. Antisystemic struggle during this time was critical in transforming the world so greatly. From the social compromises gained by newly ascendant political parties throughout core regions of the world-economy to the explosion triggered in the colonial world by struggles for independence and revolutions following World War II, change was driven by the actions of a disparate collection of movements. During this time, we see the breakdown of empires, the reconstitution of the world ruling class, and the reconfiguration of nationalist as well as individual identities on a global scale. Herein, we seek to link, spatially and temporally, patterns of antisystemic resistance to global domination and exploitation across geographic and temporal boundaries.

The late nineteenth and early twentieth centuries marked the emergence of clear opposition to the processes of world capitalism. For the first time in history, this opposition took the form of established, often global movements that ideologically and politically challenged the domination of workers, people of color, and the peasantry. The acceptance of liberal ideology, a double-edged sword visible in an embrace of state power as *the* avenue for change, became the principal impetus for and sometime source of solidarity between workers' movements, nationalism, and Pan-Africanism. The right to self-determination—through political participation in the form of the extension of civil and/or voting rights as well as the gaining of state power for the first time—along with the notion of universal human rights and the right of livelihood, became the driving force of the "property-less masses" to challenge imperial and colonial power relations and the global division of labor operating within the capitalist system. The Bolshevik Revolution (1917) that opens the period was only one early instance of the many manifestations of systemic crisis within the capitalist world-system during 1917–1968.

The history of antisystemic movements from 1917 to 1968 can be told in two periods centered around global movement conjunctures, 1917–1945 (World War I/Russian Revolution) and 1945–1968 (World War II/Chinese Revolution). This twofold history highlights major shifts in the world-system that occurred during this time. Economic and political turmoil marks 1917–1945, a period of quiet relative *only* to what follows World

War II. Following World War I, a wave of antisystemic activity shook the world-system in the form of widespread labor unrest and socialist agitation as well as an important peak in an emergent and increasingly global black nationalism. Important antisystemic moments also occur around the Spanish Civil War and the Italian invasion of Ethiopia. However, following the flurry of activity at the opening of the period, labor and socialism drew closer to systemic embrace. In the United States, the emerging world hegemon, labor was increasingly institutionalized and made safe for the ongoing operations of capitalism.

The period 1945–1968 demonstrates the outcomes of movement strategy of the nineteenth century. Overall here, World War II presents a critical break. Movements that had emerged during the late nineteenth century in the centers of world power, important labor movements and socialist organizations, realized long-held goals at this time. In North America and Europe, labor and socialist struggles were fully institutionalized following the war, gaining access to state power and significant political and economic benefits *at the very cost of their antisystemic nature*. Social compromises and Fordist arrangements meant better quality of life for workers as long as the status quo was agreed upon and maintained.

At the same time that these powerful movements lost antisystemic momentum, all across the colonial world struggles for independence placed critical strain on metropole powers. This forms a central part of our thesis—the rise and fall of labor and social-democratic organizations as antisystemic actors at the same time that antisystemic struggle was taken up by radical nationalists in the colonial world. Following World War II, independence movements in Asia and Africa became radical world actors for a brief time;[2] of course, this says little of revolutions, such as those in China and Cuba, that fundamentally troubled the balance of the world-system at this time. By 1968, the vast majority of the world's population was free of colonial rule, and those still under colonialism were in active resistance. Driven by antisystemic movements, independent states became the norm across the globe at this time, and the interstate system began to look much as it does today. Yet, following a similar path of the older labor and socialist efforts, these movements across the colonial world pursued state power as an ultimate objective, becoming independent nation-states firmly ensconced within the capitalist world-system. This fundamental dilemma of movement strategy lies in large part behind the often *systemic* outcomes of *antisystemic* activity. By the close of the period in question, an entire set of "new" movements led by students, oppressed people of color, women, and others would call into question this strategy. A "New Left" or "new" antisystemic movements would emerge in 1968 to pose new challenges to the existing order, including the once antisystemic movements now in power.

Labor and Socialism: Unrest at the Centers of Power, 1917–1945

The first part of the history of antisystemic struggle follows the continuing evolution of labor and socialist struggles in core regions during this time. Two events stand out for their impact on labor and socialism—World War I and the Russian Revolution. Labor, growing in strength, size, and organizational sophistication from the second half of the nineteenth century, entered this period with a bang. The labor unrest following World War I clearly defines workers' struggles. The close of hostilities and the liberal rhetoric of the victorious states ushered in a brief window of time where antisystemic possibilities again were open. Arrighi's assessment captures something of the pathbreaking essence of this postwar peak:

> *Both* world wars did in fact generate global waves of class struggle. Overall strike activity declined in the opening years of the two wars only to escalate rapidly in their closing years. The resulting peaks in world labor unrest had no historical precedent and have remained unmatched to this day. And each peak was associated with a major socialist revolution—the first with the Soviet Revolution and the second with the Chinese Revolution. (1990: 65; see also Arrighi 1983)

The work of the World Labor Unrest research working group (Silver, Arrighi, and Dubofsky 1995) confirms this startling surge. The peaks for strike waves worldwide following World War I present the highest surge on record. Major, watershed strike waves follow the war in Italy (Arrighi 1995), the United States (Dubofsky 1983, 1995; Edwards 1981; Babson 1999), Germany (Casparis and Arrighi 1995), in locales as far apart as South Africa (Beittel 1995), Japan, and China (Selden 1983), as well as a host of other countries. On China, Selden confirms that "the labor unrest of the years 1922–27 ... best illustrates the conjuncture of labor with international issues of imperialism and nationalist revolution" (1995: 74). Both Japan and China were heavily influenced by the Russian Revolution, and the effects of World War I, as well as anarcho-syndicalism.

Without question, the close of World War I awakened a somewhat quiescent labor movement. In the United States, the Great Steel Strike of 1919 reflected a larger mass strike wave across the country, and again "labor in North America seemed to be a potent political force" (Dubofsky 1983: 33). In the textile districts of New England, the railroad yards across much of the country, the coalfields of the Midwest, as well as the dockyards of the West Coast, workers rose up to make claims on the postwar state (Brecher 1997). In Seattle, longshoremen demonstrated affinity with the Bolshevik Revolution in Russia by refusing to load arms destined for Kolchak and the counterrevolution in Siberia—the effect of which "was to suddenly bring American labor struggles into the context of the revolutionary conflicts sweeping the world in the wake of World

War I" (Brecher 1997: 128). Across Europe at the same time, labor rallied against the state in a crucial wave of strikes, factory occupations, and mass demonstrations that shook the continent (Arrighi 1983). In Germany, strikes in the metalworking industry and the mines of Silesia, a navy mutiny, worker-soldier councils, and military defeat combined to put Germany in a "revolutionary situation" (Casparis and Arrighi 1995). In Spain, labor organization grew rapidly from 1914, divided between socialist and anarcho-syndicalist strategies (Smith 1995).

Yet, this upsurge in militancy would not last. In the United States and across Europe, labor's immediate postwar gains were quickly stymied in the 1920s. In the United States, the 1920s present a relative lull or a "lost decade" in labor activity (Nelson 1997), as trade unions went into relative decline and strikes fell to the lowest levels of the industrial era (Brecher 1997; Dubofsky 1983). At this time, "the power of the government came down heavily on capital's side" (Brody 1993: 62)—American capital *rose* as labor movements *fell*. In Great Britain, home to the exceptional General Strike of 1926, 8.3 million workers were organized in trade unions at the start of the 1920s; by the opening of the 1930s, that number had fallen to 4.4 million (Williams 1995). In a somewhat different manner, the rise of fascism in Italy as early as 1922, as well as in Spain and Germany, spelled doom for labor struggles there as such organizations were ruthlessly crushed. In many of the hotbeds for labor unrest following World War I—Germany, Great Britain, Italy, Spain, the United States—the late 1920s and 1930s were devastating for this state-driven repression.

Interestingly, the correlation between labor, socialism, and the Bolshevik Revolution in Russia often lent the state *justification* for its actions. The attainment of state power in Russia, held out as a source of hope for workers around the world, was used as a reason for states, democratic or otherwise, to repress labor and reverse the gains of the postwar period. The dilemma was such that "for much of Europe (and indeed the world) during these years, the Russian Revolution served as a model of future trends. But the same revolution that served as a positive example for left-wing militancy served equally as a spur to anti-left activities among those who feared communism" (Chirot 1977: 94). The Russian Revolution clearly dealt a "crippling blow" to the socialists organized in the Second International (Dubofsky 1983). Labor organizations like the radical and globally minded Industrial Workers of the World were also crushed at this time. Mussolini and Franco justified their power grabs by the need to fight the spread of communism in their countries (Halliday 1999). Nationalism, in its extreme form as fascism, was thus used in the consolidation of capital to the detriment of radical labor and socialism (Polanyi 1957). Here, we see a critical paradox at work in the struggles between the forces of historical capitalism and those who oppose them. The relative success of antisystemic struggle, the Russian Revolution here, provides inspiration and support for some while serving as a powerful weapon against future efforts for others, most notably the state, at this time.[3]

Latin American Unrest Following World War I and the Russian Revolution

On the heels of the Russian Revolution and the larger revolutionary wave at the start of the twentieth century, Latin America was a hotbed for the evolution of Communist parties—Mexico in 1919; Argentina in 1920; Brazil, Chile, and Uruguay in 1921; Ecuador and Cuba in 1925; and Peru in 1930 (Young 2001). Also a part of this radical history, "the years between 1914 and 1927 saw a surge of labor mobilization" (Skidmore and Smith 2001: 49). As national economies of Latin America were increasingly integrated within the world-economy, the social landscape was altered by increased immigration policies. Working-class imports brought egalitarian ideas of workers' justice to all parts of the region. Even though these laboring classes, along with the peasants, did not gain a political foothold early on, they set up a historical tradition of labor unrest and instability that challenged the ruling elites throughout Latin America during the period 1917–1968. As industry grew throughout the 1940s, an organized labor force emerged with significant political influence.

Latin America presents a clear case of geopolitical asymmetry. Its social, economic, and political landscape has been characterized by a complex history of unequal development, economic dependency, and political instability. In the context of its regional development, Latin America, because of its proximity to the United States and the region's dependent status, has become a political playground for overt and covert American involvement in state affairs.

Bolivia offers an immediate example. As one of the poorest nations in the Western Hemisphere, it had as many as twenty-nine regime changes between 1880 and 1952 (Guevara 1997: 313). With its unstable history, what began as labor strikes in May 1936 led to "toppling the Tejada government" (Lora 1977: 17). After a long history of labor unrest, strikes, and violence, concessions were finally (albeit temporarily) made in the interest of workers. However, it was the military that seized the moment in order to overthrow the government so that "the revolt against poverty acquired unexpected dimensions because of the extreme political instability which prevailed. The army, at the instigation of Colonel Busch, promised not to intervene against the workers, so the repressive capacity of the government was enormously reduced" (Lora 1977: 174). All this came about directly on the heels of the Chaco War, at a time when the traditional parties and socialist parties were in disarray. As in much of Latin America, military and national politics became intertwined. The radical demands of the workers provided only the catalyst for the military to co-opt power and install a similarly repressive government under Colonel Busch.

Considering its position within the world-economy, Bolivia, like all Latin American countries, was dramatically affected by the Great Depression. According to Skidmore, "Both unit price and the quantity of Latin American exports dropped, with the result that their total value for the years 1930–34 was 48 percent below what it had been for 1925–29" (Skidmore and Smith 2001: 51). Even shifting to an import-substitution industrial economy did not quell or alleviate political instability, so that, as Stavrianos so aptly put it, "bad business helped to make bad governments intolerable" (1981: 577). Hence, military rule became standard operating procedure in Bolivia and throughout Latin America.

Interlude: Internationals, the Spanish Civil War, and Movement Cooperation/Competition

Within this history of organized labor's gains and setbacks can be found interesting examples of antisystemic linkages across borders and the cooperation and antagonism that such ties fostered. With massive surges in membership and begrudging acceptance by the state, the nascent labor struggles of the previous era, 1848–1917, at this time became the sustained, often massive *organizations* familiar even today. Movements' development into these sustained organizations only facilitated the development of transnational linkages, whether complementary or antagonistic. As movements became organizations that lasted, ties between movements and leaders became easier to form and maintain. Such international organizations had, of course, been around for some time, but the First International, for example, was short-lived due in no small part to its being a "weak collection of weak movements" (Wallerstein 1990: 18). The Second International that followed was, in contrast, composed of nationally based parties and trade union federations. Yet, World War I devastated even the Second International (Stevis 1998; Dubofsky 1983), weakening member groups both organizationally and ideologically. Thus, international movements started the period 1917–1968 at something of a disadvantage.

However, with the attainment of power in Russia, socialists had a "success" to emulate elsewhere and from which to gain support. On the heels of the Revolution, "the Bolsheviks would place the 'national question' squarely at the center of the international communist movement" (Griffler 1995: 12). Following their own revolution, Russian socialists were quick to turn their attention to revolution elsewhere in the world, establishing a new International with the express hope of developing movements that could overthrow states everywhere. The path to power again was attainment of the state. Along these lines, "at the Congress of Baku in 1921 ... Lenin in effect proposed a formal alliance between the anticapitalist social movements of the core and the anti-imperialist nationalist movements of the periphery" (Wallerstein 1990: 25). Indeed, the Communist International (Comintern) at this time was organized precisely to guide revolutionary efforts around the globe (Katz 1997). In this role, the Comintern held seven congresses and until World War II was "a major factor in the politics of many European states and those of China and much of the colonial world" (Halliday 1999: 106). For example, the Soviets provided important support for the development of the prolonged Chinese Revolution (Pantsov 2000), and Filipino radicals, who would play a "central leadership role" in the development of Philippine communism, studied and trained in Moscow in the 1930s (Morris 1994).

In 1936, civil war erupted in Spain between Republicans and Franco's forces. The Spanish Civil War as an event demonstrates the increasing linkages that brought movement struggles together. This struggle in Spain became "a test for the moral convictions of the Left everywhere in the Western world" (Diggins 1992: 177). The Soviet Comintern fought on the side of the loyalists—as did communists from *throughout* Europe. Even entering the conflict on the side of the loyalists were 3,200 Americans. These struggles and their internationalism highlight the positive dynamics of antisystemic linkages. At the same time, the "antifascist nationalism" evident in the Spanish Civil War served to bring nationalism and the Left together (Hobsbawm 1990a). Fighting against fascism in the 1930s, radicals of all sorts came together to oppose reactionary regimes. This connection between nationalism and the Left, forged in Spain, grew stronger after World War II.

Yet, the interwar years are important for another reason—the *divides and negative ties* that also emerged among the Left at this time. In 1919 at Berne, Switzerland, European social democrats took steps to restore the Second International under the express ideal that the Bolshevik Revolution was *not* relevant for the development of socialism (Callaghan 2001). With the near contemporaneous development of the Third International oriented toward communism and the Soviet state,[4] two separate internationalist movements emerged "vehemently opposed one to the other" (Arrighi, Hopkins, and Wallerstein 1989: 32). Among labor, similar divisions became readily apparent. Condemning here, "by 1922, the divisions within the world's labor movement broke down its prospects of becoming a hegemonic organization within socialist civil society" (Stevis 1998: 58). The International Federation of Trade Unions, founded in 1919, and the communist-led International Council of Trade and Industrial Unions, founded in 1921, competed with each other throughout the 1920s and the 1930s. Following World War II, these sorts of divisions would only *strengthen* among labor organizations under the demands of the Cold War and U.S. hegemony.

Labor also had uneven relationships with other movements at this time. During the interwar years, labor and black radicals in the United States reached an uneasy alliance of sorts (Griffler 1995). As Griffler points out (and discussed at greater length in the next section), "The decade following World War I displayed a vibrancy in Black radicalism in the United States that no decade before or since could match" (1995: 13). Owing to massive migrations to the industrial North (the "Great Migration"), black workers were also important for a developing labor movement at the same time. Labor organizations were thus compelled to address the "Negro Question,"[5] pushed and linked to workers' struggles by black radicals. At the Sixth Congress of the Comintern in 1927, Stalin even weighed in on the "Negro Question," declaring that "one of the most important tasks of the Communist Party consists in the struggle for a complete and real equality of the Negroes, for the abolition of all kinds of social and political inequalities" (Griffler 1995: 84). The recognition of the importance of race and racial inequality was clearly pushed by black radicals at this time, and labor and socialists were compelled to address this fact. Such a meeting of movements displays the cooperation and conflict inherent in antisystemic activity.

Here, the African Blood Brotherhood (ABB), another radical black nationalist organization, merits consideration for its influence as an ideological bridge between an emergent black nationalism and communism/socialism in the form of the Communist Party of the United States (CPUSA). Founded by Cyril Briggs between 1917 and 1919, the ABB was one of several radical organizations of the "New Negro" movement in the United States. As a paramilitary organization, it sought the protection of blacks against increased mob violence committed by whites[6] and called for the formation of an international cross-racial alliance between all oppressed groups as well as an open alliance with Soviet Russia (Bush 1999; James 1998). As a revolutionary nationalist organization, the ABB called for a separate black nation *within* the United States (Robinson 1983). Furthermore, the close ties between the ABB and the CPUSA reveal, once again, the ideological contradiction in the race/class dichotomy between black nationalism and socialism/communism. Yet, in spite of these differences, the brotherhood's legacy is manifested in its ability to radicalize the black population for protection and for pursing the agenda of a unified liberation struggle.

The CPUSA thus had a substantial impact on blacks throughout the United States as an instrument of labor mobilization *and* racial solidarity.[7] Prior to the 1920s, socialism/communism for the most part had no formal policy toward blacks as a constituent part of American society. In fact, "at the beginning of the twentieth century, the socialist movements and black nationalist movements were separate and distinct groups, often bitterly opposed and with quite divergent programs" (Bush 1999: 64). All this was to change by 1921, when the party began to actively recruit blacks into the CPUSA. Ultimately, this connection between race and socialism/communism reflects a larger concern at this time. In South Africa, for example, communists also "made strenuous efforts to place themselves in the forefront of black protest against white supremacy" (Fredrickson 1995: 179). The Comintern in 1928 put forth declarations for the establishment of a "Black belt" in the Deep South and a "native republic" in South Africa. West confirms that "in the 1920s the internal colonial thesis, as the demand for a black nation-state on American soil became known, received the strong backing of the Comintern which directed the [CPUSA] to work for the creation of a black Republic" (1999: 83; see also Kelley 1994).

Despite the ideological limitations of such thinking,[8] the CPUSA did play a vanguard role in the black fight against racism by making a formal commitment to interracial solidarity. This led the CPUSA in 1925 to establish the American Negro Labor Congress (ANLC), whose specific goal was to end lynching, Jim Crow, and industrial discrimination (Bush 1999). Such efforts, despite their relative lack of success, reflect an increasing connection between socialism and race/nationalist struggles after World War I and the Russian Revolution. Communist positions on the "Negro Question" unintentionally helped to open up the space for black nationalism (Kelley 1994).

The Impact of Garveyism and the Radical Black Nationalism Wave after World War I

Much like labor's upsurge, immediately following the war an important wave of black nationalism erupted in 1919 (West 1999; Shepperson 1960; Assensoh and Alex-Assensoh 1998; Hodges 1995). Hundreds of thousands of black men had joined the army and otherwise supported the war effort. Hundreds of thousands had also migrated to the American North hoping for better work and lives. Yet, the postwar hopes that went with such effort were quickly dashed.

Key to this wave, Marcus Garvey's Universal Negro Improvement Association (UNIA) is the most extensive "and the most advanced concept of Pan-Africanism in the period after World War I" (Campbell 1994: 290). Born in Jamaica in 1887, Garvey came from a long tradition of black radicals from the Caribbean going as far back as the Haitian Revolution, the maroon societies of Jamaica, and the Morant Bay Rebellion. Garvey and UNIA's ability to mobilize the black masses and to forge a common identity between black people on three continents raised the political stakes by inspiring a racial consciousness that brought conflict to the surface and created aspirations for social equality and economic justice. Garvey presented the opportunity for American blacks to become a part of the global majority as opposed to an isolated, impoverished black minority.

Through the widely disseminated *Negro World* and local UNIA chapters in multiple locales worldwide, Von Eschen points out that:

> it was Marcus Garvey and his Universal Negro Improvement Association that brought the notion of the links between the Black world and Africa to a mass audience, creating a new working-class diaspora consciousness. By linking the entire Black world to Africa and its members to one another, Garvey made the American Negro conscious of his African origins and created for the first time a feeling of international solidarity between Africans and peoples of African descent. (1997: 10)

Part of a larger "three-way process" of exchange between the Caribbean, continental North America, and Africa associated with other prominent nationalists like Edward Blyden and George Padmore (Shepperson 1960), Garvey and his movement were rightly perceived as a direct challenge to white hegemony. Magubane (1994) credits Garvey with establishing the "first truly international organization of Africans and people of African descent" and goes further to credit Garvey with being the first to make the link between Africans and African Americans in terms of economic exploitation. Under Garvey, black nationalism, often an affair of educated elites, was a mass movement for the first time (West 1999).

In the person of Garvey, one gains a glimpse of the connections between antisystemic actors and locales at this time. Garvey, an extensive traveler, arrived in the United States in 1916, having already established the first branch of UNIA in Jamaica in 1914. Two years prior, he had been in London where he worked in Mohammed Ali Duse's editorial office of the journal *The African Times and Orient Review*.[9] While in London, he published his first article on Jamaican history, and in this, Garvey's vision of the future is first evident (Geiss 1974). While the idea of nationhood and a return to Africa was not a new concept, Garvey made his concept revolutionary through his ability to mix key elements of Christianity with racial pride, self-interest, and economic determination—all of which had mass appeal to the socially and economically oppressed (Thomas 2001; Martin 1993). The impact of this idea raised racial consciousness to a level that linked blacks throughout the diaspora to the "African Motherland." On the African continent, the message of Garveyism and the Black Star Line elevated Garvey and his diasporic followers to the status of liberators and redeemers of the African continent (Kodi 1993; Phiri 1993). In South Africa, for example, Garvey and UNIA had a tremendous impact—establishing seven branches by 1926 and forming open ties to Clements Kadalie's Industrial and Commerical Workers' Union of Africa (ICU) (Fredrickson 1995). As Fredrickson points out, "UNIA and the ICU, both populist movements, capitalized on the betrayal of liberal-reformist hopes in the post–World War I era" (1995: 174).

The impact of Garvey's movement is undeniable. Movement links were particularly extensive, as in a ten-year period, he set up more than 1,100 branches of UNIA in more than forty countries (Martin 1993).[10] Seven hundred of these branches were founded in the United States where branches mushroomed particularly in the southern states (in all probability because of the increased repression and lynching of blacks in the South after World War I). He also established branches on almost every island of the West Indies; and in South and Central America, he had branches in Costa Rica, Nicaragua, Guatemala, and more than 40 branches in Panama alone (Martin 1993). UNIA branches were also established firmly in West Africa, as well as southern Africa and even extended as far as Canada, Europe, and Australia.

Of course, not all ties were positive. Prior to Garvey's arrival in the United States, Harrison had garnered the title "Father of Harlem Radicalism" for his radical socialist activity and his commitment to a race-first consciousness.[11] As Garvey came into the picture, his flamboyant style eclipsed Harrison's popularity as a radical black nationalist (James 1998). In fact, the relationship between these two black nationalists represents divergent segments of the "New Negro" radicalism of the 1920s. Although Garvey and Harrison were radical black nationalists, Harrison's intellectual development came out of the Marxist tradition, making him a black socialist and nationalist, while Garvey's appeal remained firmly populist. Similarly, Cyril Briggs's African Blood Brotherhood formed strong ties to Garvey and UNIA only to be expelled by Garvey in 1921.[12] At the 1921 Pan-African Congress, Du Bois and some of the other delegates attempted to disassociate themselves from the activities of Marcus Garvey (Geiss 1974).

For all intents and purposes, Garveyism, however, has to some degree or another influenced virtually all black nationalist organizations. His "Africa for the African" approach awakened the consciousness of the black working class and set the tone of self-determination for a new generation of black nationalists in the post–World War II period. Kwame Nkrumah, nationalist leader in Ghana's struggle for independence, claimed that Garvey influenced him more than anyone else while in the United States (Shepperson 1960). Powerfully, UNIA's "conception of African redemption spoke a language that the poor understood and the colonial overlords feared" (Campbell 1994: 291). The contacts and alliances made in this earlier period became an important element to realize change in imperialist colonial policy after World War II.

Pan-Africanism after World War I

When compared with the Garvey movement, the early Pan-African Movement to 1945 appears to be less successful in appealing to the working masses. Pan-Africanists were often considered a conservative organization of intellectuals. Universally, however, the Pan-African movement was more successful in its ability to build a conceptual framework and a political infrastructure that eventually incorporated *coalitions* of Africans, Asians, and Latin Americans who were involved in the same liberation struggle. This marks one of the key fundamental differences between Garveyism and the Pan-African movement at this time.

The Pan-African movement, as a historical process, grew out of a tradition in black political consciousness that goes back well into the nineteenth century.[13] Within the framework of black nationalist politics, Pan-Africanism developed out of what Hanchard (1991) refers to as the racial asymmetry created by the dialectical relationship between dominant (whites) and subordinate groups (blacks).[14] Seen in this light, Pan-Africanism was, by and large, an integral historical process resolute in practice to transform the political, economic, and psycho-social dimensions of this dialectical relationship. The politics of racial identity served to broaden the spatial and temporal boundaries of blacks throughout the diaspora and at the same time provide the rationale to challenge the global racialized system. As Magubane notes, "That the birth of Pan-Africanism took place 20 years after the dismemberment of Africa by Europe and 25 years after the political expulsion of the Black from the democratic process in America is important. It is further important that this movement conceived the emancipation of Africa from white rule as a prerequisite to the emancipation of the Black in America and wherever foreign rule was perpetrated on the African" (1994: 135). A brief look at the historical formation of the Pan-African movement will reveal how these challenges came about.

As previously noted, the first Pan-African conference was held in London in July 1900. Organized by Henry Sylvester Williams and W.E.B. Du Bois, the conference was composed of elite intellectuals from Africa (which was underrepresented), the United States, the West Indies, and a few participants who actually resided in London (Geiss 1974). This first meeting led to the five Pan-African congresses of 1919, 1921, 1923, 1927, and 1945, and the institutionalization of a political movement. The 1921 Pan-African Congress can be seen as a high point of the early Pan-African movement (here again, the earliest years of 1917–1945 have a place of importance). On two points it was successful. This congress laid the groundwork for more African participation and direct appeals within the movement. Thus far, Pan-Africanism had limited participation from Africans; yet, in this conference of 113 delegates, one third came from the continent. At the 1921 congress, delegates were even able to draft a petition to the League of Nations appealing for an end to racial discrimination worldwide.

Later, the 1927 congress in New York presents another example of the early successes achieved by Pan-Africanism. The 208 delegates and 5,000 participants from twenty-two states—including India, China, Egypt, Liberia, Nigeria, Sierra Leone, and the Gold Coast—were able to draft resolutions calling for native rights and education for all children. They also called for development and the reorganization of commerce and the nondiscriminatory treatment of people of color (Marable 1996).

Perhaps more than anything at this time, Pan-African leaders such as Du Bois had a notable impact on an emerging African nationalism. The congress movement in South Africa, for example, was influenced heavily by Du Bois and other Pan-Africanists at this time (Cell 1999). Likewise, Du Bois' *African Roots of the War,* published in 1915, emphasized the link between World War I and colonialism in Africa,[15] a message many Africans understood and appreciated. Emerging from the Francophone colonial world, negritude, associated most closely with Aimé Césaire, "sought to grasp the cultural unity of Africa" (Campbell 1994: 294). What can be seen at this time—through the political Pan-Africanism of Du Bois, the cultural Pan-Africanism of Césaire, or the populist Pan-Africanism of Garvey—is an increased awareness of a shared plight and condition throughout Africa and the diaspora. Such thinking played an important role in radical liberation struggles that followed World War II. Boahen affirms, "[T]he Pan-Africanist activities of Sylvester Williams, Du Bois, Marcus Garvey and others and their congresses in the metropolitan capitals ... not only internationalized the anticolonial movement but also inspired the nationalists in Africa and won them some converts" (1987: 78). Yet, by the late 1920s and 1930s, the stock market crash and the global instability created by the rise of fascism prevented any further Pan-African congresses until 1945. By that time, the turbulent winds of change had shifted in the direction of the masses and struggles for independence exploded across Africa, again changing the character and content of Pan-Africanism.

Anticolonial Resistance in Asia and Africa, 1917–1945

Before moving on to the critical decades following World War II, we must note that the struggles for independence that followed the war really came after decades, if not centuries, of antisystemic activity throughout Africa and Asia.[16] The parties, guerilla movements, and other groups that led struggles for independence often came into existence in the interwar years. By the opening years of the period at hand, Indian resistance, led often by the congress movement, was placing major strains on British colonialism. Demonstrating the complicated nature of nationalism, especially when driven by elites, the congress movement in India worked by this time to bottle up more radical demands for change. Yet, by the early 1930s, Gandhi-led campaigns of civil disobedience, the salt march and rent strikes, for example, were also happening alongside bombings, widespread violence, and the Chittagong Arsenal Raid in Bengal (Cell 1999). The year 1942 brought the Quit India Movement, and British authority in India was placed under serious pressure (although still able to repress such movements until *after* the war).

In 1919, the May Fourth Movement took place in China as workers, students, and other Chinese demonstrated against ongoing foreign influence in their country (Altbach 1970).[17] In reality, China was in the throes of unrest throughout 1917–1945. This is especially true when one takes into account the 1931 Japanese invasion of China, the effective beginning of World War II in that part of Asia. Elsewhere, in 1924 American members of the Communist International entered the Philippines, and several years later, the Communist Party of the Philippine Islands was proclaimed—on November 7, 1930, the symbolic date of the anniversary of the Bolshevik Revolution (Morris 1994). The Vietnamese Nationalist Party was founded in 1927 "on the model of the Chinese [Guomindang]" (Wolf 1969: 180; see also Short 1989) and by 1930 led a significant uprising at Yen Bay. Vietnamese communists, unified under Ho Chi Minh in 1930, sponsored an uprising at Nghe An in 1929. The years 1926 and 1927 saw communist revolts in Java and West Sumatra, both part of the 1920s *pergerakan* in Indonesia that "met its death in an attempt to seize state power" (Shiraishi 1990: 339). In 1926, Indonesia's Sukarno wrote "Nationalism, Islam, and Marxism," voicing a "new consciousness" that drove Indonesia's independence struggle of World War II (Shiraishi 1990).

Resistance to colonialism in Africa follows a similar path following World War I. Africans had faced conscription in the war and fought alongside European soldiers in the name of metropole powers. Expecting rewards and recognition for their efforts following the war (a similar tale), Africans returned home to face little in the way of positive change. In fact, much of this early period, 1919–1935, is even described as "colonial imperialism's last territorial drive in Africa" (Boahen 1987). In the face of ongoing imperialism, resistance by Africans continued; a vast number of uprisings took place during 1917–1945 that served to challenge the operation of colonialism in Africa (see table 3.1).

Despite the high volume of continued resistance to colonialism at this time, the interwar years were difficult ones for resistance efforts in Africa. By this time, colonialism was highly consolidated in many places, and the colonial state exercised severe powers of repression and control. The military reverses by colonial powers forced much resistance underground at this time (Campbell 1994).[18]

Well above the "background hum" of ongoing resistance to colonialism stands the Pan-African reaction to the Italian invasion of Ethiopia in 1935. During the height of the Great Depression and following the collapse of Garvey's movement in 1925, the invasion caused a "wave of agitation" as "Africans at home and abroad rushed to the aid of Ethiopia (West 1999: 87; see also Asante 1977). Similar to the Spanish Civil War around the same time, the invasion served as a test for the convictions of black nationalists and Pan-Africanists throughout the world. The widespread response and degree of outrage also indicate just how effective Pan-Africanist early efforts had been in elevating awareness and

Table 3.1: Select African Resistance to Colonialism, 1917–1945

Resistance	Date	Location	Reason
Bondelswarts rebellion	1922	Southwest Africa	Tax increase
Rehobothers rebellion	1925	Southwest Africa	Harsh treatment
Peasant rebellions	1920–1922	Belgian Congo	Tax increase
	1930–1931		Commodity prices
Zambesi Valley rebellion	1917–1921	Mozambique	Forced labor, tax increase, conscription
Mahdist uprisings	1922	Sudan	Religion
Dinka uprisings	1919–1920	Southern Sudan	End colonialism
	1927–1928		
Local uprisings	1920, 1922, 1925, 1927, 1932, 1935	Somaliland	Colonialism
Aba women's rebellion	1929	Nigeria	Direct taxation, courts

Source: Boahen 1987.

forging linkages, political, cultural, and otherwise, between Africa and the diaspora. Yet, despite the impressive rally against the invasion and ongoing efforts to resist colonialism elsewhere, in 1935, "the colonial system looked virtually impregnable and seemed likely to last forever. Yet, it did not" (Boahen 1987: 90–91).

The second half of our argument examines the reasons that colonialism collapsed following World War II. For now, the postwar revolutions, anticolonial and otherwise, clearly emerged from extended histories of protest and (often failed) resistance throughout Latin America, Asia, and Africa. The economic, social, and political impacts of decades of colonialism—negative changes in labor regimes, agricultural production processes, and land tenure high among them—meshed with the contestation and end of Japanese occupation and the postwar weakness of metropole powers (still keen to hold on to colonial possessions) to unleash a wave of independence efforts following World War II. These many earlier struggles played no small role in establishing the conditions and providing the buildup for such change.[19]

Labor and the New Deal:
The Routinization and Institutionalization of Unrest in the 1930s

Before moving on to the 1945–1968 period, a brief examination of the fate of labor in the years leading up to the war is in order. In Europe, by the close of the 1930s labor had experienced a "significant erosion" of the gains made following World War I and the early 1920s (Salter and Stevenson 1990). Yet, in many ways, the labor-capital arrangements facilitated by the Roosevelt administration in the United States provided a *prelude* to the institutionalization of labor throughout the core countries that followed World War II. This window of time was when "American trade unions reached their twentieth-century apogee, whether measured by organizing success, economic power, or political influence" (Lichtenstein 2002: 12; see also Nelson 1997). After a rather extended period of quietude, American labor came to life in the mid-1930s: realizing the biggest organizing victories in its history, witnessing the formation of the Congress of Industrial Organization (CIO), and demonstrating the power of the sit-down strike in a wave of related, massive labor protests, including the important General Motors strike in 1937 (Babson 1999; Nelson 1997; Brecher 1997). The result of this conjuncture of labor activity "produced a major transformation in the dominant pattern of labor-capital relations in the most capital-intensive sectors of the United States economy … [T]rade unionism had come to stay in that sector of the economy, and capital began to bargain with labor's representatives" (Dubofsky 1995: 133).

Behind this activity, however, lay the trends of a shift that marked the absolute demise of labor as an antisystemic force in the centers of power in the capitalist world-system. Section 7A of the New Deal's National Recovery Act guaranteed the workers' right to organize, an important, if loaded, victory for organized labor. The 1935 Wagner Act affirmed this right for unions in the United States, and labor was a recognized force in the production process in the United States. These were accomplishments of a major magnitude, realizing goals set forth for decades by labor. The National Labor Relations Act of 1935, establishing the National Labor Relations Board, set up a government body for mediation of the labor-capital relationship. Most interesting, at this time, unions, including those in the CIO, began to play something of a double game—"champion" of the sitdown movement to workers, while, "to management, the CIO was able to sell itself with equal honesty as a mechanism for disciplining the workforce" (Brecher 1997: 235).

In the 1930s, one thus witnesses the institutionalization of labor in the United States, as workers' demands were channeled into organizations and forms of protest acceptable to capital and the state. Workers and their unions even became linked to the "established bourgeois party" of the Democrats rather than any true left-wing party (Dubofsky 1983). Edwards provides a powerful summary of this key period in the 1930s, explaining that "rank and file protests came increasingly under institutional control as the New Deal progressed. Union recognition and collective agreements with employers were made the main aims, and the conservation of CIO leaders and the revival of the AFL [American Federation of Labor] illustrates the absorption of rank and file militancy by union structures" (1981: 171). In the United States, emerging hegemon in the world-system, labor organizations thereby subsumed the radical power of the workers who filled their ranks—making labor protest "safe" for systemic forces. This development was realized on a much larger scale following World War II, *even with the assistance of these same movements.* Organized labor's days as a truly antisystemic force were at an end.

After World War II: The Demise of Labor's and Socialism's Antisystemic Character

> In every instance in which workers confronted state power directly it was the state rather than the labour movement which emerged triumphant ... By and large, workers achieved significant gains only in cooperation with *the state, not in opposition to it.*
> *Salter and Stevenson 1990: 4*

The years following World War II present a surge in antisystemic activity similar to that following World War I. The accomplishments of movements after World War II eclipse those of World War I, however. The immediate postwar period brought to fruition the organizing gains of labor and a related socialism in many parts of the world. Decades of struggle, going back to the nineteenth century, found these important antisystemic actors well positioned to realize serious gains. The year 1945 can be seen as a "psychological turning point," as these movements, as well as important nationalist/anticolonial struggles, seemed stronger and closer to success than ever before in their history (Wallerstein 1990; Arrighi, Hopkins, and Wallerstein 1989).[20] Part of a larger Marxist-Leninist revolutionary wave stemming from the Russian Revolution (Katz 1997; see also Arrighi 1990), numerous communist governments came to power in Europe (as well as in China and North Korea). This revolutionary situation was seemingly strengthened by the presence of Communist parties in France, Italy, Greece, and Czechoslovakia, and by such parties in political coalitions in much of Western Europe (Callaghan 2001). In England, the labor party won the 1945 election, and Attlee succeeded the war-hero Churchill on the foundation of an agenda for real social change. Social Democrats in much of Western Europe also saw success on unparalleled levels.

At the same time, in the United States, Europe, and much of the rest of the world, one of the largest strike waves on record followed the war. Major strike waves followed the war in the United States (Edwards 1981; Dubofsky 1983, 1995), while in Germany and Italy, with the collapse of fascist regimes, labor was given room to maneuver for the first time in years (Arrighi 1995; Casparis and Arrighi 1995). China and Japan also experienced significant working-class protest after the Pacific war's end—Japan almost approaching a "revolutionary situation" owing to working-class unrest (Selden 1983). In Africa, working-class struggles combined with nationalist impulses to bring an end to colonialism after the war. Finally, significant worker actions played a major role in shaping the emerging socialist states in much of Eastern Europe in the 1940s and 1950s.

Yet, the close of World War II also marked the beginning of U.S. hegemony and the accompanying Cold War between the United States and the Soviet Union. With Europe devastated, the United States stepped into a rebuilding role on the continent looking to shape postwar Europe to its desires. The Marshall Plan offered European states much needed support with serious strings attached; Europe was to be made safe for the growth of (American) capitalism. A crucial component of this included fashioning a labor-capital relationship in much of Europe similar to that which existed in the United States in the 1930s. The Truman Doctrine made the U.S. desire to contain the spread of communism blatant. In fact, a large component of U.S. hegemony included a counterrevolutionary thrust aimed directly at antisystemic movements at home and abroad; anticommunism became an "ideological carapace" of the newly constituted hegemon (Arrighi, Hopkins, and Wallerstein 1989).

In this era of polarized world politics, labor and socialism in the United States and much of Europe compromised—realizing the final closure of their time as antisystemic forces. Victory came at the expense of antisystemic impetus, and the outcomes of movement activity resulted in movements that strengthened the system. O'Connor nicely captures the shifts that had now occurred.

> By the third quarter of the 20th century, the national leaders of social democratic, communist, and nationalist parties succeeded to power and privilege. The price that they had to pay—or, more accurately, the price that they made their working classes pay—was the abandonment of class politics. Struggles for political goals or *ends* were regarded as more or less completed (the left's own "end of history" thesis) and politics largely became *means* to the end of realizing economic and social demands. Working class political parties became parties of national rule and they themselves became the left-wing of the establishment or the establishment itself. (1994: 9)

Labor was now a major pillar of support for the state. The 1947 Taft-Hartley Act in the United States made the state's intentions (and labor's acquiescence) even clearer—radical opposition had no place in organized labor.

In 1952, the AFL for the first time formally endorsed a major party candidate, Adlai Stevenson. The 1955 merger of the AFL and CIO created a massive and powerful labor organization, "but one committed irrevocably to the two-party system" (Brody 1993: 70; see also Dubofsky

1983). Under the Fordist reorganization of labor-capital relations, labor accepted higher wages, greater levels of employment, and the benefits of the welfare state in return for the routinization of protest under collective bargaining agreements. Similar, if even wider social accords were also struck throughout much of Europe. In the worldwide picture at this time, under U.S. hegemony, "while pro-communist parties and movements were repressed, core working classes were *co-opted*" (Silver 1995: 174).

Part of this co-option meant that labor began to play an increasing international role in *controlling* the direction of labor politics worldwide. Negative ties grew increasingly common between movements at this time. In postwar Germany, policy-makers were fearful of radical labor reemerging, especially given the proximity of Soviet power in Eastern Europe, and "aided by the AFL ... acted vigorously to ensure the tractability of German labor" (Eisenberg 1983: 306). This pattern was repeated again and again over the coming decades as the AFL established regional labor offices in all parts of the world that became tools for the spread of American state policy. The AFL and the CIO also joined the Dies Committee and the House Un-American Activities Committee (HUAC) in purging their own unions during the anticommunist campaign after the war (Rose 2000).[21] At the transnational level, the World Federation of Trade Unions (WFTU), organized in 1945, "brought together the vast majority of unions in Europe, South America, and Asia, with the notable exceptions of the AFL and Christian unions" (Stevis 1998: 59). The AFL was extremely hostile to the WFTU, distrusting the member British Trade Unions Council (TUC) and other socialist unions, and in 1949 helped form the adversarial International Confederation of Free Trade Unions (ICFTU). In the polarized world of the Cold War, the ICFTU and WFTU then became "transmission belts for the priorities of the interests of U.S. and U.S.S.R labor-state alliances" (Stevis 1998: 60).

Under conditions of economic prosperity and with collective bargaining now a part of the labor process, the 1950s and 1960s saw the "withering away of the strike" (Silver 1995). Remarkably, these movements, which had only emerged in the second half of the nineteenth century, had succeeded in roughly a century's time in realizing many of their goals. The postwar world was a markedly different place, and these movements—at first in opposition, now in cooperation—played a major role in the transformations that occurred. The Russian Revolution at the opening of the period inspired and supported a wide array of socialist revolutions and insurgencies. In the capitalist states, labor unrest and the growth of Socialist and Communist parties threatened the very process of capital accumulation. The social accords that were struck with militant labor assured workers of significant gains *under the agreement that the status quo be maintained.* The eventual détente that was reached between the United States and the Soviet Union (not to mention China) secured much the same on a global scale. These arrangements were affected precisely because of the threats posed by this legacy of antisystemic activity. However, as the movements became institutional-ized, it became impossible to describe their activities as "antisystemic" (perhaps "systemic-reformist" fits best). Arrighi agrees, "After the Sec-ond World War, therefore not only did the politicization of the labor movement progressively decline, also the radicalization of labor parties' political platforms tended to disappear" (1983: 47). Movements turned parties or closely tied to parties are questionable antisystemic actors.

The goal of state power, set out by these movements in the previous era, 1848–1917, had been achieved to a greater or lesser degree, "resulting in a complex pattern of antisystemic mobilization combined with con-stant co-optation" (Wallerstein 1983: 19). Labor ultimately undermined itself in the core, because multinational corporations would eventually seek the advantages of lower wages and lax governmental control in the periphery and begin shifting labor-intensive work to new locales. Accordingly, as labor power relatively began to diminish in the core, it picked up in the periphery and helped tilt the balance in favor of the anticolonial and nationalist projects. At the same time that labor and many socialist parties were losing antisystemic thrust in much of the core, the seeds of nationalism were coming of age throughout the colo-nized world. The dilemmas of change would thereby be placed before the many nationalist and anticolonial movements that flowered after the end of World War II—a crucial history to which the rest of the text is devoted.[22] The struggles against empire and oppression tell the most important story of 1917–1968.

Revolution and Independence in Asia, Africa, and Latin America

> [T]he general movement towards independence and decoloniza-tion, especially after 1945, was unquestionably identified with socialist/communist anti-imperialism, which is perhaps why so many decolonized and newly independent states and by no means only those in which socialists and communists had played an important part in the struggle for liberation, declared themselves to be in some sense "socialist."
>
> *Hobsbawm 1990a: 149*

In the first decade after World War II, the United States solidified its position as hegemon in the world-system: Europe and Japan would be rebuilt and a new world economic order based on militarism and an unstable interstate system would dominate the globe. This would not only have dramatic implications for labor in the core but would also have major repercussions in colonies and the peripheral states of Latin America. By this time, however, nationalism and decolonization were critical movements, and revolutions in China and Cuba became new antisystemic ideals. This signals a major shift after World War II away from established movements in the core regions of the world-economy to the nationalist, revolutionary struggles in the colonies and on the margins of the world-system.

With the onset of the Cold War, the United States initiated changes in its policy agenda toward Latin America states. With American companies (Standard Oil, United Fruit Company) among the largest capital investors, American intervention in Latin American politics was a foregone conclusion. Citing Bolivia as an example, prior to the Cold War the United States had been opposed to the National Revolutionary Movement (MNR) for its "fascist leanings, rather than its reformist policies." Nevertheless, Washington supported the "politically undesirable" regime rather than risk what Milton Eisenhower (U.S. special ambassador to Latin America) referred to as "a Communist takeover" (Guevara 1997: 317).

This policy shift characterizes U.S.–Latin American relations throughout the Cold War period. Guatemala experienced a popular uprising in 1944, which ousted the dictatorial regime of Jorge Ubico. José Arévalo's administration (1944–1950) began instituting political and social reforms, which threatened the oligarchy. Ten years later (1954), during the Jacobo Arbenz administration (1951–1954), the United States financed and directed a coup to oust Arbenz and subsequently install a succession of military dictators—who immediately reversed reforms initiated by the two previous administrations (Guevara 1997). As a consequence, only one "civilian" administration was seen in Guatemala between 1958 and 1984.

A few additional examples from the region highlight the tension between radical movements and the U.S.-supported regimes. Venezuela is case in point. The Trienio administration (1945–1948) implemented a reformist program—refining their oil industry leases and initiating agrarian reform—until a military junta in 1948, in which the authoritarian dictator Marcos Pérez Jiménez was installed and supported by the United States. In addition, Colombia (1946–1958), Nicaragua (1958–1963), and Peru (1962–1963) all experienced guerilla activity and peasant uprisings with the United States involved in one way or another in state affairs in each case. After World War II, the Cold War struggle and emerging U.S. hegemony carried significant repercussions for antisystemic activity around the world. Yet, by the turn of the twentieth century, the seeds of an often radical nationalism were firmly planted around the globe (the United States was also eager to control decolonization in its interests). The antisystemic movements aimed at freedom from colonial rule and, often with strong ties to socialism and communism, became the radical actors that altered the world from 1917 to 1968.

Rebellion and Revolt in Asia Following World War II

Throughout a larger Asia from 1945 to 1968, independence and revolution swayed the balance of power from intrusive, colonial powers to a large and important set of newly independent, often radical states. The sheer population of countries like China, India, and Indonesia, for example, that witnessed revolutions and/or movements for independence makes Asia a highly significant section of the world at this time. The close of the war was significant in Asia for several reasons. Radical movements across Asia used the relative weakness of colonial powers following World War II to achieve independence. The defeat of an aggressive Japan in the Pacific also provided a window of opportunity for movements that fermented under occupation. Finally, in the postwar, polarized world, the United States turned its full counterrevolutionary and anticommunist attention to Asia, invading Korea and Vietnam, while also playing a major role in the politics of countries such as the Philippines. Revolution and counter-revolution describe much of Asia after World War II.

Revolution in China

Almost coincident with the struggle of the Bolsheviks in Russia, in Asia the Chinese Revolution covers much of 1917–1968, a decades-long struggle opening with the Republican Revolution in 1911 that eventually resulted in the formation of the communist People's Republic of China in 1949 under Mao's leadership.[23] China thereby bridges the two periods outlined here in many ways. For example, the conditions that pushed China's revolutionary path from 1911–1949 ring familiar with many locales around Asia during the same time—continual foreign encroachment, the spread of industry and trade, and agricultural discontent among them. Such changes combined to push a "rising anti-foreign nationalism" in China (Wolf 1969) evident in the formation of the nationalist Guomindang and the Chinese Communist Party (in 1921). Interesting as well, *both* world wars again had an impact on Chinese discontent when the May Fourth Movement, "a significant advance in the growth of Chinese nationalism" (Lazzerini 1999: 13), erupted alongside a major strike wave (Selden 1983) to condemn allied decisions after the close of World War I. The civil war in China recommences in 1946 *after* the close of World War II; the end of the struggle against Japan and its long occupation of much of China meant that attention could again turn to issues at home.

The long road of revolution in China offers something of a microcosm of larger issues of cooperation and antagonism between antisystemic movements. For instance, in 1923, the Guomindang established a formal relationship and exchange of advisers with the Soviet Union.

Even with Chinese communists as something of a "second party" in the early nationalist-Soviet relationship (Wolf 1969),[24] the Bolsheviks had a profound impact on Chinese communists in the early years. Displaying the antagonisms inherent between parties in a revolutionary situation, the nationalists and communists in China parted ways in 1927 after Chiang Kai-shek's turn against the communists. The communists' famous Long March in 1934 under Mao was an effort on their part to escape Guomindang encirclement. The revolutionary process in China demonstrates the ways in which internal and external antisystemic actors worked together and against one another.

China's antisystemic impact extended throughout Asia and eventually around the world. From the ashes of the Nationalist Revolution and Chiang Kai-shek's coup, Mao and the communists adopted a new strategy for revolutionary change that focused on the peasantry. This strategy gained favor throughout Asia (and eventually around the globe) and the many struggles for independence that came during 1917–1968. One cannot discount the overall impact of China's revolution on antisystemic movements elsewhere. The very success of the revolution in attaining state power in Asia echoed loudly the accomplishments of the Russian Revolution, again reinforcing the state-power strategy for antisystemic movements (Arrighi, Hopkins, and Wallerstein 1989).

In many ways, China became the revolutionary ideal at this time, the *true* revolutionary state for antisystemic movements around the world. Mao's belief in violence and revolution to realize change presented a radical option for aspiring revolutionaries throughout the world-system at a time when reformist parliamentarianism was increasingly common. For Mao and many who read his *Little Red Book*, "participating in the parliamentary activities of the bourgeois state, as French and Italian communists were doing, simply served to legitimize bourgeois institutions and dampen the revolutionary ardor of the masses" (Morris 1994: 82). When disillusionment with the Soviet Union began to grow in the 1950s—Khrushchev's speech denouncing Stalin and the Soviet invasion of Hungary in 1956 being particularly damaging—the Sino-Soviet split drove home the importance of China among many antisystemic movements. With the Cultural Revolution in the late 1960s, China's place of importance was again emphasized for a "new" set of antisystemic actors. Driven by a resurgent working class taking aim at a "dictatorship of the officials" (Arrighi, Hopkins, and Wallerstein 1989: 106; see also Selden 1995), the Cultural Revolution occurred at a time when the "New Left" was emerging to challenge the decisions and choices made by those from the "old" antisystemic movements who were now the "officials" in positions of power. As Russia waned as a revolutionary ideal and labor and socialism were co-opted in much of the world, revolutionary China took on increasing importance for radicals in Asia and around the world after 1945.

War and Independence in Asia and the Pacific

The story in Asia goes well beyond China at this time as the many European colonies erupted with anticolonial sentiment after World War II. With many one-time antisystemic movements now occupying political office in Europe as organized parties, the struggles here grow all the more complex; to the point, for example:

> Communism, socialism and anti-colonial revolutions have been among the leading protagonists of the twentieth century. Sometimes they have been complementary, at other times opposed. During the First Indochinese War (1945–1954), they were both. Communists in Vietnam were in the forefront of the anti-colonial struggle, while Communists and Socialists in France responded in a variety of convergent and divergent ways. (Rice-Maximin 1986: ix)

The revolutions in Vietnam, Indonesia, and elsewhere in Asia challenged colonial powers and assumptions about movement desires at home and abroad. Radical organizations in one location were often forced to choose between colonial demands for independence and their own aspirations for state power and political participation at home. Under the growing Cold War between the United States and the Soviet Union, many struggles in Asia became battlegrounds between revolutionary and counterrevolutionary forces. The U.S. invasion of Vietnam stands out in this regard. As in the colonies of Africa, a nascent anti-imperialism exploded following World War II and resulted in independence and the formation of new states.

The impact of World War II holds great importance again. The very experience of Japanese occupation *during* the war links many movements against empire *after* the war throughout Asia and the Pacific. The demands of such occupation, including forced rice deliveries to support Japanese troops in Indonesia, the Philippines, Indochina, and elsewhere, placed strains on rural peasantries as well as urban populations that ignited resistance. In Malaysia, the Malay People's Anti-Japanese Army came to prominence because of its adamant resistance to Japanese imperialism. The insurgencies across Asia enjoyed widespread support among rural populations, keying on similar social structural factors that echoed Mao's focus on the peasantry in China. Nationalists in Indonesia, the Viet Minh in Indochina, the Hukbalahap in the Philippines, for example, enjoyed key support among peasant populations in their countries, lending significant weight to postwar efforts at change. In China, the Philippines, and Indochina, the Japanese invasion provided a major catalyst in bringing the peasantry to the side of the communists who were seen actively resisting Japan's advances while other groups and their leaders collaborated (Wolf 1969; Bradley 1999, 2000).

Combining these conditions with the political and economic strains on European powers, all across Asia rural insurgencies and larger revolutionary possibilities made it seem "as if for one brief moment the societies of Southeast Asia could begin to shape their own futures without dictation from the outside" (Anderson 1972: xii–xiii). Of course, mitigating circumstances—the strong desire of weakened but still powerful European states to hold on to colonial possessions, the Cold War struggles between the Soviet Union and the United States—meant such openings were brief, but resistance and revolution in a larger Asia resulted in the end of empire after 1945.

The postwar wave of anticolonial, nationalist, and/or communist struggles in Asia presents a remarkable history. After prolonged struggle, India gained independence in 1947. In 1945, a nationalist revolution driven by the young swelled in Indonesia, ending in 1949 when the Dutch transferred legal sovereignty to the Indonesians under Sukarno. The revolution in Indonesia is interesting because the collapse of the Dutch colonial regime combined with the Japanese occupation to awaken demands for revolution. Sukarno, who came to embody nationalism in Indonesia and around the world, emerged from the *failures* of the revolution (Anderson 1972). Sukarno also drew the counterrevolutionary attention of the United States and eventually faced a military coup with backing from the United States. Yet, by the early 1960s, the Indonesian Communist Party (PKI) would be the largest *nonruling* Communist Party in the world. Linked to the PKI, the Filipino radical, Jose Maria Sison, formed the Communist Party of the Philippines in 1968 after coming in contact with the PKI while on scholarship in Indonesia (Morris 1994). The years 1946–1953 brought the Huk Rebellion to the Philippines, this time a "failed" struggle against a relatively weak state supported again by the United States.

After decades of anticolonial resistance, the August Revolution took place in Vietnam in 1945. On September 2, 1945, Ho Chi Minh proclaimed Vietnam free of colonial rule, "marking the successful culmination of the August Revolution that brought to power the revolutionary leadership of the first postcolonial independent Vietnamese state" (Bradley 1999: 23; see also, Bradley 2000; Short 1989). The outcome of World War II is significant because the colonial power in Indochina, France, was significantly weakened by the war. Likewise, the Japanese occupation was actively resisted by the Viet Minh who were left in good position at the end of Japanese rule (Wolf 1969).

Of course, in Vietnam, matters were not so simple, and 1945 would be only the beginning of a prolonged anti-imperial struggle that enveloped neighboring states as well. At Potsdam in 1945, Truman, Churchill, and Stalin divided Vietnam at the sixteenth parallel leaving the North to China with American aid and the South to Great Britain. This division and outside involvement helped to set the stage for the war in Vietnam.

In 1946, fighting broke out between the Viet Minh and the French, who had returned to Indochina after the departure of the Chinese.[25] In 1954 at Dien Bien Phu, the French suffered "a defeat of such magnitude that it impaired their ability to continue the war" (Wolf 1969: 187)—another hugely symbolic moment in the history of antisystemic resistance. The United States, with the avowed aim to contain the spread of communism, then fully entered the war on the side of the Diem government in the South, ultimately to withdraw in humiliating defeat only in the 1970s. Of no small consequence, the loss of Vietnam severely shook U.S. hegemony in the world-system, as the Cold War superpower fell to a communist guerrilla insurgency fighting against tall military odds. The very process of waging the war and contending with antiwar resistance by a new wave of activists at home tested the resolve of U.S. leadership—keeping in mind that Democratic Presidents Kennedy and Johnson (of the "Good Society" welfare state) drove the United States into the war and then escalated military operations, respectively. As Halliday confirms, "Vietnam … was the most acute crisis of United States hegemony, at the military, economic, and political levels, of the post-1945 period" (1999: 199).

These emergent struggles, many gaining independence in the years after the war, could trace origins of discontent to an intersection between changes wrought at the national level, often under colonialism, and the neocolonial ambitions of imperialist powers after World War II (Walton 1984). The postwar succession of independent Asian states represents a critical wave of interrelated antisystemic struggles. By 1968, some of the most populous countries in the world had won independence. Communists in China, Vietnam, and elsewhere openly pressed systemic forces and at the same time provided new antisystemic models and symbols for radicals around the world.

The Cuban Revolution

> The outcome of today's struggles does not matter. It does not matter in the final count that one or two movements were temporarily defeated because what is definite is the decision to struggle which matures every day, the consciousness of the need for revolutionary change, and the certainty that it is possible.
>
> *Guevara 1997: 161–62*

Alongside China, and Vietnam, the Cuban Revolution (1956–1959) demarcates a watershed moment in antisystemic and world-systemic history drawing out distinctions between radical and hegemonic outlooks. Any discussion of antisystemic activity in the Western Hemisphere after 1945 must include the Cuban Revolution (1956–1959), if for no other reason than its stark impact on national liberation struggles around the world as well as its strategic challenges to U.S. hegemony. As the second successful Third World revolution (the first being China in 1949), Cuba's legacy imparted three fundamental lessons to revolutionary movements and their leaders: one, that armies could be defeated by popular forces; two, that an insurrection can make the necessary conditions for a successful revolution; and three, that making use of the countryside is the best option for armed resistance and guerrilla warfare (Castro 1999). However, the implications of guerrilla war were less important than the impact of Castro's ability to seize power, stay in power, and construct a successful social revolution in the Western Hemisphere (Stavrianos 1981). Perhaps the fundamental impact for international revolutionaries who were engaged in or on the verge of violent liberation struggles, Castro and Guevara represented the vanguard. In many ways, this again echoes the revolutionary impact of China for antisystemic struggle after World War II.

Ideologically, the Cuban Revolution was revolutionary on two fronts. First, it again broke with the ideological dogma of the Soviets that emphasized the urban proletariat as the revolutionary force. Influenced by Mao's Chinese Revolution, Guevara, like most leaders of liberation movements, had embraced a variant of Marxist ideology in viewing socialism as a means of achieving social justice and economic parity.[26] This combination imparted on the Cuban revolutionaries the importance of "culturally and economically de-linking from the world system," and for them socialism was the means to achieve that end (Young 2001).

Closer to home, the Cuban Revolution set precedent in Latin America in two fundamental ways. First, Cuba made it apparent that historic subservience to the United States was not automatically required. The best example here is the Agrarian Reform Law of 1959 with which Castro expropriated American-owned property without compensation and further nationalized public utilities, banking, and transportation (García 2001). Second, the "David and Goliath" style of Castro's challenge made it apparent that radical reform was in fact possible throughout Latin America. Even more directly, "Castro aided exile invasions of Panama, Nicaragua and Haiti but denied it; however, he acknowledged responsibility for a thwarted invasion of the Dominican Republic in June 1959 and promised more efforts to export his revolution" (Wright 2001: 31). Looked at collectively, the entirety of Latin America was overwhelmingly affected by the Cuban Revolution. As Wright again notes, "Political mobilization following the Cuban Revolution was greater than those of the first two waves (World War I; the Depression), and the impact of fidelismo was more widespread throughout Latin America" (2001: 45).

Internationally, the 1966 Tricontinental Conference in Havana presents perhaps the largest influence of the Cuban Revolution on the international community. This conference represented, like Bandung, which is discussed in a later section, a global struggle to be waged against European colonialism and U.S. imperialism across three separate regions of the world (Africa, Asia, and Latin America). Young notes that Guevara's final statement to the Tricontinental[27] "constitutes the first moment where a general internationalist counter-hegemonic position was elaborated by a dispossessed subject of imperialism, powerfully and persuasively invoking others throughout the three continents to open up a new front of resistance, in a global strategy of guerrilla warfare conceived from an internationalist perspective" (2001: 213).

As Castro and Guevara saw it (and like Mao before them), an anti-colonial/imperial struggle could not be based on passive resistance. Armed guerrilla warfare was a crucial element in ensuring liberation. Here again, the epicenters of revolution were moving from old centers, Russia in particular, toward places like Cuba and China. Given the historical specificity of this revolution, Cuba stands in its own right as a defining moment in the history of antisystemic struggle at this time. From Asia and Latin America, the discussion now moves to the third essential region of the world for antisystemic activity following World War II.

Nationalism, Pan-Africanism, and Independence in Africa, 1945–1968

Viewed through the prism of nationalism and Pan-Africanism, the struggles of black people throughout the diaspora, whether reformist or revolutionary, conceptually provided a medium for building solidarity between diverse groups of people. Most of the independence struggles in Africa that followed World War II can be seen as antisystemic because they not only altered the political terrain of the modern world-system through decolonization (see table 3.2) but also created the space and opportunity for subsequent movements to emerge (Wallerstein 1984: 84). World War II plays an important role again as the war delayed the end of colonialism but also made it inevitable (Boahen 1987). Much as in World War I, hundreds of thousands of Africans were conscripted to fight and after the war were again disappointed by the metropoles' rewards for their efforts. In other words, World War II "helped to weaken European powers so seriously, and to arouse political consciousness among colonized peoples so effectively, that the end of the war inaugurated the beginning of decolonization" (Mazrui 1977: 86–87). Anger over the war combined with still simmering outrage over the Italian invasion of Ethiopia in 1935 and a resurgent Pan-Africanism to drive nationalism and a wave of independence in Africa after 1945.

Understanding nationalism as an antisystemic force in Africa requires that certain qualifications be outlined before proceeding. Decolonization took many forms in Africa, from relatively peaceful to prolonged, violent struggle, from reformist efforts to revolutionary ones. Nationalism, for example, means different things to different people at different times:

Table 3.2: African Independence, 1945–1968

Year	Countries
1951	Libya
1956	Sudan, Morocco, Tunisia
1957	Ghana
1958	Guinea
1960	Cameroon, Togo, Mali, Senegal, Madagascar, Congo (D.R.), Somalia, Benin, Niger, Burkina Faso, Côte d'Ivoire, Chad, Central African Republic, Congo (P.R.), Gabon, Nigeria, Mauritania
1961	Sierra Leone, Tanzania
1962	Rwanda, Burundi, Algeria, Uganda
1963	Zanzibar, Kenya
1964	Malawi, Zambia
1965	The Gambia
1966	Botswana, Lesotho
1968	Mauritius, Swaziland, Equatorial Guinea

"Nationalism is seldom an independent variable, but rather a *form* through which a variety of responses, aspirations and interests are expressed. Its force is not internal but depends on the intensity of sentiment of various social groups. That is why self-conscious nationalist politicians never get very far unless they can harness the aspiration of the masses for a better life" (Füredi 1994: 21).

As such, nationalism can be seen as the overarching framework for organizing movements and articulating the motivations and aspirations for change of a larger populace. Attention will be paid here to *radical* nationalist struggles, revolutionary anticolonialism, and armed resistance—places where the path to state power for the leadership of these movements was through protracted armed struggle and often resulted in declared "socialist" states. Also, black nationalism and Pan-Africanism cannot be seen as entirely separate and dichotomous movements for they are linked ideologically, through movement leaders and by the actions of followers. For example, the black nationalist and Pan-Africanist struggles discussed earlier are antisystemic in part because they formed the foundations and created the organizational infrastructures for the anticolonial challenges after World War II.

At the forefront of the African liberation struggle two patterns emerged with decolonization, the "relatively" peaceful transition to independent government and armed struggle. This is significant as we juxtapose the strategies and tactics implored by colonial administrators in order to preserve control of their territories and the response of African nationalists in their demands for liberation. These administrative strategies, regardless of their nature, on the one hand only increased instability in an already unstable environment and on the other hand actually aided Africans in mobilizing politically. To arrive at this point we must look at how the ideological foundations of Pan-Africanism coupled with labor mobilization and changes in colonial policy following World War II formed the basis for organization, resulting in the widespread end of colonial rule.

The Fifth Pan-African Congress in 1945 clearly marks the "diasporic production" and the uniting of the political strains of Pan-Africanism: the early congresses of Du Bois and Williams; the negritude of Senghor and Césaire; and the populist version of Garvey.[28] This congress also marked the full emergence of a tradition of colonial resistance and forged the inroads for an intercontinental movement for decolonization (Cooper 2002; Young 2001). This congress organized by Padmore, Nkrumah, and Makonnen[29] philosophically redefined the movement. Nkrumah, Kenyatta, and other African nationalist leaders took center stage and called for the liberation of Africa for the first time. Geiss confirms, "After a series of failures and disappointments, Pan-Africanism reached its climax with the Manchester congress" (1974: 411). A new generation of radical African nationalists, Nkrumah (Ghana), Touré (Guinea), Kenyatta (Kenya), Lumumba (Congo), Ben Bella (Algeria), and Banda (Nyasaland) to name but a few, were ready to challenge the colonial status quo.

Using the Atlantic Charter, the congress's leadership challenged the colonial powers, in a weakened position after the war, to grant self-government. Churchill's response, that the Atlantic Charter applied only to Axis aggression (Stavrianos 1981: 666), served to incite action toward realizing independence without colonial government acquiescence. The official endorsement of nonviolence/noncooperation based on the Gandhian method became a central theme in direct appeals to the masses for decolonization. In an interesting parallel, the growing civil rights movement of the United States around this time also pursued change through "nonviolent protest action" or what Nkrumah called "positive action." The early liberation movements in Africa and the civil rights movement in the United States demonstrate similarities in leadership styles and movement tactics where both "used similar Gandhian tactics that had worked well in India's nationalist struggle against British colonialism and imperialism" (Assensoh and Alex-Assensoh 1998: 26; see also Fredrickson 1995). In Nkrumah's own account of the congress:

> We listened to reports of conditions in the colonial territories, and both capitalist and reformist solutions to the African colonial problem were rejected. Instead the Congress unanimously endorsed the doctrine of African socialism based upon the tactics of positive action without violence. It also endorsed the principles enunciated in the Declaration of Human Rights and advised Africans and those of African descent

wherever they might be to organize themselves into political parties, trade unions, co-operative societies and farmers' organisations in support of their struggle for political freedom and economic advancement. (1957: 52–53)

An ideological basis of nonviolence constructed in the framework of African socialism provided a seeming "third way."[30] The common ideology of Pan-Africanism at this time was a socialism that developed out of the black Marxist tradition and communist anticolonial activism (Young 2001). Africans' unique brand of socialism developed out of the historical specificity of Africa's colonial situation. This situation also included an interesting anticolonial role for organized workers, urban populations, and associated elites throughout Africa whose place in colonial economies granted them tremendous power.

Postwar Transition: Workers and Colonial Elites in Early African Independence

The European conception of colonial societies in the early twentieth century was archaic and static. By the 1920s, the "civilizing mission" was over, and the colonial authorities had written off Africa as a grouping of "tribes and traditions" and an exploitable labor force not to be invested in by the metropole (Cooper 2002: 18). Yet, from the earliest years of colonial rule, even small numbers of urban wage workers not only threatened the colonial economies but aided in building the organizational infrastructure for resistance in the post–World War II period (Young 2001). Blossoming throughout the 1930s and 1940s, the instability created by strike waves and labor unrest in mines, railways, and ports persisted and expanded after World War II.

Counter to their intent, development strategies, such as better wages, education, health care, and social services, and the subsequent changes in colonial policy, undoubtedly *aided* Africans in mobilizing politically.[31] Several patterns emerged that transcended colonial boundaries. Increased urbanization, a rising, educated middle class, and traditional religious affiliations in some form or another were common threads that fostered and cultivated political mobilization and solidarity in Africa (Hodgkin 1957: 31).

In British and Belgian colonies, there was no political representation of the colonial subject in government, and there was no citizenship for the colonial subject or the slightest indication that citizenship was forthcoming. In these colonies a new type of colonial administrator emerged. These administrators' withdrawal of support from traditional chiefs in favor of the educated, urban elite made it possible for this new African leadership to develop its own political constituencies. As colonial administrators vacillated between patriarchy and developmentalist colonialism, a new nationalist leadership was working toward mobilizing the masses. The principal goal was attaining state power and "once in power, to strengthen its own state-structure within the interstate system" (Wallerstein, 1984: 83).

In the Gold Coast, Nkrumah, for example, was quick to create a political base. By 1948, widespread unrest, strikes, and rural agitation were challenging British colonial rule. Nkrumah's political base initially came out of the United Gold Coast Convention (UGCC), but he later found support among urban workers and the less educated. Nkrumah's breakaway Convention People's Party, formed in 1949, advocated "self-government now," and Nkrumah's nonviolent transition approach to independence found favor with British administrators. As Robinson explains, "'Nonviolent mass action' threw the Black struggle into the hands of the petit bourgeoisie, albeit a radical petit bourgeoisie. It was they who would mediate between the mass movement and the representatives of imperialism" (1983: 274).[32]

In 1957, the Gold Coast gained independence in Ghana, and the independence had major repercussions throughout Africa and the larger diaspora. Martin Luther King, Jr., and other civil rights leaders were even in Ghana by invitation to witness the independence (Assensoh and Alex-Assensoh 1998). Much of British West Africa followed a path to independence similar to that of Ghana. In the French territories, Senghor of Senegal, Houphouët-Boigny of Côte d'Ivoire, and Touré of French Guinea all amassed a following and political support through the language of citizenship and identity. Working *within* the colonial system, these important leaders of independence struggles eventually were placed at the head of the postcolonial political apparatus through elections.

In essence, proletarianization, urbanization, and political mobilization such as mass strikes and civil disobedience created instability in these colonial territories that was impossible for colonial administrators to control. These factors, combined with the global pressures created by the growing anticolonial position in the United Nations and the Cold War position of the United States against *ongoing* colonial empires, led to rapid and relatively peaceful decolonization (Macqueen 1997). South of the Sahara, Ghana was the first to have been decolonized, and by the mid-1960s all of British West Africa had been decolonized. By the end of the 1960s all the colonies of French West Africa and French Equatorial Africa had won their independence—with all but one becoming members of the United Nations (Stavrianos 1981: 667–68). Between 1957 and 1967, 32 countries attained their political independence and came under African leadership.

In 1958, Nkrumah attempted to revitalize Pan-Africanism with the first All African Peoples' Conference in Accra, an important meeting because it brought together resistance movements and allowed for more difficult struggles (Kenya and the Congo) to forge links with other movements (Campbell 1994). Yet, with the formation of the Casablanca group in 1961, which eventually merged into the Organization of African Unity (OAU) in 1963, Pan-Africanism came full circle. As "State-centered Pan-Africanism became institutionalized as the OAU" (Cooper 2002: 184), Nkrumah suspended his campaign for a "United States of Africa." The euphoria of independence was over, and colonial ties of dependence to a metropole power paled by comparison to neocolonial burdens placed on the new states of Africa.

What inevitably emerged from political independence under transition were nationalist regimes tied economically to their former colonies. Ghana, Mali, Tanzania, Zambia, and a few other newly independent states openly claimed to adopt socialism—but found the goals of egalitarian social policies or nationalized industry difficult to achieve under the preponderance of neocolonialism (Hughes 1992). Another problem with the vision of most nationalist leaders was that they accepted colonial boundaries for their new states. What occurred out of decolonization, according to Young, was a "balkanization that left a collection of separate states" (2001: 240).

By the close of the period here, many of these regimes were in serious difficulty, and the Pan-Africanists and the socialist Nkrumah lost power through a military coup in 1966. Signs of difficulty were visible even earlier. In 1960, the year of "triumph" for Pan-Africanism and its "fatal defeat," nearly half of Africa was independent (triumph), but the Congo crisis of the same year eventually led to the assassination of Patrice Lumumba (defeat) (Masilele 1994). Concerning the decolonization process, however, Britain and France's experiences with guerrilla warfare (Algeria and Kenya) made them more "willing" to decolonize. Nevertheless, such "willingness" sets Britain, France, Belgium, and Italy apart from Portugal and southern Africa where a more protracted armed struggle eventually led to decolonization and national independence in the 1970s or later. The discussion now turns to this armed resistance to colonialism in Africa.

Armed Struggle and Anticolonial Nationalism in Africa, 1945–1968

The changes in power throughout the core regions driven home by antisystemic movements there after World War II certainly appear to have created the disequilibria necessary to step up nationalism and closely related labor activity in the colonial world. The all-out embracing of liberal ideology fostered under world war became a major incentive for solidarity between nationalist, Pan-Africanist, and other organizations. Themes of universal liberty had been echoed by the imperialist powers as they sought the aid of colonial subjects in the war effort.[33] Hence, the returning war veterans on *both* sides of the Atlantic sought economic and social justice. With the heightened political consciousness of colonial peoples at this time, minute compromises at the local level were insufficient to stave off the sweeping tide of change. With nationalism at its peak following World War II, Africans were all too ready to demand liberation by force.

Examples are abundant to highlight the instability on the African continent (and really throughout the colonial world). Armed struggle was the outcome of inflexible empires that at all costs sought to maintain the status quo in their respective regimes. Very often, the presence of large numbers of settlers pushed the decolonization process toward violence. While Egypt was the first to gain independence after a military coup in 1952, Algeria fought a bloody revolution from 1954–1962 to gain independence from France. The revolution in Algeria is impossible to understand outside the context of revolutions happening elsewhere in the world. The French defeat at Dien Bien Phu in Vietnam was a major signal for Algerians that resistance was possible (Gilly 1965). Yet, the Algerian Revolution signaled a change to the decolonization process in Africa and elsewhere as well. Frantz Fanon, who came to embody the Algerian struggle, gives voice to this shift, stating, "The process of liberation of colonial peoples is indeed inevitable. But the form given to the struggle of the Algerian people is such, in its violence and in its total character, that it will have a decisive influence on the future struggles of the other colonies" (1967 [1988]: 104). In the violence and the prolonged nature of the conflict, the relatively peaceful and often abrupt path to independence seen elsewhere in Africa was at an end.

Kenya's decolonization was also a protracted, violent affair (mostly for Kenyans despite the rhetoric of and fear inspired by the British administrators). Mau Mau in Kenya, as the resistance became known, was rooted in a long history of land appropriation that left Africans restricted to less than half of the cultivable land (Rotberg 1963). In 1952, with growing urban unrest and increased violence in the countryside, a state of emergency was declared in the colony. It took until 1963 for independence to be declared under Jomo Kenyatta. As in Algeria, Mau Mau was also brutally suppressed.

Taken together, Algeria and Kenya both represent examples of protracted, armed struggles that forced France and Britain, respectively, to rethink their prevailing attitudes in the use of "violence" and "force" as a political solution aimed at anticolonial nationalists (which worked to the benefit of nationalists elsewhere in Africa). Although the transition to independent government came late in Algeria and Kenya—retarded by the presence of large numbers of settlers—it is this experience, combined with global pressures, that forced the French and British to negotiate a process of "controlled" decolonization (Füredi 1994; Wallerstein 1986).

Guinea-Bissau presents a third instance of armed struggle. Guinea-Bissau is particularly interesting because of the widespread pervasiveness of repression in the Portuguese colonies at a time when the political regime in Portugal was a dictatorship. Because of the repression, for the most part political mobilization in all three Portuguese colonies (Angola, Mozambique, and Guinea-Bissau) was conducted as an underground movement. When Lisbon's response was to tighten control even further, revolutionary nationalists as agents of change met colonial violence in kind.

From a global perspective, Guinea-Bissau also provides a striking example of the marked ideological contradictions between the colonial power, the world-economic hegemon (namely, the United States), and anticolonial nationalists. Most interesting concerning the armed, violent road to independence in Algeria and Guinea-Bissau, revolutionary protagonists like Fanon in Algeria and Amílcar Cabral in Guinea-Bissau emerged to advocate and theorize a vision of revolution *in practice* much different from earlier nationalists like Nkrumah. Fanon's advocacy of violence as a liberating force in *The Wretched of the Earth* (1963) provided motivation anew for a new generation of radicals. In South Africa at this time, Nelson Mandela, Robert Sobukwe, and Walter Sisulu were emerging as a new generation of leaders to demand a more militant struggle against settler rule and apartheid. In the United States, blacks were also increasingly frustrated by the nonviolent, Gandhian approach to change of older civil rights leaders. Both Fanon and Cabral also argued for the importance of the peasantry as a revolutionary force (echoing again Mao and Guevara). Fanon's critique of the petite bourgeoisie—he saw them betraying the revolution after independence—flew in the face of earlier elite-driven decolonization processes in Africa (while also proving rather prescient, as many leaders became ineffective presidents and at worst petty dictators after independence). Amílcar Cabral's successful struggle to obtain global support for Guinea's liberation also highlights the cracks in the edifice of empire. In France, Algeria and Vietnam combined to challenge the will of the French state, including French communists now in office. In Fanon's estimation, "Every challenge to the rights of the West over a colonial country is experienced ... as a weakening of the Western world" (1967 [1988]: 124).

With nationalism on the rise, most of the African continent was decolonized by the close of the period here. Yet, the Portuguese empire and the settler colonies of southern Africa would prove stubborn to the tide of independence in Africa; independence would not come to these states until the 1970s or later. Here again, violence and confrontation would be the path to change. Interestingly, once independent, the Portuguese colonies alongside Somalia, Ethiopia, and a few other states would declare themselves in some sense "Afro-Marxist," a "second wave" shift to socialism in Africa (Hughes 1992). The Algerian Revolution and the Guinean Revolution are arguably two key events and Fanon and Cabral two key thinkers in the development of this distinct African version of Marxism (Masilele 1994). Despite the antisystemic implications of such a development, the discussion now moves to the rather systemic outcome of much of the independence efforts discussed to this point.

Bandung: Afro-Asian Alliance and the Nonaligned Movement

The (often newly) independent nation-states in Asia, Africa, and Latin America entered a polarized world in which the United States and Soviet Union faced off in the aftermath of World War II. Cold War realities placed a heavy burden on many of the newly independent states in Asia; the war in Vietnam (as well as Cambodia and Laos) and Suharto's coup in Indonesia present two of the most obvious examples of U.S. involvement in the region. Many of these newly independent states were loath to accept a polarized view of the world, opting instead to pursue a movement of nonalignment in an increasingly aligned world, a difficult or even impossible contradiction for such states.

Growing to embrace countries in every part of the world, "nonalignment was born in the circumstances of the Cold War" (Kohli 1985: 15) while also greatly "influenced by the forces of postwar nationalism expressed in terms of anti-colonialism and anti-imperialism, and the pressing problems of economic underdevelopment" (Kofele-Kale 1978: 253; see also Keuneman 1976). The appeal of nonalignment to many newly independent states reflected a shared set of conditions that compelled struggle during the Cold War era. For these countries nonalignment meant that:

> a country's policy should be independent, based on principles of peaceful co-existence and non-alignment, or it should sympathize with such a policy. A country should support the movement for national liberation, it should not join any collective military alliance, it should not enter into a bilateral alliance with any Great Power and should not permit any foreign power to establish any military bases on its territory. (Bondarevsky and Sofinsky 1975: 50)

Nonalignment as such signaled these newly emerging states' recognition of the perils inherent in attaining power and entering the world stage (or the interstate system) as an "independent" state.

Emerging forcefully with the Bandung meeting of Afro-Asian states in 1955, the immediate roots of nonalignment also extend back to the postwar years. In 1945, Ho Chi Minh proposed to the government of Indonesia "a declaration on uniting the efforts of both states in the struggle against colonialism" (Kovalenko 1980: 18). Also in 1945, the Fifth Pan-African Congress in its "Declaration to the Colonial Peoples" "affirmed the right of all colonial peoples to control their own destiny" (Mathews 1987: 47).[34] In 1947, the first All-Asian conference was held in New Delhi, and in 1949, the Conference on Indonesia took place, again in New Delhi, where sixteen states would demand Dutch withdrawal from the colony (Muni 1982; Kovalenko 1980). Nonalignment ultimately emerged from the shared vision of many different states and their leaders: India and Nehru, Indonesia and Sukarno, Egypt and Nasser, Yugoslavia and Tito, Ghana and Nkrumah, among others.

At Bandung, a large collection of (once) antisystemic movements-turned-leaders of independent states came together to make common claims and set common goals for their states (as well as those still striving for independence). Bandung carried "great symbolic importance because it was the first time that so many nations—from Asia and Africa—many of them newly decolonized—came together in the absence of the great European powers and the Soviet Union and the United States to discuss international affairs" (Waters 2001: 154; see also Wallerstein 1990). Because of this, Bandung greatly troubled core states and "imperialist capital" (Amin 1990b). In the eyes of John Foster Dulles and the U.S. State Department, Bandung "could conceivably lead to the eventual establishment of an intensely anti-Western, anti-colonial bloc from East Asia to Africa" (quoted in Waters 2001: 165; see also Prasad 1983).[35] For the hegemonic, neocolonial United States engaged in a Cold War struggle with the Soviet Union, such a possibility was troubling indeed. Such concerns only worsened when the Soviet Union openly backed nonalignment for its anti-West leanings, and the Non-Aligned Movement displayed similar leanings toward the Soviets (Muni 1982).

Troubling for American policy concerns as well, communist China also took an active interest in nonalignment, hoping perhaps to shape the process of Afro-Asian solidarity more toward China's predilections. Zhou En-lai participated in Bandung's proceedings and would later tour Africa in 1963–1964 visiting ten states to push the idea of a second Afro-Asian conference. In Ghana, Nkrumah and En-lai issued a joint communiqué stating "that all anti-colonial movements in the world should close their ranks and wage a united struggle against the forces of colonialism and neo-colonialism" (Shinde 1978: 66).[36] In such ways, China as well as the Soviet Union, despite profound differences evident in the Sino-Soviet split, tried to engage nonalignment to push critiques of U.S. hegemony at this time. Not to be outdone, nonaligned states and their leaders "played the East against the West to their advantage" (Kofele-Kale 1978: 258). Bandung and the several Non-Aligned conferences that followed in Belgrade, Cairo, and Lusaka witnessed the emergence and growth (from twenty-five member states at Belgrade to fifty-four at Lusaka) of these newly independent states across different continents.

A key dilemma for antisystemic struggle before and ever since, their strategies, including nonalignment, were based on the legal fiction of state sovereignty versus the economic reality of dependence (Kofele-Kale 1978). Nonalignment, like the strategies pursued by labor and socialism in core regions, suffered weaknesses drawn from the very sources from which it emerged. In different ways, labor and socialism's embrace of state power in the core and the emergence of nonaligned states in the recent colonial world were outcomes of an embrace of state power as *the* avenue of change. In the era of the Cold War and the end of colonialism, choosing a path as nonaligned states somehow clear of the two superpowers was easier in theory than in practice. Many of these young, nonaligned nations found themselves from the earliest days accepting economic and military aid with strings firmly attached. The newly formed states, despite the best intentions of the generation of liberation movement leaders who brought them independence, were from the beginning firmly ensconced in the machinations of the interstate system and the ties of unequal exchange. The pursuit of state power was again a strategic trap upon which nonalignment hinged. The liberation movement turned political parties of the many newly independent states after World War II toward following the footsteps of labor and socialism. As Amin describes it, Bandung "was the national bourgeois project of the third world of our time" (1990b: 113).

Decolonization in Africa and Asia was antisystemic in that it broke down the last vestiges of European empire. With African socialism as an ideological base alongside the principles of the Four Freedoms and the Atlantic Charter, Africans and Asians rose up and mobilized the masses; they demanded an end to discrimination, economic and education reform, and elections with universal suffrage (Cooper 2002). The global pressures of liberation struggles and a related labor unrest in Africa, Asia, and Latin America compelled changes in the strategy of European colonial authorities. Without question, these movements placed pressure on reticent colonial powers that brought a rather abrupt end to empire. In the immediate period following independence, the leaders of these new states pursued socialist goals and a path of nonalignment that clearly hoped to reject the economic primacy of capitalism as well as the polarized politics of the Cold War. For a seemingly brief moment, nonalignment as well as Cuba's Tricontinental provided a network for unifying anti-imperialist struggles throughout the globe.

Yet, independence also *strengthened* the capitalist world-system and the United States as hegemon. The one-time liberation movements, now political parties, much like labor and socialist organizations in Europe and North America, were brought firmly within the orbit of state power and the machinations of the modern interstate system. In the years to come, these new states, from Angola to Vietnam, would serve as battlegrounds for the struggles of the Cold War. Without question, the world in

1968—with (often nonaligned) independent states where there were once colonies, communism in China and Cuba, and important social accords benefiting labor and socialist ideals across the core—was a fundamentally different place from that inherited in 1917. The difficulties experienced by labor, socialist, and national liberation struggles at this time serve only to remind us of the difficulties at work in antisystemic struggle. Many (most) of the antisystemic movements over 1917–1968 ended the period close to a rather systemic power. Remarkably, as the period came to a close, an entirely different set of antisystemic actors turned a critical gaze on the "old" movements now in power. The revolutionary fervor of 1968 marks the rising challenge of the "New Left" at this time to which the discussion turns in conclusion.

1968 and the Challenge of a "New Left"

It was not by chance alone that the Tet offensive in Vietnam occurred in the same year as the Prague Spring, the May events in France, the student rebellion in West Germany, the assassination of Martin Luther King, the takeover of Columbia University, riots at the Democratic National Convention in Chicago, and the pre-Olympic massacre in Mexico City. These events were related to each other.

Katsiaficas 1987: 4

Black Power to us means that Black people see themselves as a part of a new force, sometimes called the Third World: that we see our struggle as closely related to liberation struggles around the world. We must hook up with these struggles.

Stokely Carmichael quoted in Fredrickson 1995: 295

By 1968, the world was a very different place, and antisystemic movements were very different social actors. The world-system was fundamentally altered by the antisystemic movements, and the movements in turn were shaped by the world-system. In an interesting dialectic, systemic and antagonistic forces had worked in opposition to establish a fundamentally altered world, yet one that was somehow the same. The older movements themselves had in many places taken new roles as governing parties or were firmly enmeshed in the day-to-day operations of the capitalist world. These "fallen" antisystemic movements were now waging wars (or supporting the states waging wars) *against* national liberation movements in Vietnam and Algeria. The nature of this new dilemma helped to trigger political crises in the United States (Vietnam) and France (Algeria). The revolutionary possibilities apparent in 1968 presented the coming-out party for a new set of movements, a "New Left" that challenged the seeming complacency and compromises of the prior movements. In other words, "The popular uprisings of 1968—in the United States, in France, in Italy, in Czechoslovakia, in Japan, in Mexico—were directed not merely against the existing world-system, the capitalist world-economy, but against the 'old' antisystemic movements in power in the system" (Wallerstein 1990: 39).

To be fair, the "New Left"—antiwar/peace and antinuclear campaigns, women's movements, students' movements, struggles around identity—did not originate with 1968. The roots of many of these important anti-systemic actors extend back years to decades before 1968. Questioning of the "old" Left can be seen in the 1962 Port Huron statement of Students for a Democratic Society in the United States. The Berkeley student strike in California happened in 1964. Khrushchev's denunciation of Stalin and the Russian invasion of Hungary in 1956 "convulsed the world Communist movement. . . . In Britain, the [Communist Party] lost around one-third of its membership and a 'New Left' was born" (Callaghan 2001: 18). Black power in the United States had roots in the early civil rights movement initiated in the late 1940s and early 1950s by a number of black-initiated struggles in the Deep South;[37] Rosa Parks and the Birmingham bus boycott happened in 1955 (West 1999). The notion of "identity politics" was in turn anticipated by black power's insistence on racial pride and self-esteem.

By now, these ties across time and space should not be surprising. As antisystemic movements matured over time, grew in strength and size, ties only became more common. The "New Left" of 1968 recognized the importance of historical precedent at the same time that it questioned the choices made by historical movements. As Katsiaficas explains, "The historical parallels of the May events [in France] were recognized in the written statements of the strikers when they called on the tradition of 1789, 1848, the Paris Commune, and the Russian soviets of 1905 and 1917 to define their movement" (1987: 7). What the new antisystemic movements asserted in 1968 was a rejection of the capitalist world-system including the old movements who were now seen as an integral part of that very system. Following the massive postwar economic expansion, "New Left" critiques targeted capitalist consumption habits (part of the Fordist compromise reached between capital and laborers). The attacks against the Vietnam War by antiwar activists and student movements called into question U.S. hegemony (and the Democratic Party and affiliated labor movements that backed the war). Antinuclear movements, "the consuming passion of the New Left" in the late 1950s (Callaghan 2001), openly challenged the spiraling nuclear arms race inherent in the Cold War (and in part, Soviet Russia's role in the arms race). Quite simply, this new generation saw the old labor and social-democratic movements as no longer antisystemic (Arrighi, Hopkins, and Wallerstein 1989)—they had lost sight of the true goals of 1789, 1848, the Paris Commune, and the Russian Revolution.

Interestingly, these new movements, as they progressed from their early years to the confrontation of 1968, adopted an increasingly militant and/or violent approach to social change. This parallels the turn to armed struggle among national liberation movements in Africa and Asia discussed earlier. Malcolm X, the Black Panthers, and the larger black power movement that emerged in the 1960s in the United States advocated confronting power with power, meeting violence in kind. Carmichael and Hamilton's *Black Power* was powerful because it made the connection between the condition of blacks in the United States and that of colonized peoples elsewhere in the world—"a revolutionary model of national liberation from colonialism" (Fredrickson 1995: 295). Yet again, this shift in tactics among these movements in the late 1960s called into question the notion of reform and nonviolent protest that an earlier generation of civil rights leaders supported. When the Civil Rights Act of 1964 and the Voting Rights Act of 1965 had no immediate impact in the lives of most blacks in the United States, the time was right for appeals to a more militant approach to realizing the movement's goals (West 1999).

In 1968, the world was again privileged to a revolution that called into question the ongoing operation of capitalism and, unique to 1968, the place of "old" movements in the existing order. Without question, the complaints leveled by the "New Left" against the "old" prove the demise of the antisystemic nature of labor, social-democratic, and socialist movements after 1945. Their very success at achieving many long held goals had drawn them into state power within the existing interstate system of capitalism. In 1968, these movement choices and goals were being called into question by students, by women, by peace activists and supporters of black power, or brown power, or even red power. The year 1968 ushered in a new set of antisystemic protagonists:

> If 1968 was anyone's year, it was the year of the students. From Peking to Prague and Paris to Berkeley, students sparked the movements which marked 1968, and more than any other group, it was their international practice ... which made the New Left a global movement. In conjunction with the movements for national liberation, particularly in Vietnam, the student movement became a force in international relations, compelling world policymakers to modify—and in some cases to cancel altogether—their grandiose plans. (Katsiaficas 1987: 37)

Students had been important in antisystemic struggles for a considerable time, but when many one-time opposition leaders became government officials, they turned on students. This divide speaks volumes about the changes wrought in the world-system and in antisystemic movements over the course of 1917–1968.

Notes

1. Hobsbawm demarcates, for this periodization, an age of catastrophe 1914–1945, the golden age 1947–1973, and the landslide from 1973–1991 (1994: 6).

2. This shift can even be recognized in the turn of much of the Left from the Russian Revolution to the Chinese Revolution of 1949 and the Cultural Revolution as *the* global beacon for radical change.

3. This paradox can be seen at work in the inspiration that antisystemic struggles such as the Haitian Revolution or the Paris Commune provided for others seeking radical social change. These same efforts were used by national and international interests to brutally repress slave rebellions in the Caribbean and radical organization in Europe, respectively.

4. So complete was the orientation of the Third International to the Soviet Union that it quickly transformed "from a network of parallel movements into a hierarchical structure adjusted to the needs of a particular state power" (Wallerstein 1990: 25). Cooperation in such a case becomes domination, and linkages turn into one-way conduits of exchange.

5. The Industrial Workers of the World, it should be addressed, was one of the few labor organizations that from inception sought to organize workers regardless of race. However, the Wobblies suffered fierce repression during the years of World War I and were thus greatly weakened relative to other labor organizations that had grown during the same period (Brecher 1997).

6. Bush (1999: 88) notes from 1916 to 1923 there were more than four dozen race riots in the United States, and in the Red Summer (1919) alone there were twenty-six.

7. The American Communist Party, according to Robinson, was constituted out of the "rebellious left wing of the Socialist Movement" (1983: 218), which here is identified as the CPUSA.

8. Lenin's lack of understanding of the racial dynamics entrenched in American society caused him to overestimate black people's ability to readily substitute their racially conscious mind-set for the class-conscious movement of the Communist Party.

9. Bush (1999) notes that Garvey's association with Duse while in London put him in contact with Hubert Harrison, John Bruce, William Ferris, and Arthur Schomberg, all Caribbean intellectuals who would later become active in UNIA. Harrison, according to James (1998), would also be linked to the African Blood Brotherhood.

10. Bush (1999: 96) notes a total of 859 branches.

11. This latter commitment eventually led him to quit the Socialist Party in 1914, evidence of the sometimes tense links between different movements. Harrison, like many radical black nationalists who believed in socialism, was disgusted by the Communist Party's lack of commitment to black workers and the New York leadership's racist treatment of him (James 1969: 125). A. Philip Randolph, on the other hand, advocated the "class first" position of the Socialist Party which, as Bush notes, pushed him politically to the left of Du Bois and to the right of Garvey and Harrison (1999: 92).

12. It appears, even if not explicitly so, that the attempted coup d'état by the African Blood Brotherhood at UNIA's First International Convention was an attempt to oust Garvey and at the same time recruit for the CPUSA. It should be noted, however, that although Robinson (1983) states this incident took place at the First International, Bush (1999) says it took place at the Second International of UNIA. We can only surmise from this discrepancy that the antagonism between UNIA and

ABB may have been such that incidents of this nature may have taken place on more than one occasion.

13. Geiss (1974) has a chapter on nineteenth-century forerunners that implies that Pan-Africanism had a definitive starting point. Any top-down analysis would make this assumption. Instead, we see Pan-Africanism as a consciousness as well as a political movement. In places where there are large ex-slave populations such as Brazil, Haiti, and Cuba, African descendants have synthesized some of their cultural traditions with Europeans; but for the most part, they have retained those spiritual ties that link them to the continent.

14. He further observes that "racial consciousness represents the thought and practice of those individuals and groups who respond to their subordination with individual or collective action designed to counterbalance, transpose or transform situations of racial asymmetry" (Hanchard 1991: 86).

15. Du Bois' argument anticipates much of Lenin's *Imperialism: The Highest Stage of Capitalism*. Lenin's work also provided part of an ideological basis for revolt against colonialism and imperialism for a growing body of nationalists in the non–Western world (Stavrianos 1981).

16. In the Philippines, for example, the Huk Rebellion from 1946–1953 arguably has origins in longer histories of protest dating back to the early years of Spanish colonization (Walton 1984).

17. Interestingly, Altbach (1970) explains that students were important for an emerging nationalism throughout Asia in the 1920s and 1930s.

18. Yet, this was also a period during which important associations, organizations, and trade unions formed in much of Africa—for example, the Tanganyika African Association in 1929, the Railway Workers Union (Sierra Leone), the Mechanics Union (Nigeria), and the Native Defense Union (The Gambia) in 1919 (Boahen 1987). However, *reform* of the colonial system was a common goal of many of these associations at this time.

19. Walton's assessment of the situation for the Huk Rebellion in the Philippines resonates for much of a larger Asia, in that "the prewar years witnessed a general organization and mobilization of workers, significant increases in labor unrest and militant protest, and all of this was based on a broad coalition of rural agricultural and urban industrial workers" (1984: 57). In such a manner, revolutionary actors were created.

20. The postwar years really are the era of the "success" of national liberation movements around the world.

21. According to Rose, "Anti-communism was also used by the government to contain the peace movement and other progressive activities" (2000: 81–82).

22. It should be pointed out that the movements that emerge in the next period starting with 1968 target the very movements here that "succeeded." These movements targeted the very failure of the strategies and the co-optation of these movements. The 1962 Port Huron statement of Students for a Democratic Society, for example, openly challenged the "old" Left.

23. Wolf (1969) traces the impetus for China's revolution back to the Taiping and Nien struggles of the mid-nineteenth century, what he calls "rehearsals of a still greater event, the peasant-based Communist revolution of the twentieth century" (1969: 118–19). There can be little doubt that in China and places throughout the world, earlier struggles carried lessons and helped to form the issues and protagonists that would push resistance in later times.

24. Such concern with revolutionary nationalism is, of course, indicative of Soviet Comintern desires at this time, but it is also interesting to note that the "Chinese

Question" played an important role in Soviet intraparty conflict, as Lenin, Trotsky, and Stalin all weighed in with different opinions on China (Pantsov 2000).

25. It is interesting to note that the presence of the Chinese and Americans in Vietnam following the end of the Pacific War played no small role in facilitating the Viet Minh's rise to power. As Worthing relates, "The presence of the Chinese and Americans delayed the return of the French and ensured that Ho Chi Minh had time in which to consolidate his control over Vietnamese politics and to prepare for future negotiations with the French" (1997: 127). Interestingly, Ho Chi Minh had worked with the United States as an agent against the Japanese during the war, and for some time afterward, the Viet Minh leadership would continue to look toward the United States for help (Bradley 1999, 2000).

26. Castro would not declare himself a Marxist-Leninist until 1961, hence completing the "fidelista-communist merger" in 1965 (Wright 2001: 23).

27. Because this date (1967) comes after the Tricontinental Conference, hosted by Cuba in 1966, I think this statement was placed in the Tricontinental journal that was a result of the conference.

28. The conference was also strategically timed to coincide with the communist-led World Trade Unions Conference of 1945, which thereby added a distinctly nationalist element organized around trade union activity (Young 2001: 238).

29. Robinson (1983) credits Makonnen—as publisher of some of the works of Eric Williams, Padmore, and Jomo Kenyatta—with being as instrumental as Du Bois, Padmore, and Nkrumah in organizing the 1945 congress.

30. This is again analogous to the Non-Aligned Movement and the 1955 Bandung Conference discussed later. The reactions of these movements, centered on different world regions, directly reflect movement realities at this time and their immediate rejection of historical capitalism and the violence of colonial domination.

31. Hodgkin further notes that public investments from 1945 through 1953 were "estimated roughly at £275 for the French, £160 for the British, and £75 for Belgian, Africa; and, though many economists would argue this is well below the desirable minimum, it is certainly on a much larger scale than pre-war" (1957: 29). Stavrianos notes similarly for this period, "British West African producers more than doubled the value of their exports between 1938 and 1946. Likewise the value of Congo exports increased fourteen times between 1939 and 1953, while government revenues rose four times" (1981: 666). This economic expansion led to improvements in housing, sanitation, and schools.

32. Robinson cites Azinna Nwafor as offering, one of what he refers to as, "the most forceful critiques of the Pan-African movement." In essence, Nwafor concludes that the choice of revolutionary liberation was not offered to the masses as an option. It was the Pan-Africanist, he claims, that "represented themselves to the colonial authorities as the only force capable of curbing the violence of the masses." Nkrumah would actually work to stifle more radical nationalists in Ghana (Hughes 1992). Nwafor further credits the leadership of this movement, who actually came to power, with establishing the Organization of African Unity (OAU) as a vehicle for maintaining the "status quo" and the subsequent and continuing disarray of contemporary Africa.

33. Geiss (1974) notes that 372,000 Africans from the British colonies and 141,000 from the French colonies fought in the war effort.

34. The same author is keen to point out that African nationalism and Pan-Africanism, discussed elsewhere in this text, had a serious nonaligned element. African leaders such as Nkrumah and Nasser certainly demonstrate the overlap of such concerns.

35. In great detail, Waters aptly demonstrates how Bandung and the Non-Aligned Movement in general challenged a worried Australia, a state with colonial possessions of its own, a race-based immigration policy, and many Bandung attendees as rather close neighbors.

36. The discussion here benefits greatly from Shinde's excellent and detailed history of Chinese involvement in nonalignment and Afro-Asian solidarity. As Shinde relates, China "came to view Afro-Asian solidarity as the most important force in the united front against imperialism" (1978: 65), although China's idea of Afro-Asian solidarity did not necessarily coincide with the nonaligned states.

37. Fredrickson (1995) points out that the term "black power" was first used in a widely noticed way in 1954 as the title of Richard Wright's account of his trip to Ghana to observe the nationalist movement of Nkrumah.

*

Chapter 4

Transformations of the World-System and Antisystemic Movements: 1968–2005

Fouad Kalouche and Eric Mielants

Antisystemic Movements

Because the world-system is in a constant state of transformation, anti-systemic forces may transform and shape the system in ways that are deemed oppositional at a particular social-historical intersection but that may not be oppositional in the long run. This can make "antisystemic" an elusive term over long periods of time. It is against this observation that we examine the interplay of systemic and antisystemic forces in relation to the contemporary world-system from 1968 to 2005. This period has been especially marked by the permeation of the world-systems' multiple cultural systems by dominant capitalist social imaginaries, provoking reactions and adaptations that have become inherent to the world-system itself. Social imaginaries encompass sites of both intangible and material forces pertaining to psyche (affects, desires, intentions, representations, etc.); social institutions underlying ethics and norms; political institutions underlying power relations; economic interactions encompassing production, consumption, distribution, and exchange; and other social and environmental relations enveloping varied ways of living.[1]

The term "movement" entails by contrast conscious and self-reflective teleology. Many movements are, it should be remembered, not antisystemic per se but can be described as "antirepressive," aimed at the repressive state apparatus. They may contribute to the well-being of the oppressed without being antisystemic, as in "liberal reform" movements. As Wallerstein has suggested, most antirepressive and liberal reformist movements are clearly motivated by systemic forces permeated through a "capitalist civilization" that demands "more" for "us" (Wallerstein 1978: 1–10).

Most antisystemic movements after 1800—including labor, socialist, and communist movements—situated themselves in relation to the "state," with the purpose of evading, abolishing, or controlling it. But while antisystemic movements were actively looking to control the "state," systemic forces have responded more recently by perfecting ways of producing desires and needs and shaping "subjectivities" (Foucault 1982, 2000; Deleuze 1990, 1995). In this respect systemic forces now operate by dominating social imaginaries and inhabiting cultural worlds at the base of a less stable interstate system. These developments distinguish our epoch from previous ones: by the time of our epoch, both systemic and antisystemic forces have undergone significant transformation.

Part One: Antisystemic Movements 1968–1989

If 1968 was a period of disillusionment with the historic antisystemic movements (nationalist, socialist, labor, and social-democratic; see Amin, Arrighi, Frank, and Wallerstein 1990; Arrighi, Hopkins, and Wallerstein 1992: 221–42; Wallerstein 1991a: 65–83; and Wallerstein 1999b: 109–25), it was also a time of transformation for antisystemic struggles across the globe. While it is impossible to present a comprehensive overview of all major antisystemic events, we consider a pool of significant representative events. We proceed chronologically to point to possible effects, links, and transformations.

World-Historical Events circa 1968

Three major world-historical events were influential in determining forms of popular struggle throughout the 1968 period: the Chinese Cultural Revolution, the Cuban Revolution, and the Vietnam War. The "Cultural Revolution" emerged in 1966–1967 as the Red Guards conducted destructive attacks against the People's Liberation Army (especially high-ranking officers) and the Communist Party bureaucracy. Only in 1968 did it change to a struggle supposedly carried out by peasants and workers rather than armed militants. The Cultural Revolution was meant to reshuffle the cards of class struggle and to enhance the self-importance of certain strata of the population that were oppressed by other strata. But the violence of the destruction that was meant to destabilize an entrenched system resonated around the globe. Armed struggle was deemed necessary in continuous class warfare, where the masses could take on the task of shaping their future rather than trusting specialized bureaucrats or party apparatchiks. The antibureaucratic struggle was thus a way of ensuring that the masses, voiceless and shapeless, took an active role in self-government.

This orientation was echoed in Cuba where Ernesto Che Guevara, a member of the Castro government from 1959 until 1965, decided to disseminate the practice of "guerrilla warfare." Around the same time that the Red Guards and other revolutionary groups were actively engaged in armed struggle in China, Guevara was engaged with Latin American peasants in rebellions aimed at regaining control of their future. Like the Red Guards, this engagement was halted in 1967 when Guevara was killed in Bolivia. Interestingly, as early as February 1963, Guevara wrote a piece entitled "Against Bureaucracy" in which he presented a form of reeducation, invigorated with nationalism, as the median between what he called "guerrillarism" and the *Junta Central de Planificacion* (Guevara 1968: 121–27).

Nationalism, of course, was behind the Vietnamese successes in opposing their French and American aggressors. But this nationalism was characterized by a socialist ideology and was related to a struggle against "imperialism" that used any means necessary to achieve "liberation." In the Tet offensive of 1968, for example, the romantic construction of a David versus Goliath scenario permeated the imagination of an entire generation that felt empowered to struggle against all authoritative and dominant powers and to liberate itself not only from imperialism but also from other forms of oppression.

These three processes were combined with numerous other struggles that inspired "popular" movements around the globe, and a variety of movements would flourish throughout this period. While nationalist struggles often took on ideologies of socialism, the popular imaginary in core countries started veering toward what we will call "identity" movements—paralleled in later periods, particularly in the periphery, by orientations toward "ethnic" and "religious" identities.

The Decline of Traditional Antisystemic Movements and Rise of "Identity" Movements

Reshuffling the cards of class struggle enhanced the self-importance of certain oppressed strata of society. In Cambodia, this process led to taking class struggle to its logical limits. The Khmer Rouge took the Cultural Revolution's aims of "transforming education, literature, art and all other parts of the superstructure which do not correspond to the socialist economic base" literally, and decided that the only logical attainment of such aims would be through a single class system. This led to the systematic elimination of the intelligentsia, the class thought to carry within it the ingrained bourgeois values that sustained the capitalist superstructure. Most core-based imaginaries, however, interpreted this aspect of the Cultural Revolution as a new crisis of legitimacy of authority, accompanied by a prevailing antibureaucratic tendency. In the core, similar struggles aimed at the superstructure occurred with the proliferation of various identity movements combating sexism, racism, as well as authority, assimilation, and integration—which in turn came to compete with nationalist or socialist identities.

A new *student consciousness* emerged in the 1960s amid the crisis of education and a growing dissatisfaction with the economic and political conditions dominated by the repressive "old" parties and an ominous Cold War. To this was added a desire for autonomy that reflected the proliferation of revolutionary and antiauthoritarian imaginaries. From 1967 to May 1968 and continuing until 1973, student unrest exploded across France, West Germany, Spain, Italy, Poland, the United States, Brazil, Mexico, the United Kingdom, Argentina, Algeria, and Senegal. This was soon extended to other countries including Canada, Japan, South Korea, Greece, India, Zambia, Pakistan, Colombia, Costa Rica, Ecuador, and Venezuela (Katsiaficas 1987: 37–57). However, as an identity group aimed at empowering itself, the "students" as an independent movement did not last beyond the 1980s (Altbach 1981), although some elements became part of other movements or causes.

By this time the Soviet Union could no longer be counted on to offer an alternative system, much less a replacement for the capitalist world-economy. This resulted in reforms and reassessment of the roles and functions of the Communist and Socialist parties worldwide. Communist parties split into factions, with many marginalized and persecuted in the semiperiphery by Socialist or Social Democratic parties. Maoism inspired a few Communist parties in power (e.g., Albania, Cambodia) but mostly left its mark in the periphery. It inspired peasant-based and localized, cultural, socialist approaches to government. Combined with Che Guevara's guerrilla *"focos"* strategy, Maoism inspired guerrilla warfare and armed propaganda struggles across the globe. During the late 1960s and 1970s, guerrilla warfare became a socialist as well as a nationalist instrument of armed struggle aimed at taking control of the state. But by this time it was no longer as effective. While it may have worked earlier in Cuba (and elsewhere in decolonization struggles), few socialist armed struggles successfully took over a state.

One successful example was the Sandinista National Liberation Front (*Frente Sandinista de Liberación Nacional*) of Nicaragua in 1979. The front relied on a complicated "practice of social transformation" that involved combining socialist goals with nationalist, antirepressive, indigenous, and other aspirations (Coraggio 1985: 203–31). A monolithic socialistic strategy would probably not have been as successful in defeating both Somoza's forces and in holding back the U.S.-supported Contras. As elsewhere, when social self-identification or "identities" proliferated (women, men, peasants, urban dwellers, students, workers, unemployed, international socialists), social movements were transformed. Socialist or nationalist movements that could not cater to, and combine the interests of, numerous strata of the population were not able to sustain their struggles effectively. In El Salvador, for example, the Popular Liberation Forces (*Fuerzas Populares de Liberación*) aimed at a "prolonged popular war" by building on strong peasant support. While at times militarily effective, they were not able to engage the "masses" (Green 1997 [1991]: 150–54). One result of these trends was that more guerrilla warfare–style armed struggles started turning toward desperate terrorism.

The 1980s prepared the way for the 1990s, as finance and speculative capital advanced wildly and state socialism was tossed out the window. While Reagan and Thatcher were unleashing the "blind fury" of conservative forces against the "evil empire," socialism was collapsing and new forces came to motivate the masses. American direct and indirect interventions—as in Nicaragua, Honduras, El Salvador, Grenada, Colombia, Afghanistan, and Panama—showed that capitalist forces were ready to save hundreds of thousands from the clutches of socialism—even if it took killing most of them. Militarily, capital was able to create soldiers for itself everywhere through the production and support of "right-wing" identities built on pure ideologies of the free market (e.g., Colombia, Nicaragua, El Salvador) or through "Muslim" defenders of a pure faith fighting infidels (Afghanistan).

By the 1990s, states and corporations increasingly used mercenary armies (such as Executive Outcomes or DynCorp), led mostly by American ex-military personnel. The economic policies implemented by the Washington consensus throughout the 1980s, along with those of the U.S.-dominated international financial institutions, had a lasting impact, ranging from U.S. pressures exerted on Japan, to extensive international regulation and manipulation of trade, foreign currencies, tariffs, and the widespread use of the dollar, to the imposition of "liberalization" schemes (and "structural adjustment") on Third World countries (Arrighi 1994: 323; Harvey 2003). State socialist policies everywhere (including France in the early 1980s) could not last in this global environment, and the Soviet Union and its satellite states were led to collapse through compounded causes including the ever-accelerating arms race. As state socialism was expiring, new religious and ethnic "identities" developed.

The 1979 Iranian Revolution reflected what was happening across various geocultural spaces in the world-system. In the 1980s, identity, religious, and ethnic movements flourished as forms of resistance to an "internationalization" or "regionalization" that grew more and more capitalistic. Afghanistan reinforced Vietnam as yet another David fighting another Goliath and joined the Iranian Revolution in inspiring antisystemic religious ways of relating to a world repressed through modernist, socialist, and liberal discourses.[2] Religion became an effective component of various social movements in the Middle East, North and West Africa, as well as in India, Europe, and the United States, where Muslims, Hindus, Jews, and Christians organized themselves politically and economically in order to confront the changing face of their societies. Nationalist and socialist struggles were greatly affected by these transformations. In 1989, the Soviet withdrawal from Afghanistan contrasted with the Vietnamese withdrawal from Cambodia; the first was leaving behind a "specter" while the second was abandoning a cadaver.

In this climate the fall of the Berlin Wall was widely proclaimed to be the success of liberal dreams in fostering imaginaries of "freedom" and the "equality of rights," while surpassing any dreams of "justice" and "economic equity." Reaganism and Thatcherism provided for a counterresistance that not only undermined communism worldwide, but also changed the meaning of socialism itself. The reign of Mitterrand in France and the sweeping victory for socialists throughout Europe ironically marked a reformation and liberalization of socialism. Meanwhile struggles against European unification revealed a growing opposition to centralization and an imaginary that demanded less centralized control and more localized interests. "Freedom" became the catchword of this era, and with it the expansion of markets and elimination of restrictions on capital.

Under these pressures internationalism was transformed into an empty discourse of rights that overrode discourses of equity and distribution. Freedom brought with it the proliferation of global investments, the formalization of international intellectual property rights, and the increasing role of international institutions promoting privatization and deregulation. These capitalistic forces also revived, however, oppositional forces that drew on a left-oriented ideology: anarchism, antiauthoritarianism, squatters' movements, and antiracist and pro-immigrant groups started to multiply in the core, especially in Western Europe.

Following the Chinese model of reorganization into collectives and cooperatives, pockets within countries such as France or Italy reacted to the growing social crisis by calling for workers' autonomy and self-management (Calvi 1977; Castoriadis 1984 [1957]). Although they fell short of generating autonomy, various cooperatives, collectives, and communes flourished throughout the West and the Third World, advocating self-management and nonhierarchical relations; sometimes these reactions were combined with other communal, religious, or identity movements. Throughout the 1980s and into the 1990s, local communities interested in cooperative efforts and communal autonomy flourished everywhere, out of necessity in the periphery and semiperiphery, and as a political engagement in the core. Neo-Luddite or anticonsumer sentiments emerged as alternatives to capitalism, as did many identity-based communities, with their antisystemic drive made more effective through collaborative efforts and active resistance to capitalist values. Some of these communities built their identity on an oppositional ideology that was neither ethnically nor religiously based; cults proliferated (from Guyana, to Switzerland, to Waco) as did military or semimilitary associations or hate groups (antistate militias, white supremacists, anti-immigrant groups). Some communities were also built on anarchist principles (especially in Italy, the Netherlands, France, Greece, Spain, Mexico, Argentina, and the East Coast and Midwest of the United States), while others flourished as squatters (especially in Germany, Italy, France, Mexico, and the United States).

At the height of the 1980s, homeless individuals, impoverished people, immigrants, destitute families, and young migrants found refuge in parks and abandoned buildings in core countries. Millions of the impoverished and destitute of the periphery and the semiperiphery, in addition to increasing numbers of refugees fleeing a variety of wars and conflicts, started building shantytowns or *bidon-villes,* mostly in urban areas (from Rio de Janeiro to Cape Town). Inevitably, confrontations between these poor populations and the state followed and movements were formed. In Europe, the height of confrontations with the state and supporting demonstrations emerged in the 1980s (esp. 1975–1977 in Italy; 1980 in the Netherlands; 1980–1981 and 1985–1987 in Germany and France; and 1989–1990 in Germany, France, and the United States) (Katsiaficas 1998; Hamel, Lustiger-Thaler, and Mayer 2000; Kriesi et al. 1995).

The global nature of these movements was also extended through a new "internationalism" associated with new identities. The struggle against the war in Vietnam and against the Cold War and the possibility of a nuclear holocaust brought people together in peace movements, which reached their peak in Europe during the mid-1980s. Meanwhile environmental movements aiming at the protection of human, animal, and earth rights came to the fore. Coalitions among these movements and their cooperation on transnational issues reflected the internationalization and the proliferation of similar problems across national boundaries. These kinds of coalitions initially emerged as alliances of nation-states under the banners of such internationalist tendencies and sometimes against dominant ideologies. The nonaligned movement, for example, inspired various movement-based coalitions to evolve into cartels of power politics based on regional economic and political interests. Although most regional state coalitions emerged in the 1950s–1960s (e.g., Organization of American States, Organization for Economic Cooperation and Development, South East Asia Treaty Organization, the Arab League, Economic Community of West African States), international institutions that were either independent (Bretton Woods institutions, General Agreement on Tariffs and Trade/World Trade Organization) or part of the United Nations system (World Health Organization, U.N. Development Programme, U.N. Children's Fund), and that flourished on the basis of post-1945 internationalism, started to become effective global forces in the 1980s.

The freedom and human rights campaigns of the 1980s also had numerous unexpected consequences, as new internationalist and egalitarian orientations started inhabiting international institutions and creating hundreds of international nongovernmental organizations (NGOs) with antisystemic orientations. The United Nations started investigating the importance of "economic" and "social" rights. In the late 1980s and early 1990s, mass movements of solidarity for the humane and/or equal treatment of immigrants, minorities, and the poor started to spread in the core and formed a constellation of new movements calling for policies opposing traditional mechanisms of upholding the interstate system and the capitalist world-economy. These ranged from pro-immigration rights movements, antiracist movements, and movements calling for the elimination of debt and redistribution of wealth. These movements of the 1980s would become the backbone of today's global egalitarian and antiglobalization movements.

The Decline of Antisystemic Labor Movements

While these new movements based on new identities were emerging, older movements died. Most prominent were labor movements in the core and in a few countries of the "rising" semiperiphery—including "communist" countries such as Poland or Czechoslovakia—which became more preoccupied with their self-interest associated with the professionalization of workers. Indeed, in the core, the labor movement was predominantly guided by liberal-reformist tendencies interested in reforming the system institutionally in order to guarantee certain rights and privileges for those already legally residing within the core, rather than transforming the system as a whole.[3] In the 1980s and 1990s, labor movements in the core ceased to generate any antisystemic activities and many of their constituents felt as if they belonged to a "professional class," that is, an amalgamation of "white-collar" with "blue-collar" workers, all working toward higher levels of credit and purchasing power.

During the same period, labor movements in the periphery and other "rising" semiperipheral countries, especially in Southeast Asia and Latin America, were mushrooming into antirepressive struggles. The "outsourcing" policies of core countries, which benefited semiperipheral nations first, initially led to a growth of unionization that was in many cases antisystemic in orientation. Only in the 1990s, with "subcontracting" to smaller and nonunionized factories and with yet another wave of "outsourcing" from the semiperiphery to the periphery did the piecework system replace assembly lines in the semiperipheral countries. This led to the decimation of labor unions and to more repressive work conditions encouraged and allowed by the "savage" capitalism of the 1990s, which reintegrated in the world-system the extraction of absolute surplus value or "new slavery" (e.g., sweatshops, sexual slavery, indentured labor). The majority of the peasants or farmers living in the periphery and the semiperiphery were hit hard in the 1990s after the dismantlement of Fordist policies and the implementation of structural adjustment programs or neoliberal trade policies that undermined farm subsidies and, in some cases, food subsidies. Some may become "professionals" but most will become "casual laborers." The worst off and their families may end up trapped in "migrant-importing" or "slave-exporting" schemes, thus swelling the ranks of the "new slavery" (see the section "1989 and Beyond: 'Savage' Capitalism and U.S. Hegemony" in part two of this chapter).

Our aim is not to map the antisystemic labor movements across our period; a good start for such an endeavor would be the excellent survey of "labor unrest" across the world-system conducted by a research working group a decade ago (see Silver, Arrighi, and Dubofsky 1995). Representative cases to support our observations are now many. In Latin America, the state-controlled trade unions in Argentina, Mexico, and Brazil gave way to new forms of labor alliances with various antirepressive movements. In Brazil, for instance, a new Brazilian Workers' Party (PT or *Partido dos Trabalhadores*) was formed in 1979, through an alliance of rural unions, radical Catholics, left-wing intellectuals, and shantytown movements (Green 1997 [1991]: 155). Invigorated by the metalworkers' strikes in 1978–1980 in São Paolo, and in 1980 in São Bernardo, the PT became an important movement precisely because it reached out to other popular movements not representing workers but a variety of oppressed people (landless peasants, homeless and unemployed, women's groups, indigenous movements, etc.). Unlike other labor union–based parties, the PT increased in popularity and power in the 1980s and 1990s, culminating in the election of PT leader Luis Inácio "Lula" da Silva as president in 2002.

Peru's trade unionists also combined their efforts with popular neighborhood movements (*barrios populares*) in their nationwide strikes between 1977 and 1979 (Henry 1985: 127–46). The factors that made Latin America a hotbed of antisystemic activities in the 1970s and 1980s included: a) repressive military regimes; b) radical Catholic "liberation theology" and "Base Christian Communities" established after the 1968 Medellín Conference of Latin American Bishops; and c) the increasing pauperization of mass urban populations and the disruption and destruction of peasants' livelihoods. When labor combined its forces with other movements, it was able to grow as a movement as had happened in Brazil. However, Latin America was also a popular site for socialist guerilla movements backed by labor and/or the peasantry. While 1979 was the year of the founding of the Brazilian PT, it was also the year of the successful Nicaraguan Revolution. Grenada and Iran were other sites of change in 1979, and like Nicaragua, they revealed that "labor" could no longer function independently of other movements, be they social-ist-based (Nicaragua), religious-based (Iran), or identity-based (e.g., the women's movement in Grenada).

These lessons spread. A reinvigorated internationalist orientation of labor, with special links between the core, the periphery, and the semiperiphery, was reestablished in the late 1990s but its mobilization power remained negligible. Massive efforts of international institutions (not limited to the International Labour Organization) and NGOs were undertaken to support workers' rights in various outsourcing sites in the (semi)periphery. In the core, a reinvigorated but dwindling labor force in industrial production opted for joining the ranks of those dissatisfied with regionalization and deregulation efforts, and would play a major role in the emerging "antiglobalization" movement.

The Transformation of Nationalism and Socialism and the Rise of Terrorism

Nationalist movements were only antisystemic in the anticolonial stage as they undermined the resources and threatened the economic as well as the political and sociocultural stability of core capitalist countries. Fewer were considered antisystemic when the outcome of their liberation struggle created a socialist space, or provided an egalitarian, distribu-tive, and communitarian form of government that countered exploitative capitalist conditions. Most nationalist movements that achieved control of the state ultimately participated in the consolidation of the interstate system, even as they ended up as the playground for American and Soviet realpolitik and fell victim to the so-called Cold War.[4]

The Soviet Union's withdrawal of support for world socialism and its entrenchment as a bureaucratic system engaged in a Cold War with capitalist centers meant limited support for state socialism and for so-cialist liberation struggles (although Cuba filled that gap in many parts of Africa). The demise of Soviet support also meant a reassessment of socialist doctrines and an attempt to realize socialist goals in a capitalist-dominated world (an impossibility, as socialism was supposed to succeed and flourish as a historical system in its own right). The neoliberal policies implemented in the 1980s by an aggressive United States also served as a secondary set of forces that undermined socialism.

Nationalist movements unable under these conditions to take over the state, along with socialist and communist forces that were disillusioned

by the state, forged the necessary mix of direct action and countervio-
lence to become "terrorists." Immersed in desperate situations, dwindling
members of these movements resorted to desperate means. But instead of
smashing the state machine, as recommended by Marx in *The Eighteenth
Brumaire,* they perfected it—through a fabricated need for security. It is the
interstate system, under U.S. hegemony, that smashed most antisystemic
terrorists (those terrorists who targeted capitalist institutions or centers
of power and who were motivated by socialist or communist ideologies),
using the new tool of controlling imaginary significations, along with
the application of the military and economic muscle necessary for any
hegemon to control the means of terror and mass genocide.

"Terrorism" is a charged word with a long history of use and abuse
(Onwudiwe 2001: 28–49). We use it here to designate "a strategy that
generates fear and anxiety, through violent methods, in order to achieve
political aims." In most cases then, terrorism is proper to state institutions
and to the state's ideological or repressive state apparatuses. The terror of
random violence, when it is not applied through dominant state powers,
becomes the "weapon of the weak" (see Onwudiwe 2001; Chomsky 1986,
2000; Herman 1983). Such a form of desperate resistance that proliferated
in the 1960s and 1970s, and reached unprecedented heights in the mid-
1980s (reported "terrorist" incidents increased from 572 in 1975 to 3,525
in 1984 [Katsiaficas 1987: 182]) as socialist, communist, and nationalist
promises started to wane, seems to have been born again.

When faced with desperate situations and devoid of hope for the success of their movements (e.g., in taking over the state), some individuals
or groups have taken it upon themselves to appropriate that strategy as in
czarist Russia, in Nazi-occupied Europe, in China's liberation wars, and
in Algeria's decolonization struggle. The strategy was appropriated by
desperate national liberation movements, such as the Palestinian liberation movements, the Irish Republican Army (IRA), and yet other groups
desiring a separate nation-state based on a shared religion, ethnicity,
language, or another identity trait. Socialist strategies also started appropriating terrorism in an attempt to counter the violence of capitalism,
as was the case with Baader-Meinhof, Action Directe, Brigate Rossa, the
Black Panthers, Tupac Amaru, the Japanese Red Army, Sendero Luminoso,
etc. Socialist activists also appropriated various dimensions of "terrorism" and spread them across the globe in the 1970s and 1980s, as in the
targeting of chief executive officers and rich politicians for kidnappings
or assassinations, and the targeting of symbolic locations, meetings, companies, and brand names for destruction or disruption. These strategies
were soon reappropriated in different contexts and performed in the
name of a different set of meanings and goals; some became associated
with religious and ethnic movements—which replaced socialism and
nationalism as dominant movements—while others became associated
with "antiglobalization" tendencies.

Rise of Religious Nationalism

In the aftermath of 1968, "liberation theology" merged with many socialist and nationalist antirepressive struggles across Latin America and in Mexico where leading Catholic figures, as well as common practitioners of the faith, reaffirmed a social commitment to helping the poor and to assisting the oppressed. This commitment materialized itself in a large-scale organizational attempt at offering assistance, education, and in building communities. In South America and Mexico, countless people hoped to liberate themselves from military regimes and repressive governments. In Central America, liberation did not come easily; priests, bishops, nuns, and scores of believers and lay people were massacred by right-wing militias and armies trained, financed, and supported by the U.S. government. In El Salvador, Guatemala, and Honduras, armies and militias trained by the U.S. Army and its School of the Americas helped to defeat the liberation theology of those clergy within the Catholic Church who made the mistake of choosing "the preferential option for the poor" (Chomsky 2003: 48–51). As archbishop Dom Helder Camara of Recife, Brazil, famously put it: "When I give bread to the poor, they call me a saint; but when I ask why people are poor, they call me a communist" (Chomsky 2003: 48–51). At the same time, in the 1970s and 1980s, a different set of religious beliefs took hold of oppressed populations in the Middle East, India, and elsewhere. The face of nationalism was changing, especially as it reflected the plight of the impoverished by increasing neoliberalization; it was no longer socialist in orientation, but often religious or ethnic.

In the Middle East, postcolonial governments cracked down on Communist parties and highlighted socialist versions of nationalism that soon evolved into a form of Arab pan-nationalism. Every government was eliminating radical egalitarians, even if those governments declared allegiance to socialism and allied themselves with the Soviet Union or were nonaligned. In Iraq, the socialist Baath government started an extensive purge from government and systematic elimination of members of the Iraqi Communist Party (from 1978 to 1986). Similarly, Nasser's regime in Egypt was working on land reform and creating an "Arab socialism" while exterminating communists.

At the same time religious movements—such as the Islamic Brotherhood—were also persecuted, as Arabism was defined in secular terms. The pan-Arab movement reached its peak in the late 1950s and continued through the 1960s as Egypt, Syria, Yemen, Libya, and the Sudan attempted—unsuccessfully—different combinations of unitary or cooperative schemes. These failed attempts at federation continued until the early 1970s when Nasserism and Pan-Arabism started to wither; by 1973, after the last major Arab-Israeli military confrontation and the OPEC attempt at empowerment, they declined rapidly. Nationalist and socialist movements in the Arab world were held together during the 1980s primarily for two reasons: (1) the shared commitment to the Palestinian cause (which was used by most Arab dictators as a political tool); and (2) the shared opposition to imperialism manifested in the region by the United States and its allies through direct U.S. interventions as in Iran in 1953, Lebanon in 1958 and 1982, Iraq in 1991, and through the staunch U.S. support of repressive and criminal governments (e.g., Israel from the 1960s to the present, Iran under the shah in the 1970s and 1980s, Iraq under Saddam in the 1980s). The imaginary significations of an entire generation, produced through a Pan-Arabism that was supposed to provide equality and common goals, collapsed. Revivalist Islam not only filled the meaning gap but also offered the only viable form of cultural resistance to neoliberalization and the cultural hegemony experienced by the growing masses of impoverished and oppressed men and women.

At the same time, most Islamist movements, be they Shi'a or Sunni, were offering communist or socialist ideals as part of their goal of social justice. Starting in the 1980s and extending into the 1990s, Islamist movements went into the business of welfare and took over the responsibilities of Arab states by building hospitals and schools, assisting the poor and the homeless, and providing cooperative stores with subsidized prices. The Islamic Brotherhood communities in Egypt own their own financial institutions and businesses, along with hospitals, cooperative stores, religious schools, etc. Hezbollah, in Lebanon, also has hospitals and schools and is engaged in helping the poor and needy (especially the Shi'a community in south Beirut and Southern Lebanon). Algeria's current Islamic revolution, led by the FIS (Islamic Salvation Front), has massive popular support and has generated cooperative efforts and quasi-socialist practices (e.g., resource sharing, social assistance, etc.), notwithstanding the occasional brutality in reaction to a repressive and terrorist government. All this is to show that religious movements and religious nationalism replaced socialist movements and socialist nationalism across the Middle East and North Africa.

Similar reactions occurred in India and Pakistan, often in association with the creation of an "other" upon whom one could transfer the discontent with savage capitalism's effects on local communities. After the socialist policies of Nehru and Indira Gandhi, resistance to neoliberalization in India collapsed. The Congress Party had resisted playing the divisive religious and ethnic card. However, a few old and new groupings, organizations, and parties started in the 1980s and the 1990s to make "Hindu nationalism" the backbone of their goal or platform; they aimed at recreating an identity based on the demonization of the "Muslim" upon whom the ill effects of neoliberalization and "globalization" could be projected: RSS (Rashtriya Swayamsevak Sangh), VHP (Vishva Hindu Parishad), and lately, BJP (Bharatiya Janata Party) (Van Der Veer 1994; Hansen 1999; Bhatt 2001).

While the BJP was at the forefront of consolidating this enormous and powerful "religious nationalist" movement, the RSS nonetheless expressed a desire to build an "identity" opposed to global forces that it associated with multinational corporations. As an RSS pamphlet stated, "Every morning we begin the job of cleansing our body with the help of products manufactured by these filthy companies which have a history of exploiting poor countries of the world" (Hansen, 1999: 170–72). Hindu radicalism thus creates an internal threat as it reacts to an external threat; its helplessness at reversing or affecting global forces associated with savage capitalism can only be repressed or compensated for through a campaign to create a strong and cohesive identity built on a tradition that is constantly threatened (and that does not adequately address the content of the tradition, be it in reformist or revivalist mode). This development is quite similar to that of Islamic radicalism, particularly in South Asia.

In Pakistan, Kashmir, Serbia, Bosnia, and Afghanistan, a similar desire for religious or ethnic independence reacts to global conditions that have created the impoverished masses and brings these masses together under the banner of identity. In the core, such a transformation is reflected in the extreme right and in the popular opposition to immigration and migrants—the transference of local government's failures on an "other." Anti-immigration policies will become an "occupation" of the jobless and resource-less masses who are offered the "other" as a bone: the Vietnamese to the unemployed Australians; the Turks to the discontented Germans; the North Africans to the disenchanted French workers, etc.

It is important, however, to point out that while we are trying to describe emerging sets of forces we are associating with "religious nationalism," these forces were not dominant, nor were they unique to particular religions or regions. These forces coexist and interact with numerous other forces, including old nationalist or socialist forces, or ideological or religious forces. What we are pointing to is that many social movements, potentially antisystemic or not, were increasingly driven by a combination of religious and nationalist forces, especially in places where socialist or liberal nationalisms are on the decline. This includes the various political brands of religious nationalism, be they Christian (e.g., United States), Muslim (e.g., Pakistan, Algeria), Hindu (e.g., India), or Jewish (e.g., Israel).

Some have argued that this applies to China as well, where an official revival of "Confucianism" was to lend legitimacy to a nationalist identity in transition from socialism to "market socialism." In the 1990s, the Chinese Communist Party leadership formally proclaimed Confucianism as another "guiding principle" besides Marxism–Leninism–Mao Zedong thought (Chan 1997: 244). China is indeed a contested site, for while many in the middle class or the nouveau riche may be driven by determinable beliefs or ideologies, it is difficult if not impossible to assess what drives the majority of the Chinese peasantry, as Robert Weil points out (1996: 17). The Tiananmen movement of 1989 revealed the increasing range of different and contradictory tendencies within the urban strata of Chinese society, from antistatist and socialist orientations to staunch beliefs in the "democracy" myth and the "free market" gospel. With various countries moving from socialist orientations to neoliberal experiments legitimized by free trade propaganda, it is difficult to project whether China will follow Eastern Europe and the former Soviet Union in succumbing to the so-called American dream of freedom and democracy or whether a new religious nationalism built on traditional Confucian ethics (or on racial superiority) may emerge there.

Identity Movements

As the survey above of the demise of socialist and nationalist movements and the emergence of new movements demonstrates, new forms of identity have increasingly come to define antisystemic movements. The term "identity" may be initially associated with those strata of populations whose empowerment accords with the effects of the early stages of the Chinese Cultural Revolution—whereby an "oppressed strata" gain privilege over a general class, be it the proletariat, the bourgeoisie, or capital. There have, of course, been numerous "identity" movements that preceded the Chinese Revolution or that were not influenced by it: the civil rights movements in the United States (especially from the 1963 March on Washington until the declaration of "black power" in 1965–1966 [Marable 1991]), the feminist movement (initially predominantly radical and socialist), as well as new radical environmental movements (from Greenpeace to Earth First!). Many of these are representative of a strand of movements whose antirepressive struggles became inextricably linked to antisystemic activity aimed at undermining the world-system's established hierarchies and exploitative mechanisms.

Along with these antisystemic forces should be listed anticolonialist movements that could be called "nationalist" (notably Algeria, Northern Ireland, South Africa, Palestine, etc.). Some of these anticolonialist movements were also combating social hierarchies based on identity (race, religion, ethnicity, caste, etc.). The late 1960s witnessed the proliferation of "identities" built around common interests, aims, occupations, ways of living, as well as around common histories and backgrounds not limited to ethnic, religious, or linguistic groups. These differences served to define one's being and goals and provided the means of empowerment and liberation as well as a basis of cooperation. Ethnic or religious movements emerged initially as "identity" movements, from the late 1960s until the late 1970s (in Malaysia, Indonesia, India, Sri Lanka, Thailand, Philippines, Spain, Lebanon, Turkey, Iraq, Nigeria, Morocco, China, Australia, and the United States). Many were soon transformed, especially after 1979, into movements that posed serious threats to the stability of the interstate system and, by rejecting the basic tenets of modernist capitalist values, acquired an antisystemic label.

While the peace movement that was linked to the antinuclear movement of the 1970s and 1980s is not based on an ethnicity or religion, it is an example of a phenomenon that redefines the identity of its participants: pacifists can be religious or laypeople, but what links them together is their belief in peace and their opposition to war, and that is a "part" of who they are and what they believe in. So while the peace movement may have been—in the 1970s in the United States, or in the 1980s in Europe, or elsewhere—an organized mass movement opposed to the policies of the United States and/or that of the Soviet Union during the Cold War, and while it may have included committed individuals united in one goal (peace or elimination of nuclear threats), over time it has become a manifestation of the fragmented identities of many in the core. The solidarity movement of the 1980s reflects a similar pattern: "SOS Racisme" in France, or the variety of German coalitions and movements opposing anti-immigrant policies and/or practices, express an opposition while presenting an aspect of the participants' "identity"—aspects that do not define that identity but may be reflective of "parts" of one's declared or assumed identity.

The Relevance of 1968 and the Primacy of Consumption

While identity movements blossomed, ruling elites forged ahead with their own projects as well. In this respect the period 1945–1989 was a decisive one, with 1968 being at the center. Through the interaction of various forces, a major transformation of the system became manifest as ruling elites sought to address the social needs of their peoples. At the center of this effort were the increasing primacy of consumption as *the* domain of capitalist expansion and consolidation and the projection of "consumerism" as a basic societal need and a motivation for peoples everywhere. Through a very long process, extending as far back as the preliminary individuation forces carried through "Modernity" and "Enlightenment," a major shift in economic, political, social, and cultural forces was slowly able to establish purchasing power as a universal human value, making it the motivation equated with the social needs of populations around the globe.

This long and complex process allowed capitalism to establish its center within the production of subjectivities by producing global "consumer subjects," rather than by relying on the state as its epicenter of power. That does not mean that the interstate system and the particular states forming it lost their ability to control the populace's desires and needs, but that the primordial forces controlling those desires and needs became "global" by permeating the "cultural worlds" at the basis of the interstate system and were thus able to directly influence the meanings and values embedded in the "material life" of various populations. This shift occurred with the help of the expanding networks of communication and information that were disseminating "consumerism" (associated with the ideological banners of "freedom," "rights," and "choice") as *the* way of living and relating to the world (Adorno and Horkheimer 1989; Marcuse 1966; Baudrillard 1970).[5]

The years following 1968 also emboldened capitalism after vigorous and long-term mechanisms were implemented to circumvent the possibility of a takeover of states across the world. Those antisystemic movements that posed a serious threat were put in check in the United States, Europe, Latin America, Africa, and in many parts of Asia, through targeted assassinations, covert actions, infiltrations, or the purchase of loyalties. These efforts ranged widely, from Iran (1953–1954), Guatemala (1955), Cuba (1960s), Chile (1973), and the Cointelpro programs in the United States to many other similar efforts.

At the same time capitalist powers launched a juridical effort to take over the international order and to depict it as "free," associated with a discourse of "human rights" that intensified after 1968. While the various explosions of 1968 momentarily perturbed the order necessary for the functioning of some states, capitalism flourished as new markets were opened when targeted by "brands" and lifestyles that catered to the revolutionary demands of various groups. The revolution of 1968 suddenly became "hip." Thus the media and integrated marketing strategies depicted their brands and products as directly associated with the life experiences of the sexual revolution, the hippie movement, the feminist movement, the peacenik movement, etc. It was soon the "product" that expressed one's identity, and one's individuality was expressed through the things that one consumed. This opened a vast array of possibilities for change and an incredible potential for an intensive proliferation of consumer goods without the actual need for geographic expansion (see Frank 1995, 1997; Featherstone 1991; Harvey 1990). "War by other means" became equated with a war of words and of control of interpretation and meaning.

While the global media and its control of the flow of information has always reflected the moneyed elite in core countries (see Chomsky and Herman 1988; Chomsky 1991, 2001), "advertising" became the weapon of choice for capitalist infiltration first within the core, and later globally, undermining the European communist dictatorships in the process. The "advertising" we are referring to is not merely about selling goods, but about selling images, attitudes, lifestyles, hopes, dreams, and other significations associated with capitalist imaginaries. It is precisely the period around 1968 that marked the initial expansion of this kind of advertising power in the United States, a power that has since reached unimaginable proportions, due to the expansion of informational and communicational flows that became global in reach (via various media conglomerates—including the film and music industries, cable and television networks, news, radio stations, print and Internet media, etc.—and marketing and advertising campaigns for products and services, international institutions and organizations, etc.).

Meanwhile the anti-Taylorist and anti-Fordist practices that became the norm in the 1980s and 1990s were transforming the face of "work" everywhere. Marx predicted (1977: 449), "As the number of co-operating workers increases, so does their resistance to the domination of capital, and necessarily, the pressure put on by capital to overcome their resistance," but he could never have imagined how capital would overcome such resistance. He dreamed of a "real subsumption" that, with increasing relativization of surplus-value extracted from labor, would create some "free time" for the development of the individual. As he wrote in *Grundrisse* (1973: 711–12): "The saving of labour time [is] equal to an increase of free time, i.e. time for the full development of the individual, which in turn reacts back upon the productive power of labour as itself the greatest productive power. From the standpoint of the direct production process it can be regarded as the production of *fixed capital*, this fixed capital being man himself." The transition from "formal" to "real" subsumption," as elaborated by Marx in *Capital*, volume one (including the discarded draft of its sixth section), combined with Marx's writings on "consumption" and "fixed capital," have allowed a few scholars to discover in Marx an analysis of capital's "production of subjectivities" (related to capital's investment in the aforementioned "free time") that is linked to the increasing importance of "immaterial labor"—that takes on the task of shaping and producing "fixed capital" (Read 2003).

Subjectivities are still produced through the web of social relations, but these relations are increasingly situated within the "immaterial" or "intangible" field that inhabits one's "free time." "Free time" is constantly expanding to encompass all other time, including "production time," due to the decreasing relevance of assembly lines in factories, so-called cooperative efforts in the workplace and in the household, the increasing relevance of "individuation" in the workplace, schools, and households. Consumption and the desires and needs for consumption—of tangibles (e.g., consumer goods or material possessions) and of intangibles (e.g., representational or ideological constructs, including styles, identities, and illusions of proximity, of belonging, or of possibilities)—became productive of social subjectivities, as a major productive activity (physical and mental)—in the same way factory labor was one of the major productive activities in the nineteenth century. At the same time, and through this production of needs and desires, capitalist imaginaries are inhabiting, permeating, and transforming other social imaginaries and various aspects of the "cultural worlds" of the interstate system, through various direct (but mostly "indirect") means including the media, multiple information and communication networks, and global entertainment and marketing industries (that are producing and shaping people's activities, desires, needs, etc.). Consumption became a primary player in the transformed system of the late twentieth century.

Part Two: Antisystemic Movements after 1989

1989 and Beyond: "Savage" Capitalism and U.S. Hegemony

The year 1989 witnessed yet another revolution: not that of the collapse of the communist bloc but the unleashing of the now hegemonic rhetoric of "globalization," seemingly unchecked by opposing ideologies. The savagery of systemic forces culminated in the abolition of most elementary benefits that had been "negotiated" through the opposition of systemic and antisystemic forces in the preceding period. The interstate system thereupon consolidated itself on various fronts with the help of antisystemic forces associated with what came to be interpreted as "terrorism"; the banner of "security" that was raised along with that of "human rights" aided the creation of an ever-increasing disciplinary juridical-political juggernaut that complemented (and supplemented) the consumerist system of control.

While finance and speculative capital moved to the fore at the expense of industrial capital in the 1980s, the 1990s brought new (and massive) concentrations of capital in the fields of information and communication and their corresponding technologies and applications. Paradoxically, the ever-increasing mutual awareness of the growing gap between the core and periphery did not deter the official abandonment of discourses of "development." The goal of development, pursued in previous periods through an "enlightenment of the savages" and a belief in catching-up policies following Rostow's stages of growth (1960), was now discarded as the containment of Third World radicals was no longer considered a priority after the collapse of the Soviet empire—which to many (radicals and conservatives alike) continued to embrace an alternative rhetoric until the very end. Disengaging from such "benevolent" policies showed the extent to which capitalist centers were confident with their newly acquired powers of persuasion. "Freedom" had won and the late 1980s and 1990s reinvented the meaning of "free market" as a new ideology (while some see it as essentially a return to the nineteenth-century paradigms of the night watchman state). Concurrently, the new dominant ideologies that were brought to the fore—post-Fordism and post-Keynesianism—exhibited a complete disregard for the basic needs of the world population, prioritizing instead the needs of the "economy."

The increasing power of the upper-middle class in core countries and the global elite in the periphery and semiperiphery coincided with the fall of the Warsaw Pact in 1991 and the subsequent transformation of the GATT into the WTO in 1995. The Eastern bloc disappeared and new markets were offering themselves to capitalist speculation and investment. Social movements that were communal, religious, and/or ideological struggles were replaced with intermittent struggles for individual rights and/or group interests that did not threaten the interstate system (but rather consolidated it) or the economic system of production and distribution (where technological capital complemented speculative capital). Some antisystemic trends and orientations nonetheless created possibilities for antisystemic movements. Ethnic and religious wars emerged all over the world (from Rwanda to Kosovo, from India to Chechnya), fueled by an economic hegemony that eliminated cooperation and increased pauperization.

Ethnicities and identities were further intensified through Cold War discourse on human rights through which new "international" wars were declared. The collapse of the former Soviet Union sent Russia and other Eastern European countries hurtling toward a firsthand experience of "savage capitalism," as International Monetary Fund (IMF) policies destroyed whatever was left of their economy and disintegrated their social bonds, inviting the formation of mafias and gangs, prostitution rings, and the development of human trafficking for slavery, while discontent was drowned in alcohol, religion, and racism/anti-Semitism (following the model described in the section "Rise of Religious Nationalism," where the close "other" becomes the culprit for one's misery). A few popular disturbances and clashes between workers and the police took place in 1998 and 1999 in Albania, Romania, Poland, and the Ukraine (Kagarlitsky 2001: 52–66). In Russia, Orthodox Christianity reemerged in importance as providing meaning and value, as did Islam in the Asian republics of the former Soviet Union. Flexibility has always been an important characteristic of the capitalist world-system, but by the 1990s, that flexibility had become malleable and permeable. The rigid structures of the state and the "societies of discipline" were, at least within the core, being replaced by "societies of control"—a kind of control that is noncoercive, nonabrasive, and nonapparent (Deleuze 1990, 1995).

The U.S. economy became much weaker. Not only were there problems associated with prolonged government deficits, rising unemployment figures, and stagnant economic growth, but its relevance to the global economy as a whole was shrinking (the U.S. economy is approximately 25 percent of the global economy [Monthly Review Editors 2003]). In this new era of "globalization," the various multinationals and their highly visible owners came to wield much power and influence—including over the policies of the nation-state in which they reside or to which they declare allegiance. Global capital measured in individual ownership is still highly concentrated in U.S. hands (in 2002, 271 of 540 billionaires were American), not to mention the United States' considerable military advantage over its competitors.

Furthermore, the control over the cultural aspects of the world-system and over the means of subjectivization around the globe should not be underestimated. Such control should more properly be called "domination" of social imaginaries, in this case capitalist social imaginaries, where domination functions at the levels of desires, needs, drives, and orientations that affect production, consumption, distribution, exchange, as well as a vast array of social relations that do not fall under any specific category. This kind of domination, while not purely political or economic in the traditional sense, permeates the economic and the political through the intersecting "cultural" traits, drives, or meanings. Since 1945, various forces associated with this kind of domination have been U.S.-based and/or were, for the most part, appropriated by U.S. capitalists.

An international or rather "U.S.-led" community was thus constructed in the 1990s through the establishment of enemies of "freedom"; such enemies are necessary to recreate the optimal conditions of the Cold War, especially for international "defense" industries and for old-fashioned "industrial capitalism." After Reagan's direct military interventions (e.g., Nicaragua, Grenada, Lebanon), and those of Bush Sr. (e.g., Panama, Iraq), the U.S. administration believed that it had established its control over the international arena. The Clinton administration was acting as "primus inter pares" of the "free world" (see Snow 2002), while militarily intervening whenever it could use the rhetoric of "rogue states" (e.g., Iraq and Yugoslavia) (Parenti 2000), ignoring genocides whenever it seemed appropriate (e.g., Rwanda), and undermining popular movements by supporting dictatorships all over the world for its own benefit (e.g., Algeria, Nepal). At the diplomatic level, the Clinton administration showed its hegemonic control of international institutions through manipulation of the IMF, World Bank, and the United Nations. It got rid of U.N. Secretary-General Boutros Boutros-Ghali when he wanted to reform the United Nations, including making the U.N. Security Council (UNSC) more representative of the world's population by adding permanent seats for countries with large populations (e.g., India, Brazil, Indonesia, Egypt, South Africa); Boutros-Ghali was voted for a second term by fourteen out of fifteen UNSC members but the U.S. veto guaranteed his demise.

After stealing the presidency from Al Gore (Kellner 2001), George W. Bush formed an oligarchic government whose main goal was to look after those sectors of capital that supported him—defense contractors, oil companies, old industrialists, and entrepreneurs—and he was willing to declare a "war on terror" where the demonic enemy is indeterminate, which guarantees the longevity of the war. The Bush government excelled at controlling information and interpretation, and has been producing "fear and anxiety" to direct the needs and desires of the American population. The White House capitalized on its control of the main means of information and of communication, shaping a majority of the 300 million Americans who are terrorized by it into submission (through terror alerts, the production of events such as the arrest of U.S.-based "al-Qaeda cells," attacking "rogue" states, etc.). This was also applied at the diplomatic and international level; Mary Robinson, the top U.N. human rights official was forced not to seek another term because she dared to mention the "disproportionate" number of civilian casualties during the American air strikes in Afghanistan and the treatment of Taliban and al-Qaeda prisoners, and because she allowed documents to be presented at the U.N. World Conference Against Racism in Durban, South Africa, in 2001 that criticized the United States and Israel (Olson 2002). The U.S. success in using terrorism as one of its means of controlling and shaping subjectivities and its ability to control the representation and interpretation of its policies and actions have limited the potential of antisystemic movements. Nonetheless, several movements and/or trends that have developed in the post-1989 period may carry antisystemic potential.

Post-1989 Movements and Trends with Antisystemic Potential

International terrorism. After 1989, the incidents described as "terrorist" decreased in scope and were no longer merely the effects of desperate nationalist and socialist strategies (as in the 1970s and 1980s) but rather extended in the 1990s to the desperate strategies of ethnic, and especially religious, movements. For example, the first Palestinian intifadah of the 1990s was not led by Fatah or by the Popular Front for the Liberation of Palestine (PFLP) but by Islamist organizations with local popular support: Hamas and other small religious groups, later to be represented by Islamic Jihad. When the intifadah and subsequent peace negotiations led to an impasse and to worsening conditions and oppression, "terrorism" became the weapon of choice for those with nothing to live for. Similarly, as the FARC (Revolutionary Armed Forces of Colombia) guerrillas were suffering from extensive military strikes by the Colombian Army, the U.S. Army (which is using chemical and biological warfare to obliterate the "coca-fields") and the right-wing paramilitary AUC (United Self-Defense Forces of Colombia) (which handles the assassination of hundreds of trade unionists and outspoken Catholic priests) started relying primarily on "terrorism." Nationalist, socialist, religious, and ethnic forms of terrorism are still common, although they are not an effective threat to capital.

Terrorism was "international" throughout the 1980s, to the extent that its targets were disproportionately "core targets" (Onwudiwe 2001). Nonetheless, a different kind of "international terrorism" flourished after the 1990s as symbolic and targeted actions were aimed at capitalism and the United States as the hegemonic power. Numerous former antisystemic tendencies proper to socialism and communism have been integrated into the radical outlook of a few religious or ethnic groups who view capitalism (and the United States or the "West") as responsible for the decay of religious value-systems. But if the United States (or other countries) consider the Muslim as the demonic "other" (or reduces any other large group of people, such as Confucians, or Hindus, to sub-human "enemy" status), "international terrorism" as a consistent and continuous desperate reaction could bleed capitalism enough to pose a possible threat to its stability.

Already a serious form of "international terrorism" is manifested in the symbolic and targeted actions of mass populations across the globe that attack McDonald's or other American chains or brands (as representatives of capitalist forces that detrimentally affect their lives or that of others), burn down hotels or resorts that were built at the expense of an existing ecosystem, blow up laboratories that experiment with animals, or burn down SUV dealerships, etc. Radical ecological groups (e.g., Animal Liberation Front) resort to terrorism only when their aims are not achievable through other strategies or tactics and they are confronted by violence. Squatters and anarchists started resorting to violence in the 1980s and 1990s when confronted by the state's intransigence and oppressive treatment. European and American anarchists have invested themselves heavily in the antiglobalization movement, to fight the powers accorded to international financial institutions, their authoritarianism, and their disregard for individual liberty and equality. With oppression and pauperization accompanying capitalism, the reserve army of international terrorists is growing. However, through means of capitalist control, the desperate rage of many has been targeting constructed "others" upon whom capitalist forces are transferred.

Identity, neo-Luddite, and indigenous movements. Many "identity" movements have also proliferated on the world scene after 1968, thus providing sites of association for groups and individuals who share common motivations, goals, or objectives. While the student movements, strongest in 1967–1968, came to an abrupt end with the "transformation" of the face of education worldwide, feminist movements, sexual liberation movements, ecological and environmental movements, international peace movements, as well as ethnic and religious movements thrived and continued throughout the past three decades. Each of these so-called movements is a rather complex grouping of different peoples with various orientations, some of which are concomitant or connected with, or radically opposed to, other orientations within or outside the "umbrella" designations that are not meant to point to any homogeneity. These movements are not only heterogeneous but also constantly transforming, permeating each other within the overall interaction of forces—situated within a particular social-historical intersection. Within the large umbrella of "identity" movements (post-1968 movements), there are movements with many connections and links with "new" movements that emerged in the late 1990s as antisystemic in orientation.

Squatters' movements reached their peak in the core in the late 1980s and early 1990s. In Germany, West Berlin squatters, leftists, and anarchists had to defend themselves against police attacks (1987 Hafenstrasse; 1990 Mainzerstrasse) as East Berlin went through a period of increased street activism and demonstrations (1989–1993). In Paris, a combination of anarchists and illegal and poor immigrants were able to draw public attention to their cause when a judge approved "an occupation contrary to the law but dictated by necessity" in a challenge to the all-powerful property rights (the case dealt with the "state of necessity" of twenty-three African homeless families) (Body-Gendrot 2000: 68–74). However, this exceptional instance could not translate into a legal solution for those who are homeless across the core. In New York City and in Portland, Maine, major confrontations between squatters and the police developed into confrontations (Tompkins Square Park, 1989–1990) and demonstrations (1993). These voices were silenced, and while squatting continues across the core, "property rights" are nowhere threatened in the core today.

It is somewhat different, however, in South Africa and Brazil. What scholars are calling "poor people's movements" are creating situations with antisystemic tendencies as they threaten the sacred right of property. Some of these movements may be promising, but they may also be mere temporary readjustments for societies in transition (cf. González 2004). South Africa's poor, who live in horrific conditions unaided by the ANC's liberalization and privatization drive, have been building "community movements" (Desai 2002). Brazil's MST (Landless Workers' Movement), one of the coalition movements behind the Labor leader and current Brazilian President Luiz Inacio da Silva (Lula), is trying to achieve what Zimbabwe is still struggling with, that is, a redistribution of land to landless peasants by occupying empty (or not) lots of land in a country where 20 percent of the population owns 90 percent of all arable land (while the poorest 40 percent owns only 1 percent) (Peter 2003). The MST's empowerment strategies are definitely antisystemic in orientation and seem to inspire other movements; a movement for the homeless is starting to settle homeless families in vacant buildings in São Paolo.

These movements are typical of new "identity" movements, based on a commonality of situations and goals. Many of those that are antisystemic have inheritances from earlier anticapitalist movements, opposing surplus production and the expansion of consumption, commodification, and exchange; resisting technological and industrial developments; and so on. Some neo-Luddite movements aim at delinking through various means of escaping the capitalist system, as in the Sarvodaya Shramadama movement in Sri Lanka (Sklair 1998: 291–311), while others try to counter capitalist forces by undermining the consumerist needs created through the suggestive powers of marketing and advertising. Identity movements could be communitarian or collectivist movements, but a few project (transfer meaning and significance) onto the "environment" (earth, animals, the globe, etc.). Most radical ecological movements can be considered antisystemic because they are against capitalist forms of extraction, exploitation, and the use of resources at the expense of the ecosystem (see "Radical Environmentalism" later in this section).

As for indigenous empowerment struggles, they directly undermine the racist and exploitative practices inherent in capitalist relations. Indigenous movements encompassed a wide array of struggles. Some aimed at self-determination or self-rule, associated with local government and control of natural resources: the Inuit in Canada, for example, have achieved some success in that regard when, on April 1, 1999, Nunavut was created as a new territory, governed by the Inuit, within the Canadian Confederation. The Nunavut Land Claims Agreement accords various other rights to the Nunavut Inuit, including Can$1.148 billion in compensation; a share of royalties from oil, gas, and mineral development; and equal representation of Inuit with government on a new set of wildlife management, resource management, and environmental boards (Polarnet 2005).

The Maori of New Zealand struggled for the recognition of the 1830 Treaty of Waitangi, and through the Treaty of Waitangi Act of 1975, it was given constitutional status (Waitangi Tribunal 2005). More recently, the Maori have been trying to pursue (through legal means and organized demonstrations) claims to the natural resources (including oil) extracted from what they claim to be Maori lands/seabed.

The Zapatistas are one of those indigenous movements of the 1990s that carried within them links to other movements; it has been stated that the indigenous Indian majority were joined by remnants of the 1968 student movement crushed in the Tlatelolco massacre and by Maoist groups. Bishop Samuel Ruiz's liberation theology also shaped the indigenous Indian communities whose uprising in Chiapas on January 1, 1994, started what would become an inspiring lesson on how to use information and communication to build coalitions between communities and movements (Castells 1997: 74–81).

Other indigenous movements, especially those in Latin America, are closely related to socialist or collectivist ideals that drive the politicization of indigenous populations in such places as Bolivia (where 71 percent of the population is indigenous), Guatemala (where 66 percent of the population is indigenous), Peru (where 47 percent of the population is indigenous), and Ecuador (where 38 percent of the population is indigenous). Indians of the Americas have suffered tremendously since the "discovery" of their lands, and since then they have been victims of racism and discrimination as well as of the ideological wars of the twentieth century, where more than 200,000 Indians were killed in Guatemala and Peru alone between the 1970s and the early 1990s. A "political awakening" of indigenous people in South America has occurred, resulting in Indian rights' being given a legal force through "Convention 169" of the

International Labor Organization (which required signatory governments to "guarantee indigenous people equal rights; participation in formulating policies that affect them; respect for their institutions, customary law and culture; and health and education"). It remains to be seen whether such movements may develop a specific antisystemic character.

New class structures, internationalists, and antiglobalization movements. These latter developments are part of a new trend of "global egalitarianism" that has emerged to oppose global inequality and exploitation, a trend attributed by "antiglobalization" activists to the effects of multinational companies and entities such as the WTO, the IMF, and the World Bank, among others. This trend is closely related to "human rights" discourses and can become an effective antisystemic force only when it facilitates the implementation of these rights on the global and interstate level (between core states and states of the periphery and semiperiphery). Such endeavors appear to be aiming at an internationalist juridical-political transformation by which international institutions with enforcement capabilities would proclaim basic rights and needs (human, economic, and social) attributable to individuals and to groups of individuals (including states) as a means of obligating core states, multinational corporations, and wealthy individuals to provide for other, less privileged states (including debt elimination and redistribution of wealth via a global taxation system). Internationalists could be state actors, NGOs, or individuals.

Most historically oppressed groups have been active in developing this global egalitarianism. Feminists, now represented through various NGOs (as well as increasing mass movements in the periphery and semiperiphery, in particular India), were concerned not only with the feminization of poverty but also with all kinds of exploitation multiplied through savage capitalism (Naples and Desai 2002; Rowbotham and Linkogle 2001; Ray 1999). They launched international legal campaigns and women everywhere became active in supporting local struggles toward global equality. African states and Pan-African organizations instituted the international condemnation of apartheid as a crime against humanity and devoted themselves to dealing with the consequences of years of Cold Wars fought on African soil resulting in poverty, famine, ethnic tensions, HIV/AIDS, and the reduction if not elimination of aid; they demanded reparations and aimed for empowerment, but also engaged with other states and entities in an attempt to eliminate Third World debt and the creation of more egalitarian and representative international institutions. The gay and lesbian rights movements, along with movements for indigenous rights, worked with reinvigorated labor and trade union organizations and remnants of socialism, as well as particular groups or individuals that stand for an "internationalist" agenda that does not necessarily preclude the importance of the "local," on calling for global economic equality and for North-South solidarity, the elimination of "Third World" debt, and the redistribution of wealth on a world scale via reallocation or the restructuring of national and international resources. Certain sections of the so-called antiglobalization movement that oppose various international organisms for precisely such distributive goals (and not merely for self-advancement or for liberal-reformist aims) could be considered global egalitarians. Yet antirepressive movements aimed at defining and defending human, social, and economic rights can be considered fully antisystemic only when their aim undermines the international division of labor and its corresponding class structure.

Indeed, the increasing global inequality is becoming the cornerstone of yet another massive differentiation and a continuously growing gap between rich and poor across the world-system: in 2002 there were more than 540 "billionaires" (476 in 2003), more than 70, 000 "super rich" (with individual capital in the hundreds of millions of dollars), and close to seven million "millionaires" around the globe, while the middle class in the core is getting poorer and the lower classes everywhere are becoming worse off (Pieterse 2002: 1023–46; Sutcliffe 2001; Journal of World-Systems Research 2002). A new class structure seems to be emerging that is as linked to the international division of labor as to the primacy of consumption. This new class structure may be practically designated by the terms "global elite," "professional class," "casual laborers," and "new slaves."[6]

This class structure is increasingly (but not effectively) challenged, however, by an increasing number of NGOs, institutions, and individuals associated with global egalitarianism, as just depicted, including North-South solidarity and antiglobalization trends or movements. As an example, we could look at the solidarity among Europeans in support of immigrants persecuted because of racism and xenophobia. In 1998 and 1999, these solidarity movements, especially in France, Germany, and Italy, developed into transnational networks in support of migration (Giraudon 2001). That movement in the core would join those in the periphery and semiperiphery who consider open migration as a type of equalizer (see below). As for "antiglobalization" movements, they date back to the late 1980s: in September 1988, 75,000 protesters gathered in Berlin to protest an IMF/World Bank convention. Those who take part in the historical protests and mass demonstrations associated with "antiglobalization" vary widely: from French farmers (who started their protests in Europe in 1992–1997 before some of them linked European unification to "globalization") to eco-feminists and witches (e.g., Starhawk); from United Students Against Sweatshops (USAS) to ACT-UP, Lesbian Avengers, and Jacks of Colors (Shepard and Hayduk 2002); from "Reclaim the Streets" to the Black Radical Congress; and from the Independent Media Center (IMC) to the Direct Action Network.

The first major successful demonstration was in Seattle in December 1999, when 40,000 protested against the WTO; success was achieved merely in causing an inconvenience and in "getting the message out" (i.e., having media coverage that influences public opinion). That was followed by demonstrations in Davos, Switzerland, in February 2000, against the World Economic Forum, where a McDonald's was trashed. In Washington, DC, in April 2000, demonstrators established a blockade at the World Bank and IMF talks. In Chiang Mai, Thailand, in May 2000, an Asian Development Bank meeting was protested. In Prague in September 2000, 12,000 clashed at a World Bank–IMF annual meeting. In Melbourne in September 2000, activists barricaded delegates to a World Economic Forum conference. At Nice in December 2000, demonstrations disrupted a European summit. In January 2001, the World Economic Forum was locked down and Zurich was trashed. In April 2001 at the Quebec City Summit of the Americas, witnesses reported police using tear gas and water cannons against demonstrators. In Barcelona in June 2001, the World Bank cancelled its conference while activists held their own. In Göteborg, Sweden, in June 2001, 40,000 marched peacefully at an EU summit but there was a confrontation with masked anarchists. Participants included: Italian anarchists "Ya Basta!," Tutte Bianche (White Overalls) members from Italy's 200 centers, the British equivalent WOMBLES (White Overalls Movement Building Liberation Through Effective Struggle), 600 "Global Resistance" demonstrators, and Anti-Fascist Action. There were also a few radical trade unions: French SUD (Solidarity, Unity, Democracy) and FSU (Unitary Union Federation), the Italian Cobas and the metalworkers' branch of CGIL (General Confederation of Italian Workers), the anarcho-syndicalist CGT (General Confederation of Labor) from Spain, and the major Greek Unions (Ratnesar 2001).

Some serious organized opposition, at an international level, started with the creation of the World Social Forum in Porto Alegre, Brazil, in January 2001—which consisted of 12,000 representatives from civil society organizations and political movements. This was followed by the Genoa Social Forum in July 2001 and meetings of the World Social Forum in January 2003 (Porto Alegre, Brazil) and January 2004 (Mumbai, India), which should be considered as part of the internationalist and global egalitarian trends. We need to add the Earth Summit Rio 1992, Johannesburg 2002, as well as Durban 2001 (U.N. World Conference Against Racism), and other meetings that allowed the opportunity to build coalitions and communities to oppose capitalist forces and hegemonic powers. One last thing to add here is that we should not rule out possible coalitions of states, beyond the United States and European Union, as possible future contenders for hegemony. Brazil is quite promising as a state actor in undermining economic and political hegemony, since its labor leadership has been successful at building coalitions and has already brought close to it, and sometimes to each other, Venezuela, Cuba, Argentina, and a few other Latin American countries. Lula is also trying to form alliances with Arab countries to create a sizable block of nations that can politically contest the hegemonic powers. Brazil also played an instrumental role in the WTO meeting at Cancun, in September 2003, by working together with India and South Africa (two equally important "rising" members of the semiperiphery) to press hard on the issue of U.S. and European state subsidies.

Ethnic and religious movements. What is designated as "ethnic" and "religious" movements dominated the 1980s and 1990s, encompassing Malaysia, India, Thailand, Spain, Lebanon, Iraq, Nigeria, Belgium, Australia, Guatemala, and the United States, as well as Rwanda, Croatia, Bosnia, Albania, Iran, and Fiji, to cite just a few. Those movements that explicitly reject the capitalist tenets and "Western" notions of universalism, human rights, freedom, and other discourses embedded in the liberal-modernist geoculture may pose an antisystemic threat in the near future. Such movements are quite different from those of earlier centuries (and should probably be called neoethnic and neoreligious) because they are reactive by nature and are produced as localized resistance to certain forces "external" to their ways of living and relating to the world or social imaginaries (that are becoming increasingly permeated and dominated by capitalist social imaginaries). One could include here renewed forms of religious, ethnic, and nationalist orientations that are described as "traditional." Some examples of these movements are: Christian, Hindu, and Islamic revivals in their different manifestations; right-wing and/or conservative French, Spanish, and Italian nationalisms; Chinese, Slavic, and Russian nationalisms; Nigerian ethnic consciousness such as that of the Ijaw, Ethce, Ogoni; indigenous Indian rights in the United States, Canada, New Zealand, Guatemala, Bolivia, Peru, Ecuador, and elsewhere; and other sects or groupings based on indigenous and ethnic lines such as the "Mungiki" sect in Kenya (a "multitude" of mostly Kikuyu, grouping many of the poor under an ideology that mixes socialism, Islam, and traditional beliefs).

Radical environmentalism. The radical environmental movement has grown out of the earlier mainstream conservationist movement. The "major shift in worldview" (Jasper 1999: 147) that occurred in 1968 was the basis of its transformation. In 1971, the now famous term "speciesism," referencing the belief that one's species is superior to another, was first used and reached a mass audience from the late 1970s on (Singer 1977; Regan 1983). In many ways, 1968 provided a watershed for the launch of social and political ecological movements. A conference held in Paris in 1968 symbolically inaugurated the "Man and the Biosphere Program," while the Club of Rome was also set up in 1968. This was followed in 1972 by a U.N. conference on the human environment in Stockholm and the simultaneous publications of the Club of Rome's shocking report "The Limits to Growth" (Biel 2000: 140–41). The 1968 crisis effectively transformed the mainstream ecological movement—of which the "animal welfare movement" is just an instance—from a traditional reform-minded liberal and paternalistic club of well-intentioned middle-class abolitionists and feminist activists into a radical antisystemic thrust that challenged the commodification of nature as a whole and adopted a holistic view (the ecosystem) rather than a national one, thus creating a "deep green" movement (Sutton 2000; Goldfrank, Goodman, and Szasz 1999).

From the 1980s onward, not only did the movement crystallize itself in Green parties across the globe, but it also initiated illegal activities in the United States as in the activities of the Animal Liberation Front (Finsen and Finsen 1994: 98). In 2003, for example, a string of arsons committed by the Earth Liberation Front in the suburbs of Detroit, Los Angeles, San Diego, New York, and Philadelphia caused more than $100 million in damage (Hettena and Wides 2003). The growth of the more radical elements in the environmental movement are indicated by the fact that on 10 June 1990, 24,000–75,000 animal rights activists converged in Washington, DC, for the March for Animal Rights (Finsen and Finsen 1994:72). Since the 1980s, the number of such organizations has increased substantially. In less than a decade, members of People for the Ethical Treatment of Animals (PETA) had grown to 300,000 during the "Green Revolution" (cf. Sale 1993). In the post-1968 period, "ecological resistance movements" such as Earth First! emerged in every zone of the world-economy, albeit with different emphases (Taylor 1995) including post-1968 eco-feminism (Adams 1999; Adams and Donovan 1995; Donovan 1990). The typical environmental activist in the core originates mostly from within the middle class (Inglehart 1997; Benton and Redfearn 1996), but in parts of the periphery it has encompassed a wide variety of grassroots support (e.g., the Chipko movement in India in the 1980s [Routledge 1993] or the Narmada movement in India in the 1990s [Kothari 2002; Khagram 2002]). Interestingly, the discourse of post-1968 radical ecological movements is no longer about "conservationism," but instead challenges the commodification of nature itself. Thus, as pointed out by "deep ecologists" (Dobson 2000: 40), natural resources are no longer considered mere commodities to be exploited at will (Jasper 1999: 148).

The commodification of the natural world is an intrinsic element of the capitalist world-economy. The "externalization" of costs (i.e., pollution of air, land, and water)—by means of passing on these costs to future generations—is as important a profit source for capitalists as the exploitation of wage laborers (Hornborg 1998; Ponting 1993); and a worldwide movement challenging this trend has gained considerable strength in the post-1968 period, forging new transnational alliances between the core and the periphery that hinge on the newfound social and political awareness of local indigenous rights movements (Martin 2003). The creation of such effective interethnic environmental alliances across the different zones of the world-economy may have huge implications for the future.

Worldwide mass migration. Traditionally, migration has been looked upon as a massive incorporation of low-wage labor by core countries (Boswell and Jorjani 1988: 169–71; Bolaria and Bolaria 1997: 11) because immigration legislation has been traditionally influenced by the labor requirements of capitalist enterprises (Petras 1980: 164). However, the continuing migration flow from the periphery to the core may undermine several fundamental aspects inherent to the stability of the world-system, such as the maintenance of the interstate system and the idea of progress embedded in liberal ideology. Historically, the creation of the welfare state in the core was linked with the creation of high barriers against the free circulation of labor and migration flows in general. In this respect unions, and their socialist political affiliations, had—despite their internationalist rhetoric—always been more nationalist than internationalist (Lucassen 1991: 158–73). This is not surprising because welfare states in the core simply had to keep their borders closed to mass immigration to construct and maintain a welfare state in the interstate system (Freeman 1986: 52). In addition, the notion of citizenship is by definition an attribution of legitimacy to human entitlements and rights within a *specific territorial unit* (a nation-state) of the world-system (Halfmann 1998: 523–24). A gradual undermining of the (welfare) state in the core caused by, among other things, massive (il)legal immigration may very well contribute to weakening the entire system (Wallerstein 1999a: 57–75). Although the demographic "explosion" in the periphery certainly increases the potential of mass migration to the core in the near future (Hoffmann-Nowotny 1997: 96; Rasmussen 1997: 106), the demise of liberalism and the hope of steady progress through stages of national development are probably equally as important in "triggering" a structural process of international mass migration out of the periphery (Wallerstein 1995) as the Malthusian variable in itself.

The myths of "stay-at-home development" (Martin 1992) and the possibilities for universal takeoff have been painfully exposed in the officially decolonized periphery especially after 1973. Due to the ever-widening gap between the core and the periphery, and the increasing availability of information related to this reality (Rasmussen 1997: 125–26; Baldwin and Martin 1999: 24), citizens living in the periphery will no longer be misguided by misleading hopes about the prospects of a nation-state that is located at the bottom of the hierarchically structured worldwide division of labor. Essentially, "the only realistic long-term hope for reduction of international migration is broad-based, sustainable development in the less-developed countries, enabling economic growth [there] to keep pace with growth in the population and labor force" (Castles and Miller 1998: 291). Yet, as the lure of modernization and development theories steadily diminished after 1968, the increasing disbelief in the feasibility of liberalism and reformism in the periphery may ultimately lead to gradually increasing and uncontrollable migration toward the centers of capital accumulation.

Yet increasing mass migration to the core, because the majority of it will likely be illegal, will challenge not only the welfare state (which has been devised to "take care" of a happy few in the capitalist world-economy) but also, concurrently, the political legitimacy of its existence. Because mass migration can only be discouraged, at best, the credibility of the nation-state itself is now at stake (Vernez 1996: 7–8). At the same time, when more migrants are on the move, more governments are downsizing their versions of the welfare state and intervening less on behalf of its poorest citizens, among whom immigrant ethnic minorities are overrepresented. This trimming of the welfare state is in turn inherent to the pressures operating within the world-economy (Martin and Schumann 1996), which induce states to a competitive race to the bottom (Greider 1997).

However, what started as a systemic force (the incorporation of labor on demand for certain sectors and firms) may effectively function as an antisystemic force on a global scale owing to the contradictions of the capitalist system; mass migration may become as important an antisystemic pressure on the interstate system as the ecological factor. Indeed, it is often forgotten that the two are interlinked because increasing ecological crises are likely to impact mass migration in the near future (Ghosh 1998: 48–50; King and Öberg 1993). As multiple ecological crises (environmental degradation, desertification, deforestation, soil erosion, salinity, and other effects of global warming) cause more migrations to occur (Lohrmann 1996; Myers 1993), core states will attempt to keep these growing numbers of "ecological refugees" in the periphery.

Yet traditional efforts of nation-states to control borders and to determine the numbers and types of people who enter and remain in their territory are no longer effective (Bigo 1998), resulting in a decline in sovereignty (Cornelius et al. 1994; Richmond 1994: 216–17). This is important because the sovereignty of nation-states is a pillar of the capitalist world-economy (Wallerstein 1999a: 57–75). Theoretically, the ever-increasing migration of poverty from the periphery to the core can be interpreted as a symptom of a crisis in the world-system (Vandepitte et al. 1994: 147). The number of mass migrations is greater than it has ever been (Weiner 1997: 97), and the widening demographic and socio-economic gap between the haves and have-nots (Sorensen 1996: 93) can only increase the *potentiality* of ever more migration to the core as the total migrant population today constitutes only approximately 2 percent of the entire world population (Faist 1997: 187).

As "exclusive territoriality" is being destabilized by economic globalization and mass migration (Sassen 1996), the legitimacy of the nation-state is undermined in the long run. As immigrants keep moving in the highly stratified world-economy, using ingenious strategies of relying on various affiliations and networks to overcome the barriers created by the core states (Massey and Espinosa 1997), their fight to get "legalized" and to get the same (political, economical, and social) rights as other citizens implies a double squeeze on the sovereignty and financial burden of various states. This is especially challenging to the democratic institutions that are maintained by core countries, as those who favor the protection of popular sovereignty (e.g., to bring about a redistribution of wealth within a nation-state) are increasingly confronted with "global egalitarians" (Weiner 1996: 176), that is, those who are concerned with global inequalities and the exploitation of (illegal) immigrants within core countries (Van Parijs 1992: 163–64).

This creates very specific challenges for labor unions in the core. As Martens (1999: 226) argues, to what extent will unions and their political allies in core countries show solidarity with immigrants from the periphery since most people in the core are, after all, (indirect) benefactors of "transfer value" (Köhler 1999)? This presents a dilemma: if mass migration can imperil the right to economic security of people in the receiving (core) country, whose (human) rights have priority? The rights of those already residing in the core or the rights of (potential) immigrants? The answer to this question is likely to depend on whether one takes "our own country" or "our planet" as the unit of analysis (Sutcliffe 1998: 335).

After having lured immigrants to the core during the boom years of 1945–1973, while hoping that they would be nothing more than a reserve labor army that would return to the periphery whenever the economic upturn ended (Obdeijn 1998: 130; King 1996: 48), capitalist firms from core countries have been *indirectly* inducing more immigrants to move from the periphery and semiperiphery to the core from 1973 onward. This indirect lure is brought about by the fact that multinationals increasingly reallocate themselves outside the core where (labor) costs are temporarily cheaper and exploit young laborers there only to dismiss them after a few years when they become "too expensive" after unionization sets in. This "economic redundancy" converts these uprooted laborers thereafter into "a ready pool for future migration" (Portes 1996: 165; Graham 2000: 188). Peripheral countries have become slowly "remolded by the twin processes of corporate globalization and immigrant transnationalization" (Portes 1996: 164). Thus, the exploitation of young laborers in the periphery induces them to migrate to the core while, once there, the previously mentioned (chain) migration networks are likely to facilitate more migration in the near future (Boyd 1989: 641; Gurak and Caces 1992: 159; Simmons and Guengant 1992: 113).

Only the proposition of the transferability of social rights between states for immigrants (Bauböck 1993: 45), resulting in universal entitlements and a "globalization of the welfare system" (Halfmann 1998: 528), would be an alternative strategy by core countries to deal with the massive migration from the periphery. Yet to do so requires pushing liberalism and its notions of progress and universal rights into practice and changing the very nature of the capitalist world-system. From a liberal ideological point of view, it is also difficult to construct even more barriers against immigrants; individual human rights, including the freedom of movement—as in the freedom of movement for capital, goods, technology, and knowledge—(Lim 1992: 139; Vernez 1996: 6) and the right to the pursuit of happiness, can hardly be claimed by the capitalist entrepreneur alone (Emmer and Obdeijn 1998: 12). The "very different regimes for the circulation of capital and the circulation of people" (Sassen 1998: 66)—with the exception of wealthy entrepreneurs and tourists (Bauman 1998: 89)—may not be defensible in the long run.

A continuing policy of exclusion and protectionism, which may "save" the core by maintaining a world order of "global apartheid" (Richmond 1994; Alexander 1996), is the complete opposite of the liberal ideology that is still defended by many parties in power. The rapid population growth in the periphery and semiperiphery (as opposed to the core) and the processes inherent to the capitalist world-economy (in which multinationals exploit cheap labor in the periphery, only to pull out to other peripheral locations the moment wages rise) produce masses of workers in the periphery without jobs who have high expectations that cannot be fulfilled locally (Lim 1992: 135, 145). At the same time a growing number of ecological refugees, while primarily an immediate disaster to countries located in the periphery, may threaten the stability of the interstate system as a whole. Because core states are militarily, economically, and technologically stronger than peripheral ones, it is the desperate masses of the latter that constitute the greatest threat to—and arouse the greatest fear of—core states in the world-economy (King 1998: 125).

Instead of looking at international mass migration as a threat, one should recognize it is an "expression of spatial inequality" (King 1996: 54) that could bring the system into disequilibrium in the long run. Indeed, as convergence in socioeconomic conditions between core and peripheral countries is unlikely to occur (Coleman 1997: 144; Köhler 1998, 1999), non-core countries increasingly become dependent on the revenues received from (illegal) immigrants working in core countries who send money home because the countries from which they originated are structurally incapable of creating enough jobs for their own population (Martin 1997: 20; Hammar and Tamas 1997: 6). Martin (1997: 23), for example, estimates that worldwide remittances of immigrants in industrial countries to their countries of origin were at least $75 billion per year, which outweighs the amount of official development assistance to "developing" countries and often exceeds the inflow of direct investment (Lorey 1999: 164–65; Patnaik and Chandrasekhar 1998: 361) or national budgets (Menjivar et al. 1998: 99). Once governments of peripheral and semiperipheral countries finally decide to officially promote and support the (international) migration of all their "excess populations" to the core (Levy 1999: 220; van Hulst 1995: 86), both development and neoliberal capitalist ideologies will face a severe crisis.

Alternative currencies. Another potential challenge to the current stability in the world-system, as new challenges to Davos occur (Houtart and Polet 2001), is the formation of alternative currencies. This no longer assumes any form of territorial "delinking," as advocated by Samir Amin (1990) and others. The creation and multiplication of local exchange trading systems throughout small communities within the core (e.g., United States, Australia, Canada), such as "scrips," "ithaca hours," and "time dollars," illustrate the agency local communities have to resist and limit the power of large multinationals and their relative immunity to currency fluctuations within the world-economy (Meeker-Lowry 1996). The very recent creation of "barter bucks" in Kansas, for example, despite their initial limited scope, could potentially recreate a sense of local delinking from existing financial networks and a relative empowerment of Braudel's sphere of "daily life" vis-à-vis the commanding heights of capital accumulation. There is potential, on this front, for a deliberate strategy to undermine the legitimacy and efficiency of existing currencies. In addition, the development of new measurements of progress separate from the gross national product (GNP) (Halstead and Cobb 1996) can only increase the awareness of the necessity to attempt to reinvigorate local and regional barter and alternative trading networks that benefit the community rather than multinationals operating from distant headquarters that can transfer all profits to distant shores. This movement has gained so much appeal that in 1997 the International Journal of Community Currency Research was created to academically scrutinize its impact across the globe. In addition, Alternative Investment Funds, microcredit, and other projects could fall into this category as they try to establish "self-sufficiency," which sometimes takes religious or ethnic colors (India, Egypt, China, etc.).

Alternative media. Recognizing the importance of the media in shaping the "reality" of subjects, increasing coalitions of individuals and groups have been involved in providing alternative sources of information and of interpretation of facts and events, as opposed to the ones dominated by capitalist social imaginaries or by states intent on the control and manipulation of information. Linked to the new technologies, some of these alternative media are Internet-based (e.g., IndyMedia), especially in the core and semiperiphery, and provide access to people across the globe. Other sources, however, are print based but are widely read and discussed. However, this proliferation of "alternative media" is specifically targeting misinformation campaigns by governments and is reacting to the hegemonic strategies implemented across the globe; its outcome may build an antihegemonic consciousness and not an antisystemic one—even though it may carry antisystemic orientations. It could have a potential antisystemic effect only when it becomes a major source not only of information but also of values and meanings that could effectively counterbalance the dominant (and "global") discourses of capitalist imaginaries—in the way that some religious or nationalistic discourses have been trying to do, as previously described. Only a marked increase in the possibility of disseminating meanings and values, and of interpreting events and situations, would qualify alternative media networks as an antisystemic force.

New technologies. Last but not least, new technologies created by the drive for ever-increasing accumulation can also have antisystemic potential as in the case of cyberactivism (McCaughey and Ayers 2003), linking and uniting a multitude of diverging antirepressive and other movements with each other across the globe, opening up new potentials of awareness, organization, mobilization, and different forms of support that may result in antisystemic forces, events, or even new kinds of "movements." The blending of culture jamming, semiotic terrorism, and "hacktivism" could be newly emerging sites of antisystemic movements (Jordan 2002) paradoxically enabled by capital's intrinsic need for ever-growing speed of communication of information and transportation of commodities. The more sophisticated the forms of newly emerging technologies embedded within late capitalism, the greater the potential for their disruption, causing unparalleled disruption of the space of flows.

The efficiency of protests have increased as well; despite many similar protests throughout the 1980s and early 1990s against "globalization" (primarily directed against the G7 and EU summits, IMF, World Bank, and GATT meetings), the 1999 protest in Seattle displayed for the first time an enormous disruptive potential and effectiveness (Yuen, Katsiaficas, and Rose 2001), partially because of the previously mentioned newly available technologies appropriated for the organization of the demonstrations—also witnessed in Washington, DC, Prague, and Göteborg (2000); Genoa (2001); and Florence (2002). This enabled the antiglobalization movement to create newly unprecedented mobilizing structures and tools for counterideological space (e.g., ATTAC's Web site) (Clark and Themudo 2003), at times culminating in innovative and tentative institutional settings such as the World Social Forum in Porto Allegre (Schonleitner 2003), the counterpoint to Davos. At this point it remains to be seen to what extent these divergent movements will be able to successfully challenge the existing status quo without being co-opted or suppressed by systemic forces. Yet in combination with the increasing tensions caused by the contradictions within the system itself, new post-1968 movements and their potential to disrupt the status quo should not be underestimated.

Conclusion: Twentieth-Century Transformations of Movements and the System

Our claim is that antisystemic activity has been radically recast as capitalism in the last half of the twentieth century has increasingly penetrated and permeated every aspect of the economy and of material life. Consumption everywhere is increasingly regulated through capitalist forces, rather than by daily necessities and cultural spheres of influence; everywhere capitalism effectively manipulates local sociocultural values and epistemologies. These developments have in turn reawakened identities and localized groups based on common interest, religion, ethnicity, or "tribe" (Dunaway 2003; Amin 1998; Maffesoli 1996 [1988]; Castells 1997), while the ideological forces inherent in socialism, nationalism, and communism have been weakened. The challenges of migration have, moreover, served to intensify the trend toward "identity formation" through the vilification and demonization of an "other."

While national education curricula and the national state are still effective mechanisms of producing political subjects, they are no longer as effective in counterbalancing the "global" forces of production and reproduction of meanings and values associated with dominant capitalist imaginaries. It is therefore no surprise that after 1968 protests and demonstrations have no longer exclusively targeted capital or specific national governments, but rather institutions such as the United Nations, WTO, IMF, World Bank, international NGOs, and multinational companies. These have all become effective sites of control, as well as sites of struggles for hegemony and increasing competitiveness between various forms of capital still centered in core—and some semiperipheral—countries.

As for the movements, they, too, have been transformed along with the nature of social relations and social consciousness. After the 1970s, and increasingly in the 1980s and 1990s, committed individuals with ideals that stood for moral values have participated in many demonstrations and occasional actions. Yet these actions cannot usually be described as a "movement." The peace marches of 2003, for example, as in many demonstrations in support of specific issues, have offered only a limited opportunity for more individuated selves to express shared goals with others. Unlike past movements aimed at the capture of the state, these new movement manifestations are most often aimed at lobbying policymakers or affecting public opinion. Movements that are organized toward a specific goal with antisystemic aims have thus become the exception to the rule.

Identity movements are in this respect easily contrasted with traditional "unidirectional" movements that worked toward the achievement of a general (rather than a particular) goal through generalized means. The takeover of the state that was the explicit goal of socialist movements, for example, stands in stark contrast with the movements of the 1980s and after that rarely entertained the possibility of the overhaul of the political and economic system through collective action. As imaginary significations undermined linear and determinate "realities" in this period, the social consciousness of actors became ever more complicated and diverse, lending themselves easily to multiple aims, numerous goals, and an almost infinite number of strategies.

Thus, with the withering away of the state as the "promised land" of traditional movements, social movements aimed at gaining power wherever they could locate it and "empowerment" became the aim of most movements in the 1990s. Agents were no longer participating in "one" movement; instead they were participating in as many commitments as their social consciousness called for. While we could talk of different strategies and tactics of empowerment, it would be impossible to outline contemporary movements based on their "identity," "adversary," or "societal goal" (as Castells and Touraine suggest; e.g., Castells 1997: 71), for such criteria could not elucidate the nature of movements but would rather "construct" it.

At the forefront of strategies of empowerment were concerted efforts at influencing and shaping public opinion (via information and communication), catering to the media and to a culture of numbers (polls, surveys, and votes) proper to certain so-called democratic processes (by organizing demonstrations, massively attended marches or events, etc.), and demanding transparency and more open participation (so that more diverse "interest" groups could lobby and influence policy setting). Other strategies included escaping the overall political (and sometimes economic) processes, by choice or by necessity, to pursue particular forms of empowerment (through a lifestyle, a belief system, etc.). Many other empowerment strategies could be listed, from the basic construction of a shared "identity" (ethnicity, religion, ideology, cult, etc.) to engagement in coalition and cooperative activities aimed at achieving a specific goal (antiwar demonstrations, boycott of certain brands, voting for a candidate, pushing for a project, etc.).

What has interested us here is to illuminate those that could be called "antisystemic" or have displayed strategies of empowerment that could have antisystemic tendencies. Such strategies (some of which were described previously) may pose an increasing threat to the equilibrium of the capitalist world-system. They do not yet, however, constitute an "antisystemic movement" with an organizational infrastructure that sustains the effective power of consistent, recurring, and threatening actions. Many contemporary movements, as we have pointed out, are disempowered either through the capitalist control of the same processes of communication they aim to influence, or by the ways through which capitalism has learned to flourish and ignore "pockets" of resistance or delinked sites. It remains to be seen how the worldwide interaction between these different—indeed often divergent—forces will have specific impact on the system in the decades to come. We can only hope that this analysis may contribute to rethinking current paradigms and traditional strategies for political action.

Notes

1. The term "social imaginary" as used throughout this chapter is meant to go beyond the limited significations associated with such concepts as "social conscious-ness" or "ideology." The term accentuates forces or powers associated with imagination rather than images and representations, and is intricately connected to discourses across time, space, and disciplinary boundaries. The concept of "social imaginary" has been used specifically by political philosophers and social scientists to indicate the signifying social forces that drive the beliefs and practices of populations beyond the theory-practice distinction as reflected, for example, in the Marxist dichotomy of "base-superstructure" or "productive forces-ideology." Our use of the term "social imaginary" is closest to that of the late political philosopher Cornelius Castoriadis (1987 [1975]).

2. Various manifestations of Islamist movements that can be described as antisys-temic are also reflected in other religious traditions, from Christianity to Hinduism. Varied reactions to neoliberalization can be described as: "fundamentalist" (going back to the fundamentals of a religious teaching through overreliance on recognized texts), "revivalist" (rekindling interest in a religion as a basis for a renewed identity and as a guide for how to live within a community of shared beliefs), and "radical" (rejection of the dominant social, political, and economic environment as incompatible with religious beliefs *and* commitment to radically alter these dominant conditions in a variety of ways). See Choueri 1997.

3. The majority of strikes in the United States (around 2,560 in 1968) were short term and concerned mainly with the improvement of workers' conditions. The Con-fédération Général du Travail (CGT) in France stopped its major strike in 1968 after concessions by Pompidou. The days when workers controlled the means of production expired with the last breath of the self-management movements that flourished in factories throughout Europe c. 1968–1971. Self-management and "autonomia" move-ments were predominant in countries like Italy, inspired by anarchists and radical groups on the extreme Left, while the less numerous factory-based experiments in self-management in England, France, and West Germany were led by Trotskyist and Maoist groups, with some influenced by student movements. This trend, however, was quite limited and soon expired as the communist or socialist party line, or the major labor unions, decided to limit their free ride on the wave of popular discontent and social upheavals. Eastern European reactions, especially the thwarted reformist efforts in Czechoslovakia, Poland, and Hungary, left their mark in new forms of la-bor organizations reaching their peak in Poland's "Solidarity" movement in the next decade.

4. The case of decolonization demonstrates how a linear approach to historical development impedes understanding the transformative processes of the world-system. It is insufficient to look at colonial struggles as only antisystemic movements; it is equally important to look at such movements' systemic potentials. Thus, creating independent production spaces may go hand in hand with becoming a full-fledged partner of the interstate system and creating new spaces for consumption, new identities, new ethnicities, and new "free" markets.

5. This development may mark one of the most important transformations in twentieth-century capitalism. This transformation consists of the change of modes of control of needs and desires that effectively contributed to the deep infusion of capitalistic values into the various cultural worlds and the different manifestations of "material life" at the basis of the world-system. This was achieved through various means, not least of which were the proliferation of immaterial labor, the commodification of "free time," the increasing dominance of capitalistic forces in "global" processes of production of human desires and needs—through images, significations, communicational and informational flows, etc.—and of transforming localized sociocultural values and epistemologies.

6. These "classes" designate somewhat separate domains of different fabrics of "material life"—that still intersect and where "purchasing power" is presented as the value dominating social relations in a world where everything is commodified, including human life. While such differences are not absolute, they are substantial enough to warrant a different material development of social relations and of a socialization connected to integrated global networks of information, communication, and the media.

There are four principal new classes relevant to today's new movements. First, a new global elite has emerged that engages in very little productive activity, and if any, it would be managerial or organizational. Second, a new professional class is marked by an engagement in an occupation that provides for "basic necessities" *and* more through credit and enhanced purchasing power. Basic necessities vary from core, to semiperiphery, to periphery. The professional class household is the "consumer subject" par excellence: cable, electronics, Internet, games, gadgets, etc., are essential to the household, as are fashion, style, and access to information. A third class grouping is provided by casual laborers who cannot regularly provide for their or their household's basic necessities, and who depend on external aid and support, governmental or otherwise. Casual laborers have no access to credit, more debt than income, and little if any disposable income. The measure of casual laborers is their irregularity of income and the constant fear of being downsized. Criminality, prostitution, drug dealing, and other "miracles" (e.g., lotteries) provide the only possible way of "striking it big." A fourth group may be termed "the new slaves." This group includes those who are forced into the long-term abuse of the sexual trade or other occupations such as sweatshops or criminal activities. Such use is not based on labor power (use-value or exchange-value) but on the construction of human commodities (disposable bodies) through direct coercion (kidnapping, buying, etc.) or indirect coercion (luring, repaying an indeterminate debt, or under threat of violence to oneself or to others). Usually these slaves are spatially restricted and are stripped of any "purchasing power." Those who are homeless, hungry, who have to fight on a day-to-day basis for food and subsistence, shelter, basic necessities, for themselves or their households, especially in the periphery and semiperiphery, and who do *not* receive assistance from NGOs or governments could also be qualified as "new slaves."

✳

Chapter 5

Conclusion:
World Movement Waves
and World Transformations

William G. Martin

The first, most fundamental finding of this project may be simply stated: clusters of worldwide, antisystemic activity are clearly discernible over the past 250 years. These "world movement moments," usually lasting one to two decades, stand in stark rebuke to arguments that transnational movement activity appears only with late twentieth century "globalization." This evidence also rebuts the dominant derivation of movement activity from national inequalities and conflicts, state-formation, nation-building, long-term global cycles of accumulation, or episodes of hegemonic rivalry and war. By contrast to these claims that locate protest and social movements by isolated locations and times, disconnected from each other, we have found surprising, if often short-lived, worldwide outbursts of antisystemic action.

Global clustering does not necessarily mean, of course, that local movements were connected by formal organizational ties or even indirect, informal contacts. To restrict ourselves to these common conditions severely limits our ability, however, to perceive simultaneous protests set within similar conditions, with similar hopes and dreams, and even with similar enemies. Such parallel phenomena in very disparate locations across the world-economy have been charted in each of our epochs, in sharp defiance of traditional, linear, historical narratives.

We need not limit ourselves, however, to simply parallel outbursts of antisystemic activity. For transcontinental linkages are evident in all our epochs, even centuries before the recent focus on globalization and antiglobalization movements. These ranged from corresponding organizations, as in links among abolitionist and revolutionary movements in different countries and continents, through formal black, labor, and socialist internationals, to coordinated antiwar, anticolonial, and student movements at different world movement moments. More informal networks, most notably those borne through the constant circulation of people across the world-economy, also acted to forge channels of movement communication. As discussion in preceding chapters demonstrates, transoceanic diasporas from the eighteenth to the present century were especially important channels of movement diffusion and communication, including multiple Ottoman, Asian, African, and European diasporas. Circuits of labor, faith, and trade similarly served to construct pathways carrying mobile sailors and merchants, soldiers and missionaries, and coerced and often circulating labor.

Networks and exchanges among movements did not always produce (as is often assumed) cooperative or felicitous relationships among movements. Indeed, one of our earliest and sharpest discussions in the research working group revolved around the continuing discovery of antagonistic relations among antisystemic movements located in different zones and status positions across the world-economy. Seemingly irreconcilable conflicts related to racial, gender, or class differences among and within movements were visible and debated long before the race, gender, and Third versus First World debates of the 1960s (much less the 1990s). These explicit, public antagonisms were evident in the great state revolutions, antislavery and anticolonial movements of the late eighteenth and early nineteenth centuries, the next century's organized labor and nationalist movements, and the widespread anticolonial movements of the nineteenth and twentieth centuries—to mention but a few examples.

Indeed, one can often lay bare the structural fissures and processes of the world-economy as they have been formed through contentious as well as collaborative movement relationships. The combination of common timing, similar modes of organizing, and mutual opponents readily chart shared experiences and radical consciousnesses linked by global processes. In each of our epoch studies these are evident, from the construction of intercontinental production and labor processes, as in the intertwining formation of sea labor, slave labor, and urban wage labor in the eighteenth century, to the transcontinental remaking of gender, household, and labor formations in expansive nineteenth-century anticolonial constructions, to the organically and often opposed movements tied to national liberation and state formation in core, semiperipheral, and peripheral areas in the twentieth century.

Each of our world epoch studies examines these relationships and movement activities in detail, and we need not repeat these findings here. Together their limits also point toward future research agendas, including among other items the development of methodologies suitable to world movement studies; the investigation of relations among similar and also dissimilar movements in different zones of the world-economy; concrete studies of successive movement legacies in far greater detail than we have been able to conduct given the scope of our inquiry; and the examination of specific movement conjunctures, especially those suggested by our work but unexplored as world-historical movement moments (e.g., the 1830s).

Movement Conjunctures and World Transformations

The successive epoch studies in previous chapters do provide us the materials, however, to begin to construct an understanding of how move-ment waves successively link to each other over time, how they served to undermine and transform the capitalist world-economy, and what these successive transformations imply for evaluating today's movements.

Stepping back and moving across successive world epochs reveals that protest waves have, in both their failures and successes, generated radical changes in the broader capitalist world—and beyond. This reveals two additional findings of this project: (1) successive world movement waves have changed the contours and processes that form the world-economy, and (2) in so doing they have altered the conditions within which future movements form, and the forces against which they protest.

Our first epoch offers striking confirmation of how movement waves have radically transformed the capitalist world-economy and even social formations outside it. The contours and impact of the French and U.S. revolutions are, of course, well known, from the emergence of European modernity and liberalism to the demonstration of the possibilities of collective action. From these founding revolutions of the modern world would usher the formation of revolutionary political parties and trade unions within Europe, and, well beyond the boundaries of Europe, na-tionalist movements seeking modern states for newly imagined nations.

Yet as the authors of this epoch study argue, equally important were other, "transformative" movements beyond the classic narratives of modern state and party formation. Most obvious is the impact of the Haitian Revolution and the antislavery movements that surrounded it, which not only shaped the struggle for hegemony among world powers but propelled a worldwide scramble for postslavery forms of coerced labor (even as more highly repressive forms of slavery spread to replace the loss of Haiti). Taken together with European and settler revolts it is possible to chart how parallel yet starkly different movements, in very different zones of the world-economy, led to the worldwide transformation of modes of labor, racial, and colonial control.

The scale and impact of these transformations are missed in core-centric accounts, which usually cast other revolts as either precapitalist unrest or derivative, early modern protest. Equally missing in most accounts are the social worlds created through resistance to, and even escape from, an aggressively encroaching, Euro-American capitalism. These ranged from newly freed slaves' refusal to participate in commodity production, to flight from remaining centers of slave production and the pursuit of wholly new noncapitalist social worlds, to the transformation of Asian and African societies and empires because of the resistance of merchants, workers, and state officials. Protest against the corrosive political and cultural effects of increasing relations with European states and the world-economy could and did lead to the transformation of societies alongside but outside the capitalist world-economy.

The formative response of core states and capitalist enterprises to the challenges raised by these movements within and outside the world-system resulted in a new world order as the nineteenth century proceeded. Successful cases of resistance were bypassed, as in Haiti, while unruly labor forces elsewhere were replaced with new sources and modes of labor control all across the expanding boundaries of the capitalist world-economy. Successful anticolonial and antislavery movements in the Americas came, in this way, to stabilize the world-economy. As the interstate system expanded and incorporated local elites, Britain's new faith in free trade came to propel and legitimize aggressive expansion across Africa, the Indian Ocean, Asia, and the Pacific.

By the mid-nineteenth century a new international division of labor and hegemon had emerged, with many of the targets of eighteenth-century movements absent from the scene. Decolonization had ended colonialism and created independent states in the Americas; the end of the slave trade had pushed forward even cheaper, especially indentured (or "coolie"), labor from Asia; and liberalism and its promotion of social change and progress delegitimized the eighteenth-century world while promising a new age. These radical changes did not still protest: as epoch two recounts, widespread revolts broke out across the world in the decade surrounding 1848. By century's end two striking responses emerged from below to signal vast changes to come. One challenge arose from growing urban and especially waged workers' movements within core states. The adoption of institutionalized and at times transnational forms of organizing in trade unions and political parties opened the door to formidable bids to capture state power.

A second challenge arose from the expansion of the capitalist world-economy under the "free trade" system, which stimulated in turn a new wave of antisystemic protests all across the outer rim of the world-economy. Responding to the dual driving forces of increasing armed intervention by core powers and international racism—most starkly evident in the rise of orientalism and scientific racism in this period—a new wave of anti-imperial and anticapitalist resistance emerged. This was, moreover, an increasingly organized and transnational movement. As with the rise of labor and socialist internationals in this period, new transnational organizations emerged, including Pan-African and Pan-Asian anticolonial organizations. Where these processes overlapped, particularly in locations where states and capital were weak and workers and nationalists were strong, they could produce revolutionary seizures of state power—most notably in Russia in 1917.

Despite the intensity of worldwide protest surrounding World War I, however, most revolutionary movements were defeated by the early interwar period. Divisions within and between antisystemic movements across class, zonal, and racial boundaries posed significant obstacles to movement alliances and movement successes. It proved increasingly difficult, for example, for predominantly white labor movements to support black, Asian, and anticolonial aspirations, as was made violently evident in the post–World War I strike and riot wave around the world. The banner of South Africa's 1922 Rand Revolt offered an extreme but not unknown sentiment: "Workers of the World, Fight and Unite for a White South Africa."

These divisions among and within movements did not lessen as movements came to power after World War II, fulfilling almost a century-long drive to state power: from Britain to France to Germany and even the United States, Labour, Socialist, and Social Democratic parties supported continuing control over Algeria, the Congo, Indochina, Southern Rhodesia, South Africa, Cuba, etc. Racial and gender hierarchies, so central to the international reconstruction of capitalism in the nineteenth century, remained embedded in even the most successful movements. This was never so simple a matter as chauvinism or betrayal, as commonly posed, for such positions also flowed directly from the logic of the pursuit of state power, especially in core zones where racial, gender, and colonial privilege were most closely correlated.

The assumption to power of African, Caribbean, and Asian nationalists produced a parallel outcome from the other end of the interstate system by the third quarter of the twentieth century: as movements became parties and parties became states, the transnational, Pan-African, and Pan-Asian roots of the struggle against colonial rule were abandoned. Bandung, as the study on this period charts, represented the fulfillment of a long anticolonial struggle—and its burial. Nationalism in both North and South had achieved state power, and these victories contributed significantly to the postwar boom by redistributing world income and legitimizing liberalism and U.S. hegemony. The transnational traditions that had spawned and sustained labor, socialist, and anticolonial struggles were, however, shredded through the very victory of the movements and the acceptance of a world order that had so directly responded to many movements' demands. In this sense internationalism was defeated by nationalism.

All the greater shock was "1968" for the revolt it presented to the victorious social movements that had succeeded to power in the previous two generations. The rejection of the old Left by the new Left, in all areas of the world, went well beyond the charges of "weakness, corruption, connivance, neglect, and arrogance" (Arrighi, Hopkins, and Wallerstein, 1989: 102). As charted in previous chapters, the refrain of young rebels from Europe to China, from the United States to Africa, was increasingly the same: states run by purportedly Left parties had proven no less imperial, repressive, and racist in the North and no less dependent, bureaucratic, and kleptocratic in the East and South than those they had replaced. This was a rejection of the universal claims of 1789 and was recognized as such by both the old and new Left. As poor, Third World, black, and feminist movements advanced, they insistently laid bare the correspondence between universalist movements in power and exploitation by race, gender, and location in the world-economy.

If the 1968 conjuncture was a worldwide one, it was also a brief one: everywhere anticapitalist and antistatist movements were rolled back in a flurry of fierce repression. Yet their challenge to liberal states and movements was, paradoxically, successful in most unexpected ways. Those who wielded power and wealth were forced to confront the shattered legitimacy of liberal developmentalism and were forced to contemplate alternative possibilities to tame unruly populations. This led to unexpected initiatives to reorganize, restabilize, and relegitimize the world-economy.

The first response toward these ends was explicitly brutal, as the neoliberal counterrevolution unleashed in the 1980s and 1990s reshaped the worldwide division of labor, disciplined unruly states and workers, and replaced liberalism with the harsh realities and stark promises of the "free market" and the spread of Western democracy. No longer was development and wealth promised to all through state action; liberalism was undercut by the very states, firms, political parties, and international institutions that had sustained it for over a generation. If the model was most sharply posed in Reagan and Clinton's America and Thatcher and Blair's England, by the early 1990s it had been implemented in Mandela's South Africa and Deng Xiaoping's China.

Under these pressures the surviving new Left movements, especially in core areas, fragmented, with surviving movements becoming increasingly institutionalized. As noted in the introduction to this volume, by the 1980s scholars were openly heralding the emergence of nonviolent, routinized, and bureaucratic movement society. The days of radical, violent, and anticapitalist protest seemed to have ended. As posed by the 1968–present epoch study, a new social imaginary, based on capitalist consumption and propelled by neoliberalism, had not only broken down national boundaries but penetrated all levels of material life across the planet. Revolutionary or antisystemic activity more generally had become increasingly difficult to discern. The victory of Western democracy and the free market had, the defenders of the system argued, triumphed (e.g., Fukuyama 1992).

Post-1968 Dilemmas and Postliberal Movements

As just before 1968 (Bell 1965), these predictions of the death of all movements proved to be most premature: radical, anticapitalist demands and movements emerged just as their historic burial was being celebrated. For while 1989 seemed to seal the fate of the old Left and the 1968 movements, the events following the armed Chiapas revolt on the first day of NAFTA in 1994 inaugurated an innovative, new movement wave. Carried forward to the "Battle in Seattle" in 1999 and then beyond the formation of the World Social Forum in 2001, a growing set of networks arose to link radical anti–United States, anti–World Bank, and anticapitalist activity generally. As the last chapter demonstrates, these new movements vary widely, not least in their antisystemic aspirations and potentials.

Set within past movement outcomes as composed above, today's movements raise obvious questions: Do they pose an antisystemic threat to the neoliberal world that has emerged in the past generation, in response to 1968? Do they prefigure the reconstruction of the capitalist world-economy? Or even more boldly: do they signal a long successive wave of movement toward a different social world, one more diversely local and noncapitalist—as some assert?

Many senior scholars committed to the long-term, world-scale analysis of capitalism foresee at least an age of transition: Wallerstein speaks of the end of the world as we know it (2004; see also Hopkins and Wallerstein 1996); Arrighi charts an age of global turbulence, chaos, and uncertain transition (2003; see also Arrighi and Silver 1999b: 271–89); and Amin speaks of the transition to world socialism (1999: 31–32). A broader argument revives Karl Polanyi's (1957) double movement thesis for core zones, whereby an unconstrained, self-regulating market so debases human communities that movements arise to demand, once again, social protection from the ravages of unfettered capitalism (Mittelman 1996; Bello 2003: 114 passim). While the direct analogy between the crisis of the nineteenth-century British free trade system and the short American century of free enterprise is difficult to sustain (not to mention the limits of core models in explaining a global phenomenon), the argument has wide appeal, particularly for social democrats and those who look to Western Europe where social services continue to legitimize the state (not to mention competition with the United States). The case is easily put: has not neoliberalism denuded states and destroyed social contracts, and elicited in response a wide array of movements that are consciously antimarket, antiprivatization, and, in a nutshell, practicing "antiglobalization"?

It would certainly seem so to many.[1] Certainly today's movements more readily grasp the global character of capitalism and mobilize across national boundaries, as is illustrated in the networking of local protests, the wider demonstrations against U.S. military power, and the global targeting of the World Bank, the International Monetary Fund (IMF), and the World Trade Organization (WTO). From this it is but a small step to see contemporary movements as a great leap forward from past world movements. This is often held to be the case not only at the level of the coordination and modalities of today's movements, but also in movement activists' aims and their vision of alternative social worlds (e.g., Notes from Nowhere 2003).

Particularly evident is the abandonment of the expectation that emancipation can be achieved through the capture of state power, and, conversely, the positing of an intercommunal pursuit of liberation beyond both the state and the divisions imposed by the world-construction of race, gender, and unequal exchange. Not only have the transformation of movements into parties and the pursuit of state power been eschewed, but any engagement with political parties has been formally dismissed by many movements. The cases range across environmental, land, and antiprivatization movements, from the EZLN (Zapatista Army of National Liberation) in Chiapas to the meetings of the World Social Forum (where direct party participation has been excluded [a contested position]), to landless movements in Brazil and elsewhere.[2] Current movements are clearly working through the dilemma posed but unanswered by the 1968 movements, namely, how to pursue freedom in a world where states hold political power, and yet do not exercise dominion over world processes of accumulation and exploitation. The revival of anarchism (Graeber 2002), so evident in today's direct action protests, is an indicator of this process (although the rejection of party and state strategies is now embedded in a very different world-economic context and type of movement—as evidenced in local or regionally circumscribed movements).

Looking Forward: Postliberal to Postcapitalist Scenarios

If we apply these observations alongside the successive layering of world social change induced by past movement waves, it is possible to construct discrete future possibilities arising from the contemporary, post-1989 movement eruption. While these scenarios are useful for discerning possible futures among myriad possibilities, they hardly delimit the possible paths that movements might chart. They also do not take into account in any detail the changing forces attending capital accumulation, hegemony, and the cultural structures of knowledge; these are assessed in the contributions of our larger, common project undertaken by the Fernand Braudel Center's Research Working Groups on the Categories of Knowledge and the Structural Trends of the Capitalist World-Economy.

Nevertheless, focusing upon the outcomes of past movement waves suggests three plausible scenarios to consider as we face the near future.

Scenario 1: Fragmented and Consumed Identities and Movements

One is starkly suggested by Kalouche and Mielants in the preceding chapter for the contemporary period: despite the "pregnant possibilities" offered by movements in Latin America, Africa, and elsewhere, there are few signs that protest activity poses fundamental challenges to the contemporary world-system.

One the one hand, the new sociality imbued by the primacy of consumption has engendered new social relations, social consciousnesses, and forces that have been capable of contesting dominant capitalist imaginaries—as evidenced in international terrorism and many new movements, including identity, neo-Luddite, indigenous, ethnic, religious, radical environmental, and antiglobalization movements. Yet, on the other hand, the prospects of these forces cohering or operating in a cohesive, antisystemic manner seem dim. Working against an antisystemic trajectory is the continuing and worldwide unfolding of the marriage of new needs and desires with the processes of a technologically innovative capitalism that now penetrates all local cultures. Thus while the fragmentation of identities and nationalities has fostered new movements, many of them are conservative if not prosystemic movements, unable to mount a long-term, institutionalized challenge to a rampant, postliberal capitalist world. In this sense the dilemmas posed by 1968, especially the inability of noninstitutionalized, non-state-centric, and disruptive local action to effect radical social change, are even more debilitating today.

Scenario 2: Overcoming Dilemmas, Alterglobalization Rampant

A second, very counterposed scenario could be projected from the very cumulative effect of successive world-movement transformations. Movement optimists could, for example, project a future of successful alterglobalization activity, whereby attacks by the world's social and economic justice movements on the globally organized, neoliberal project coalesce into initiatives to construct alternative modes of organizing social life—and not just a reformed and cyclically rejuvenated capitalist world-economy that has been effected by past social and national movements. Here the fragmentation of past movements and the search for new, transnational, social imaginaries becomes an indicator of fundamental, anticapitalist challenges to come—hence, for example, the demands for the decommodification of land, labor, and cultural life, demands so prominent in the local, but increasingly globally integrated, struggles against the privatization of basic human needs (land, enterprises, food, water, education, health). The growing coalitions and networking among such movements—through the Internet, international conferencing and protests, and most notably at successive regional and international meetings of the World Social Forum among many other avenues—offer the potential to overcome the organizational dilemmas imposed by 1968 and noted in chapter 4. Indeed the promise of such a projection revolves around the possibility of avoiding the allure of a signal focus on state politics while seeking an alternative social and political existence through world political alliances.

Here contemporary antisystemic movements may find much to learn from earlier movements against incorporation into the capitalist world—movements that have often been dismissed as attempts to retain "precapitalist" modes of life and production.[3] As we know from varied examples—not the least of which is the rejection of plantations and commodity production in the wake of successful slave revolts—success was often tied to a vigorous rejection of the modern capitalist state, commodification, and capitalist rationalities. The present search for alternatives to communities organized by capital accumulation, accelerating commodification, and the national state demonstrates in part a broad return to the search for noncapitalist alternatives.

Such seemingly millenarian aims appear in movements on every continent. As pointed out by observers of such diverse phenomena as collapsing states, indigenous movements, land movements, and women's movements,[4] these strategies may be strongest outside core zones. In many areas of Latin America and Africa, for example, the ravages of neoliberalism have forced many to devise survival strategies outside the realm of waged labor and market consumption—even while consumption accelerates and states grow larger in core areas (Dickinson and Schaeffer 2001, Wallerstein 2002: 38–39).[5] Certainly the antiglobalization movements have had to confront, in ways the 1960s movements did not, the harsh inequalities imposed by the international division of labor and, especially, across the lines of race and gender—as revealed in widespread discussions of "third wave" feminism or, more rarely, a fourth wave of the black international (West 1999). To decommodification as an antisystemic strategy, global movement discussions and activities now openly pose the tasks of deracialization and depatriarchalization. No longer can struggles against racial and gender oppression be contained within the nation, the household, the body.[6] Post-1968 and postliberal realities have moved these differences squarely to the uneasy heart of contemporary movements' deliberations.

Scenario 3: A Postliberal World Regime?

While these first two scenarios focus upon long-term structural and cultural transformations of movements themselves, it is worth recalling one of our starkest findings, namely, that over the *longue durée* strong movement clusters may both undermine and yet lead to the restabilization of the capitalist world-economy. Radical social change in response to worldwide crises of capital accumulation, legitimacy, and material life may thus change the world and put capitalism upon a new footing. This is a different basis for projecting future choices than those that commonly rest upon economic or technological determinants. As our analysis indicates, the role of social movements in challenging the old order and defining the contours of the new is critical—and varies over successive world movement clusters.

This suggests a third possible scenario in the medium run, which may be termed the "postliberal world regime" possibility. This sketch is straightforward: novel, non-state-centric modes of challenging both capital and local states have begun to play a central role in developing and legitimizing a post-nation-state, postliberal configuration of political power suitable to continued accumulation on a world scale. Driving this project forward is the pressing challenge of tackling the demise of liberalism's promise of wealth and equality, the demise of the legitimacy of the interstate system, and the absence of development and social welfare policies.

The emergence of new world governance structures offers a potential systemic solution to these challenges, by promoting the integration of civil society and nongovernmental organizations (NGOs) with transformed international financial and political institutions. Such initiatives point to the creation of institutions of political rule that operate above and below the increasingly denuded nation-state and are in practice far less democratic. Whereas previous movement clusters ended colonialism and expanded the interstate system through decolonization, a very different, formative response could be cast today: the construction of a networked mode of political control above and below the putative democratic, liberal state. In this process the transformation of movements and civil society organizations into institutional partners of newly legitimized international institutions is central.

The signs of such a future are many, including the transition at the World Bank toward the legitimization of its work through the language of poverty relief; the relegation of aid, education, health, and other services to increasingly selected NGOs; the proposed reformation (but not democratization) of the U.N. Security Council; and the incorporation of neoliberal, semiperipheral states like Brazil and South Africa into the working levels of global financial institutions (the WTO, the World Bank) and global military intervention (as in Haiti, Burundi, the D.R. Congo, etc.). Debates and divisions within the World Social Forum also reveal these contradictory tendencies (see Sen et al. 2004), as in the tensions between those committed to "horizontal" linkages among movements and direct forms of action, reminiscent of anarchist traditions, and those who argue for more powerful, "vertical" forms of institutionalized organizing reminiscent of the old Left. The increasing prominence of wealthier organizations with ties to northern funders, particularly NGOs, has led to a similar debate: is the forum, as some activists charge, less an encounter among grassroots movements and increasingly a northern-dominated, NGO trade fair (e.g., Manji 2006)?

As these debates suggest, contemporary movements could thus well advance beyond the strategic dilemmas, limitations, and institutionalizations of past world movements—as posed by our first two scenarios—and yet be caught up in delivering a new and highly polarized capitalist world. From this line of argument it is possible to project that the very form and demands of today's antisystemic movements are being adapted, as in the past, to build the launching ground for a new, long wave of capitalist expansion.

Such scenarios suggest both the real advances of antisystemic movements in the past three centuries, their current promise, and the substantial difficulties faced by any effort to resuscitate a stable, flourishing capitalist world-economy. For scholar activists, among which we count ourselves, these tough questions suggest not only the need for imaginative thinking on future possibilities in the ongoing search for emancipation, but also the dangerous shoals that lie ahead: the lure of institutionalization into novel structures of power; the difficulty of recognizing difference while forming coalitions across the boundaries of location, status, and privilege; and the requirement to deepen and widen, across the world, democratic relationships and organization. Of one thing we may be certain: nationalism, liberalism, and even neoliberalism offer us no future. Contemporary as well as historical evidence suggests only one certainty: revolts on a world scale will play a major role in fashioning our futures and these are increasingly, we hope, pointing toward not simply a postliberal but a postcapitalist existence.

Notes

1. Patrick Bond charts and aptly categorizes the force at play in his *Against Global Apartheid* (2001: 3, and "Table 3: Five reactions to the global crisis," 2001: 94–95). For a quite different formulation from the same region, stressing community movements

"free from the ideological inhibitions of the organized labour or the tired dogmas of the Left," see Ashwin Desai (2002: 139).

2.   This is, of course, highly debated, most notably within the World Social Forum where political parties are obviously engaged. The transmutation into conservative neoliberalism of recent radical movements who have come to power, most notably the African National Congress (ANC) in South Africa and the PT (Workers Party) in Brazil, has served to highlight this debate and the distance between state power and radical movements.

3.   Newer work on the process of incorporation and indigenous movements provided conceptions and historical evidence; see, for example, Wilma Dunaway (1996), Thomas Hall (2001).

4.   In all these areas the relationships across world zones, so often missed in core-centric and nationalist conceptions, prove critical. This is as true for discussions of collapsed states and state formation along the periphery of the world-economy, which need to be related to core state formation, as it is for the relation between polarized consumption and feminist movements. As illustrations see, among others, Dickinson (1998), Friedman (1999), Bennholdt-Thomsen et al. (2001): and for African states, William G. Martin (2005a).

5.   See, for example, the arguments of Dickinson (1998), Dickinson and Schaeffer (2001), and Wallerstein (2002: 38–39).

6.   None of this means, of course, that current movements are not conflicted by patriarchy and racial difference—as revealed in critical discussions of the protests in Seattle and the World Social Forum meetings themselves. See, for example, Hardt (2002), Elizabeth Martinez (2000), Mertes (2004), Notes from Nowhere (2003), and Yuen et al. (2002).

Bibliography

Abu-Lughod, Janet L. 1989. *Before European Hegemony: The World System A.D. 1250–1350.* New York: Oxford University Press.

Adams, Carol. 1999. *The Sexual Politics of Meat: A Feminist-Vegetarian Critical Theory.* New York: Continuum.

Adams, Carol, and Josephine Donovan. 1995. *Animals and Women: Feminist Theoretical Explorations.* Durham, NC: Duke University Press.

Adas, Michael. 1979. *Prophets of Rebellion: Millenarian Protest Movements Against the European Colonial Order.* Durham, NC: University of North Carolina Press.

———. 1981. "From Avoidance to Confrontation: Peasant Protest in Precolonial and Colonial Southeast Asia," *Comparative Studies in Society and History* 23 (2), 217–47.

Adelman, Jeremy. 1993. "State and Labour in Argentina: The Portworkers of Buenos Aires, 1910–1921," *Journal of Latin American Studies* 25 (1), 73–103.

Adorno, Theodor, and Max Horkheimer. 1989. *Dialectic of Enlightenment.* Trans. by John Cumming. London: Verso.

Afary, Janet. 1994. "Social Democracy and the Iranian Constitutional Revolution of 1906–1911," in John Foran, ed., *A Century of Revolution, Social Movements in Iran.* Minneapolis: University of Minnesota Press, 21–43.

Ahn, Jae-Hung. 1996. "Ideology and Interest: The Case of Swedish Social Democracy, 1886–1911," *Politics & Society* 24 (2), 153–87.

Alexander, Titus. 1996. *Unraveling Global Apartheid: An Overview of World Politics.* Cambridge: Blackwell and Polity.

Altbach, Philip G. 1970. "Student Movements in Historical Perspective: The Asian Case," *Journal of Southeast Asian Studies* 1 (1), 74–84.

———. ed. 1981. *Student Politics, Perspectives for the Eighties.* Scarecrow.

Amin, Samir. 1987. "A Note on the Concept of Delinking," *Review* 10 (3), 435–44.

———. 1990a. *Delinking: Towards a Polycentric World.* London: Zed Books.

———. 1990b. "The Social Movements in the Periphery: An End to National Liberation," in Samir Amin, Giovanni Arrighi, Andre Gunder Frank, and Immanuel Wallerstein, eds., *Transforming the Revolution: Social Movements and the World System.* New York: Monthly Review, 96–138.

———. 1997. *Capitalism in the Age of Globalization: The Management of Contemporary Society.* London: Zed Books.

———. 1998. *Spectres of Capitalism: A Critique of Current Intellectual Fashions.* New York: Monthly Review Press.

———. 1999. "For a Progressive and Democratic World Order," in Francis Adams, Satya Dev Gupta, and Kidane Mengisteab, eds., *Globalization and the Dilemmas of the State in the South.* New York: St. Martin's, 17–32.

Amin, Samir, Giovanni Arrighi, Andre Gunder Frank, and Immanuel Wallerstein, eds. 1990. *Transforming the Revolution: Social Movements and the World System.* New York: Monthly Review.

Anderson, Benedict R. 1972. *Java in a Time of Revolution: Occupation and Resistance, 1944–1946.* Ithaca, NY: Cornell University Press.

Anderson, Bonnie S. 1998. "The Lid Comes Off: International Radical Feminism and the Revolutions of 1848," *NWSA Journal* 10 (2), 1–12.

Arrighi, Giovanni. 1983. "The Labor Movement in Twentieth-Century Western Europe," in *Labor in the World Social Structure.* Beverly Hills, CA: Sage, 44–57.

———. 1990. "Marxist Century—American Century: The Making and Remaking of the World Labor Movement," in Samir Amin, Giovanni Arrighi, Andre Gunder Frank, and Immanuel Wallerstein, eds., *Transforming the Revolution: Social Movements and the World System.* New York: Monthly Review, 54–95.

———. 1994. *The Long 20th Century.* New York: Verso.

———. 1995. "Labor Unrest in Italy, 1880–1990," *Review* 27 (1), 61–68.

———. 2002. "Lineages of Empire," *Historical Materialism* 10 (3), 3–17.

———. 2003. "The Social and Political Economy of Global Turbulence," *New Left Review* 20, 5–71.

Arrighi, Giovanni, and Beverly J. Silver. 1999a. "Introduction," in Giovanni Arrighi, Beverly Silver, et al., *Chaos and Governance in the Modern World System.* Minneapolis: University of Minnesota Press, 1–36.

———. 1999b. "Conclusion," in Giovanni Arrighi, Beverly Silver et al., *Chaos and Governance in the Modern World System.* Minneapolis: University of Minnesota Press, 271–89.

Arrighi, Giovanni, Terrence K. Hopkins, and Immanuel Wallerstein. 1989. *Antisystemic Movements.* New York: Verso.

———. 1992. "1989, The Continuation of 1968," *Review* 15 (2), 221–42.

Asante, S. K. B. 1977. *Pan-African Protest: West Africa and the Italo-Ethiopian Crisis, 1934–1941.* London: Longman.

Assensoh, Akwasi B., and Yvette M. Alex-Assensoh. 1998. "The Leadership of the American Civil Rights Movement and African Liberation Movements: Their Connections and Similarities," *Proteus: A Journal of Ideas* 15 (1), 23–28.

Atwell, William S. 1997. "International Bullion Flows and the Chinese Economy, circa 1530–1650," in Dennis Owen Flynn and Arturo Giráldez, *Metals and Monies in an Emerging Global Economy.* Brookfield, VT: Ashgate, 141–63.

Babson, Steve. 1999. *The Unfinished Struggle: Turning Points in American Labor, 1877–Present.* Lanham, MD: Rowman & Littlefield.

Baldwin, Richard, and Philippe Martin. 1999. "Two Waves of Globalization: Superficial Similarities, Fundamental Differences," in Horst Siebert, ed., *Globalization and Labor.* Tübingen: Kiel and Mohr Siebeck, 3–58.

Bales, Kevin. 1999. *Disposable People: New Slavery in the Global Economy.* Berkeley: University of California Press.

Basu, Subho. 1998. "Strikes and 'Communal' Riots in Calcutta in the 1890s: Industrial

Workers, Bhadralok Nationalist Leadership and the Colonial State," *Modern Asian Studies* 32, 949–83.

Bauböck, Rainer. 1993. "Entitlement and Regulation. Immigration Control in Welfare States," in Hedwig Rudolph and Mirjana Morokvasic, eds., *Bridging States and Markets*. Berlin: Rainer Bohn Verlag, 19–47.

Baudrillard, Jean. 1970. *La Société de Consommation*. Paris: Editions Denoêl.

Bauman, Zygmunt. 1998. *Globalization: The Human Consequences*. New York: Columbia University Press.

Beittel, Mark. 1995. "Labor Unrest in South Africa, 1870–1990." *Review* 27 (1), 87–104.

Bell, Daniel. 1965. *The End of Ideology*. New York: Free Press.

Bello, Walden. 2003. *Deglobalization: Ideas for a New World Economy*. Cape Town: David Philip.

Bennholdt-Thomsen, Veronika, Nicholas G. Faraclas, and Claudia Von Werlhof. 2001. *There Is an Alternative: Subsistence and Worldwide Resistance to Corporate Globalization*. New York: Zed Books.

Benton, Ted, and Simon Redfearn. 1996. "The Politics of Animal Rights—Where Is the Left?" *New Left Review* 215, 43–58.

Best, Geoffrey, ed. 1988. *The Permanent Revolution: The French Revolution and Its Legacy*. Chicago: University of Chicago Press.

Bhatt, Cheton. 2001. *Hindu Nationalism*. New York: Berg.

Biel, Robert. 2000. *The New Imperialism: Crisis and Contradictions in North/South Relations*. London: Zed Books.

Bigo, Didier. 1998. "Frontiers and Security in the European Union: The Illusion of Migration Control," in M. Anderson and E. Bort, eds., *The Frontiers of Europe*. London: Pinter, 148–64.

Birchall, Ian. 1997. *The Spectre of Babeuf*. New York: St. Martin's.

Blanchard, Peter. 1982. *The Origins of the Peruvian Labor Movement, 1883–1919*. Pittsburgh, PA: University of Pittsburgh Press.

Boahen, A. Adu. 1987. *African Perspectives on Colonialism*. Baltimore, MD: Johns Hopkins University Press.

Body-Gendrot, Sophie. 2000. "Marginalisation and Political Responses in the French Context," in Pierre Hamel, Henri Lustiger-Thaler, and Margit Mayer, eds., *Urban Movements in a Globalizing World*. London: Routledge, 68–74.

Bolaria, B. Singh, and Rosemary Bolaria. 1997. "Capital, Labour, Migrations," in B. Singh Bolaria and Rosemary Bolaria, eds., *International Labour Relations*. Delhi: Oxford University Press, 1–17.

Bond, Patrick. 2001. *Against Global Apartheid: South Africa Meets the World Bank, IMF, and International Finance*. Cape Town: University of Cape Town Press.

Bondarevsky, G., and V. Sofinsky. 1975. "Bandung's Historic Lessons." *International Affairs* 5, 45–53.

Bosch, Aurora. 1997. "Why Is There No Labor Party in the United States? A Comparative New World Case Study: Australia and the U.S., 1783–1914," *Radical History Review* 67, 35–78.

Boswell, Terry, and David Jorjani. 1998. "Uneven Development and the Origins of Split Labor Market Discrimination: A Comparison of Black, Chinese and Mexican Immigrant Minorities in the United States," in Joan Smith et al., eds., *Racism, Sexism, and the World-System*. Westport, CT: Greenwood, 169–86.

Boxer, Charles R. 1965. *The Dutch Seaborne Empire, 1600–1800*. New York: Knopf.

Boyd, Monica. 1989. "Family and Personal Networks in International Migration: Recent Developments and New Agendas," *International Migration Review* 23 (3), 638–70.

Bradley, Mark. 1999. "Making Revolutionary Nationalism: Vietnam, America and the August Revolution of 1945," *Itinerario* 23 (1), 23–51.

———. 2000. *Imagining Vietnam and America: The Making of Postcolonial Vietnam, 1919–1950*. Chapel Hill, NC: University of North Carolina Press.

Braudel, Fernand. 1979. *Civilisation matérielle, économie et capitalisme: XVe–XVIIIe siècle, 2: Les jeux de l'échange*. Paris: Armand Colin.

———. 1981. *Civilization and Capitalism, 15th–18th Century*, vol. 1, *The Structures of Everyday Life*. New York: Harper and Row.

Brecher, Jeremy. 1997. *Strike!* Boston: South End.

Breuilly, John. 2000. "The Revolutions of 1848," in David Parker, ed., *Revolutions and the Revolutionary Tradition in the West, 1560–1991*. New York: Routledge, 109–31.

Brody, David. 1993. *In Labor's Cause: Main Themes on the History of the American Worker*. New York: Oxford University Press.

Brown, Dee Alexander. 1970. *Bury My Heart at Wounded Knee*. New York: Henry Holt.

Brown, Louise. 2000. *Sex Slaves: The Trafficking of Women in Asia*. London: Virago.

Bush, Rod. 1999. *We Are Not What We Seem: Black Nationalism and Class Struggle in the American Century*. New York: New York University Press.

Cahm, Caroline. 1989. *Kropotkin and the Rise of Revolutionary Anarchism, 1872–1886*. New York: Cambridge University Press.

Caldwell, Gillian, Steven Galster, and Nadia Steinzor. 1997. *Crime and Servitude: An Exposé of the Traffic of Women for Prostitution from the Newly Independent States*. New York: Global Survival Network and International League for Human Rights.

Callaghan, John. 2001. "The Cold War and the March of Capitalism, Socialism and Democracy," *Contemporary British History* 15 (3), 1–25.

Calvi, Fabrizio, ed. 1977. *Italie 77: Le "mouvement," les intellectuels*. Paris: Seuil.

Campbell, Horace. 1987. *Rasta and Resistance: From Marcus Garvey to Walter Rodney*. Trenton, NJ: Africa World.

———. 1994. "Pan-Africanism and African Liberation," in Sidney J. Lemelle and Robin D. G. Kelley, eds., *Imagining Home: Class, Culture, and Nationalism in the African Diaspora*. New York: Verso, 285–307.

Casparis, John, and Giovanni Arrighi. 1995. "Labor Unrest in Germany, 1906–90," *Review* 27 (1), 137–54.

Castells, Manuel. 1996. *The Rise of the Network Society*. Cambridge, MA: Blackwell.

———. 1997. *The Power of Identity*. Cambridge, MA: Blackwell.

———. 1998. *End of the Millennium*. Cambridge, MA: Blackwell.

Castles, Stephen, and Mark Miller. 1998. *The Age of Migration*. London: Macmillan.

Castoriadis, Cornelius. 1984 [1957]. *Workers' Councils and the Economics of a Self-Managed Society*. Wooden Shoe pamphlet, Philadelphia Solidarity.

———. 1987 [1975]. *The Imaginary Institution of Society*. Cambridge, MA: MIT Press.

———. 1990. *Le Monde Morcelé*. Paris: Seuil.

———. 1991. *Philosophy, Politics, Autonomy*. Edited by David Ames Curtis. New York: Oxford University Press.

Castro, Daniel, ed. 1999. *Revolution and Revolutionaries: Guerrilla Movements in Latin America*. Wilmington, DE: Jaguar Books on Latin America, no. 17.

Cell, John W. 1999. "The Indian and African Freedom Struggles: Some Comparisons," *The Journal of Imperial and Commonwealth History* 27 (2), 107–23.

Chakrabarty, Dipesh. 1981. "Communal Riots and Labour: Bengal's Jute Mill-Hands in the 1890s," *Past and Present* 91, 140–69.

Chan, Adrian. 1997. "In Search of a Civil Society in China," *Journal of Contemporary Asia* 27 (2), 242–51.

Chase, Ashton. 1964. *A History of Trade Unionism in Guyana, 1900 to 1961.* Ruimveldt, Guyana: New Guyana Co.

Chaudhuri, K. N. 1997. "World Silver Flows and Monetary Factors as a Force of International Economic Integration, 1658–1758," in Dennis Owen Flynn and Arturo Giráldez, eds., *Metals and Monies in an Emerging Global Economy.* Brookfield, VT: Ashgate, 286–93.

Chaudhuri, Sashi Bhusan. 1957. *Civil Rebellion in the Indian Mutinies, 1857–1859.* Calcutta: World Press.

Chiang, Xiangze. 1954. *The Nien Rebellion.* Seattle, WA: University of Washington Press.

Childs, Matt D. 1998. "A Case of 'Great Unstableness': A British Slaveholder and Brazilian Abolition," *Historian* 60 (4), 717–40.

Chirot, Daniel. 1977. *Social Change in the Twentieth Century.* New York: Harcourt, Brace, Jovanovich.

Chomsky, Noam. 1986. *Pirates and Emperors, Old and New: International Terrorism in the Real World.* Cambridge, MA: South End.

———. 1991. *Media Control: The Spectacular Achievements of Propaganda.* Westfield, NJ: Open Media.

———. 2000. *Rogue States: The Rule of Force in World Affairs.* Cambridge, MA: South End.

———. 2001. *Propaganda and the Public Mind.* Cambridge, MA: South End.

———. 2003. *Power and Terror.* New York: Seven Stories/Little More.

Chomsky, Noam, and Edward Herman. 1988. *Manufacturing Consent: The Political Economy of the Mass Media.* New York: Pantheon.

Choucri, Nazli, 1986. "The Hidden Economy: A New View of Remittances in the Arab World," *World Development* 14 (6), 697–712.

Choueiri, Youssef M. 1997. *Islamic Fundamentalism.* London: Pinter.

Clark, John, and Nuno Themudo. 2003. "The Age of Protest," in John Clark, ed., *Globalizing Civic Engagement: Civil Society and Transnational Action.* London: Earthscan, 109–27.

Cockburn, Andrew. 2003. "21st Century Slaves," *National Geographic* (Sept.), 8–24.

Cohen, Paul A. 1997. *History in Three Keys: The Boxers as Event, Experience, and Myth.* New York: Columbia University Press.

Coleman, David. 1997. "Europe under Migration Pressure: Some Facts on Immigration," in Emek Uçarer and Donald Puchala, eds., *Immigration into Western Societies: Problems and Policies.* London: Pinter, 121–46.

Conlin, Joseph R. 1969. *Bread and Roses, Too: Studies of the Wobblies.* Westport, CT: Greenwood.

Conrad, Robert E. 1972. *The Destruction of Brazilian Slavery, 1850–1888.* Berkeley, CA: University of California Press.

Cooper, Frederick. 1994. "Conflict and Connection: Rethinking Colonial African History," *American Historical Review* 99, 1515–45.

———. 1996. *Decolonization and African Society: The Labor Question in French and British Africa.* Cambridge: Cambridge University Press.

———. 2002. *Africa Since 1940, The Past of the Present.* Cambridge: Cambridge University Press.

Cooper, Randolph G. S. 2003. *The Anglo-Maratha Campaign and the Contest for India.* Cambridge: Cambridge University Press.

Coraggio, José Luis. 1985. "Social Movements and Revolution: The Case of Nicaragua," in David Slater, ed., *New Social Movements and the State in Latin America.* Amsterdam: CEDLA, 203–31.

Cornelius, Wayne A., et al. 1994. *Controlling Migration: A Global Perspective.* Stanford, CA: Stanford University Press.

Davis, Mary. 1993. *Comrade or Brother? A History of the British Labour Movement, 1789–1951.* London: Pluto.

Deleuze, Gilles. 1988. *Foucault.* Trans. by Sean Hand. Minneapolis: University of Minnesota Press.

———. 1990. "Postscript on the Societies of Control," *L'Autre Journal* 1 (May 1).

———. 1995. *Negotiations: 1972–1990.* Trans. by Martin Joughan. New York: Columbia University Press.

Desai, Ashwin. 2002. *We Are the Poors: Community Struggles in Post-Apartheid South Africa.* New York: Monthly Review.

Dickinson, Torry. 1998. "Preparing to Understand Feminism in the Twenty-First Century: Global Social Change, Women's Work, and Women's Movements," *Journal of World-Systems Research,* http://csf.colorado.edu/wsystems/jwsr.html, 4, 96–111.

Dickinson, Torry, and Robert Schaeffer. 2001. *Fast Forward: Work, Gender and Protest in a Changing World.* Lanham, MD: Rowman & Littlefield.

Diggins, John Patrick. 1992. *The Rise and Fall of the American Left.* New York: W. W. Norton.

Dirlik, Arif. 1991. *Anarchism in the Chinese Revolution.* Berkeley, CA: University of California Press.

D'Itri, Patricia W. 1999. *Cross Currents in the International Women's Movement, 1848–1948.* Bowling Green, OH: Bowling Green State University Popular Press.

Dobson, Andrew. 2000. *Green Political Thought.* London: Routledge.

Donovan, Josephine. 1990. "Animal Rights and Feminist Theory," *Signs* 15, 350–75.

Dubofsky, Melvyn. 1983. "Workers' Movements in North America, 1873–1990: A Preliminary Analysis," in Immanuel Wallerstein, *Labor in the World Social Structure.* Beverly Hills, CA: Sage, 22–43.

———. 1988. *We Shall Be All: A History of the Industrial Workers of the World,* 2nd ed. Urbana, IL: University of Illinois Press.

———. 1995. "Labor Unrest in the United States, 1906–90," *Review* 27 (1), 125–36.

DuBois, Ellen C. 1999. *Feminism and Suffrage: The Emergence of an Independent Women's Movement in America, 1848–1869.* Ithaca, NY: Cornell University Press.

Dunaway, Wilma A. 1996. *The First American Frontier: Transition to Capitalism in Southern Appalachia into the World-Economy, 1690–1763.* Chapel Hill: University of North Carolina Press.

Dunaway, Wilma A., ed. 2003. *Emerging Issues in the 21st Century World-System.* Westport, CT: Praeger.

Dusch, Sabine. 2002. *Le trafic d'êtres humains.* Paris: Presses Universitaires de France.

The Economist. 2002. "Violence in Columbia: Gunned Down," March 23, 36.

———. 2004. "Indigenous People in South America: A Political Awakening." Online at http://www.economist.com/world/la. Accessed February 19, 2004.

Edwards, Paul K. 1981. *Strikes in the United States, 1881–1974.* Oxford: Basil Blackwell.

Eisenberg, Carolyn. 1983. "Working-Class Politics and the Cold War: American Intervention in the German Labor Movement, 1945–49," *Diplomatic History* 7 (4), 283–306.

Ekins, Peter. 1992. *A New World Order: Grassroots Movements for Global Change.* New York: Routledge.

Emmer, Piet, and Herman Obdeijn. 1998. "Het paradijs is aan de overzijde," in Piet

Emmer and Herman Obdeijn, eds., *Het paradijs is aan de overzijde*. Utrecht: uitg. Jan van Arkel, 7–19.

Engels, Friedrich. 1968. *The Condition of the Working Class in England*. Translated and edited by W. O. Henderson and W. H. Chaloner. Stanford, CA: Stanford University Press.

Esenwein, George R. 1989. *Anarchist Ideology and the Working-Class Movement in Spain, 1868–1898*. Berkeley: University of California Press.

Faist, Thomas. 1997. "The Crucial Meso-Level," in Tomas Hammar et al., eds., *International Migration, Immobility and Development: Multidisciplinary Perspectives*. New York: Berg, 187–217.

Fanon, Frantz. 1963. *The Wretched of the Earth*. New York: Grove.

———. 1967 [1988]. *Toward the African Revolution*. New York: Grove.

Fasseur, Cornelius. 1992. *The Politics of Colonial Exploitation: Java, the Dutch, and the Cultivation System*. Ithaca, NY: Southeast Asia Program, Cornell University.

Featherstone, Mike. 1991. *Consumer Culture and Postmodernism*. London: Sage.

Feuerwerker, Albert. 1975. *Rebellion in Nineteenth-Century China*. Ann Arbor, MI: Center for Chinese Studies, University of Michigan.

Fick, Carolyn. 1997. "The French Revolution in Saint Domingue: A Triumph or Failure?" in David Gaspar and David Geggus, eds., *A Turbulent Time*. Bloomington: Indiana University Press, 51–75.

Finsen, Laurence, and Susan Finsen. 1994. *The Animal Rights Movement in America, from Compassion to Respect*. New York: Twayne.

Foran, John. 1991. "The Strengths and Weaknesses of Iran's Populist Alliance: A Class Analysis of the Constitutional Revolution of 1905–1911," *Theory and Society* 20, 795–823.

———. 1993. *Fragile Resistance: Social Transformation in Iran from 1500 to the Revolution*. Boulder, CO: Westview.

———. 1993a. "Dependency and Resistance in the Middle East, 1800–1925," *Political Power and Social Theory* 8, 107–40.

Ford, Franklin L. 1989. *Europe 1780–1830*. New York: Longman.

Foucault, Michel. 1982. "The Subject and Power," Appendix in Hubert A. Dreyfus and Paul Rabinow, eds., *Michel Foucault: Beyond Structuralism and Hermeneutics*. Chicago: University of Chicago Press.

———. 2000. *Power: Essential Works of Foucault 1954–1984*, vol. 3. Edited by James D. Faubion. Trans. by Robert Hurley et al. New York: New York Press.

Frame, Murray. 1995. *The Russian Revolution, 1905–1921: A Bibliographic Guide to Works in English*. Westport, CT: Greenwood.

Frank, Andre Gunder. 1998. *Reorient: Global Economy in the Asian Age*. Berkeley: University of California Press.

Frank, Andre Gunder, and Marta Fuentes. 1990. "Civil Democracy: Social Movements in Recent World History," in Samir Amin, Giovanni Arrighi, Andre Gunder Frank, and Immanuel Wallerstein, eds., *Transforming the Revolution*. New York: Monthly Review, 139–80.

Frank, Thomas Carr. 1995. *Commercialization of Dissent: Counterculture and Consumer Culture in the American 1960s*, vols. 1 and 2. Ann Arbor, MI: UMI.

———. 1997. *The Conquest of Cool: Business Culture, Counterculture, and the Rise of Hip Consumerism*. Chicago: University of Chicago Press.

Fredrickson, George M. 1995. *Black Liberation: A Comparative History of Black Ideologies in the United States and South Africa*. New York: Oxford University Press.

Freeman, Gary P. 1986. "Migration and the Political Economy of the Welfare State," *The Annals of the American Academy of Political and Social Science* 485 (May), 51–63.

Friedman, Jonathan. 1999. "Indigenous Struggles and the Discreet Charm of the Bourgeoisie," *Journal of World-Systems Research* 5 (2), 399–411.

Fukuyama, Francis. 1992. *The End of History and the Last Man*. New York: Free Press.

Füredi, Frank. 1994. *Colonial Wars and the Politics of Third World Nationalism*. London: I. B. Tauris.

García Luis, Julio. 2001. *Cuban Revolution Reader: A Documentary History of 40 Key Moments of the Cuban Revolution*. Melbourne: Ocean.

Garza, H. A. 1979. "Political Economy and Change: The Zapatista Agrarian Revolutionary Movement," *Rural Sociology* 44, 281–306.

Geary, Dick. 1989. "Socialism and the German Labour Movement before 1914," in Dick Geary, ed., *Labour and Socialist Movements in Europe before 1914*. Oxford: Berg, 101–36.

Geggus, David. 1991. "The Haitian Revolution," in Hilary Beckles and Verene Shepherd, eds., *Caribbean Slave Society and Economy*. New York: New Press, 402–20.

———. 1997. "Slavery, War, and the Revolution in the Greater Caribbean, 1789–1815," in David Gaspar and David Geggus, eds., *A Turbulent Time: The French Revolution and the Greater Caribbean*. Bloomington, IN: Indiana University Press, 1–50.

Geiss, Imanuel. 1974. *The Pan-African Movement: A History of Pan Africanism in America, Europe and Africa*. Trans. by Ann Keep. New York: Africana.

Ghosh, Bimal. 1998. *Huddled Masses and Uncertain Shores: Insights into Irregular Migration*. The Hague: Martinus Nijhoff.

Giddens, Anthony. 1990. *The Consequences of Modernity*. Stanford, CA: Stanford University Press.

Gilly, Adolfo. 1965. "Introduction," in Frantz Fanon, *A Dying Colonialism*. New York: Grove, 1–22.

Gilroy, Paul. 1993. *The Black Atlantic: Modernity and Double Consciousness*. Cambridge, MA: Harvard University Press.

Giraudon, Virginie. 2001. "Weak Weapons of the Weak? Transnational Mobilization Around Migration in the European Union," in Doug Imig and Sidney Tarrow, eds., *Contentious Europeans: Protest and Politics in an Emerging Polity*. Lanham, MD, and Oxford, UK: Rowman & Littlefield, 163–85.

Glassman, Jonathan. 1995. *Revelry, Rebellion and Popular Consciousness on the Swahili Coast, 1856–1888*. London: Heinemann and James Currey.

Goldfrank, Walter. 1979. "Theories of Revolution and Revolution Without Theory: The Case of Mexico," *Theory and Society* 7, 135–65.

Goldfrank, Walter, David Goodman, and Andrew Szasz, eds. 1999. *Ecology and the World-System*. Westport, CT: Greenwood.

Gonzales, Michael J. 1996. "U.S. Copper Companies, the Mineworkers' Movement, and the Mexican Revolution, 1910–1920," *Hispanic American Historical Review* 76 (3), 503–35.

González Casanova, Pablo. 2004. "Present Systemic Trends and Antisystemic Movements" in Immanuel Wallerstein, ed., *The Modern World System in the Longue Durée*. Boulder, CO: Paradigm, 91–105.

Graeber, David. 2002. "For a New Anarchism," *New Left Review* 13, 61–74.

Graham, David T. 2000. "The People Paradox. Human Movements and Human Security in a Globalising World," in David T. Graham and Nana Poku, eds., *Migration, Globalisation and Human Security*. London: Routledge, 186–216.

Grebing, Helga. 1985. *The History of the German Labour Movement: A Survey*. Dover, NH: Berg.

Green, Duncan. 1997 [1991]. *Faces of Latin America*. London: Latin American Bureau.

Gregory, John S. 1969. *Great Britain and the Taipings*. London: Routledge and Kegan Paul.

Greider, William. 1997. *One World, Ready or Not: The Manic Logic of Global Capitalism*. New York: Simon & Schuster.

Griffler, Keith P. 1995. *What Price Alliance? Black Radicals Confront White Labor, 1918–1938*. New York: Garland.

Guarneri, Carl J. 1991. *The Utopian Alternative: Fourierism in Nineteenth-Century America*. Ithaca, NY: Cornell University Press.

Guevara, Ernesto Che. 1968. *Oeuvres III: Textes Politiques*. Paris: François Maspero.

———. 1997. *Guerrilla Warfare*, 3rd ed. Wilmington, DE: Scholarly Resources.

Guidry, John A., Michael D. Kennedy, and Mayer Zald, 2000. *Globalizations and Social Movements: Culture, Power, and the Transnational Public Sphere*. Ann Arbor: University of Michigan Press.

Gurak, Douglas, and Fe Caces. 1992. "Migration Networks and the Shaping of Migration Systems," in Mary Kritz, Lin Lim, and Hania Zlotnik, eds., *International Migration Systems: A Global Approach*. Oxford: Clarendon, 150–76.

Habib, Irfan. 1999. "Introduction: An Essay on Haidar Ali and Tipu Sultan," in *Confronting Colonialism: Resistance and Modernization under Haidar Ali and Tipu Sultan*. New Delhi: Tulika, xvii–xlvii.

Halfmann, Jost. 1998. "Citizenship Universalism, Migration and the Risks of Exclusion," *The British Journal of Sociology* 49 (4), Dec. , 513–33.

Hall, Thomas D. 2001. "World-Systems, Frontiers, and Ethnogenesis: Incorporation and Resistance to State Expansion," *Proto-Sociology* 15, 51–85.

Halliday, Fred. 1999. *Revolution and World Politics: The Rise and Fall of the Sixth Great Power*. Durham, NC: Duke University Press.

Halstead, Ted, and Cobb, Clifford. 1996. "The Need for New Measurements of Progress," in Jerry Mander and Edward Goldsmith, eds., *The Case Against the Global Economy*. San Francisco: Sierra Club Books, 197–206.

Hamel, Pierre, Henri Lustiger-Thaler, and Margit Mayer, eds. 2000. *Urban Movements in a Globalizing World*. London: Routledge.

Hamilton, Nora, and Norma Chinchilla. 1967. "Global Economic Restructuring and International Migration," *International Migration* 34 (2), 195–231.

Hammar, Tomas, and Kristof Tamas. 1997. "Why Do People Go or Stay?" in Tomas Hammar et al., eds., *International Migration, Immobility and Development: Multidisciplinary Perspectives*. New York: Berg, 1–19.

Hanchard, Michael. 1991. "Antonio Gramsci, Racial Consciousness and Afro-Diasporic Experience," *Socialism and Democracy: The Journal of the Research Group on Socialism and Democracy* 7 (3), 83–106.

Hansen, Thomas Blom. 1999. *The Saffron Wave: Democracy and Hindu Nationalism in Modern India*. Princeton, NJ: Princeton University Press.

Hardt, Michael. 2002. "Porto Alegre: Today's Bandung," *New Left Review*, 14, 112–18.

Hardt, Michael, and Antonio Negri. 2000. *Empire*. Cambridge, MA: Harvard University Press.

Hart, John M. 1978. *Anarchism and the Mexican Working Class, 1860–1931*. Austin, TX: University of Texas Press.

Harvey, David. 1990. *The Condition of Postmodernity: An Enquiry into the Origins of Cultural Change*. Oxford: Basil Blackwell.

———. 2003. *The New Imperialism*. New York: Oxford University Press.

Haupt, Georges. 1986. *Aspects of International Socialism, 1871–1914*. New York: Cambridge University Press.

Headrick, Daniel R. 1979. "The Tools of Imperialism: Technology and the Expansion of European Colonial Empire in the Nineteenth Century," *The Journal of Modern History* 51, 231–63.

Heehs, Peter. 1994. "Foreign Influences on Bengali Revolutionary Terrorism, 1902–1908," *Modern Asian Studies* 28, 533–56.

Henry, Etienne. 1985. "Urban Social Movements in Latin America: Towards a Critical Understanding," in David Slater, ed., *New Social Movements and the State in Latin America*. Amsterdam: CEDLA, 127–46.

Herman, Edward. 1983. *The Real Terror Network: Terrorism in Fact and Propaganda*. Boston: South End.

Hettena, Seth, and Laura Wides. 2003. "Eco-terrorists Coming Out of the Wild," *USA Today*, Oct. 3, 22A.

Higginson, John. 1989. *A Working Class in the Making: Belgian Colonial Labor Policy, Private Enterprise, and the African Mineworker, 1907–1951*. Madison: University of Wisconsin Press.

Hirst, Paul, and Grahame Thompson. 1996. *Globalization in Question*. Cambridge: Polity.

Hobsbawm, Eric J. 1962. *The Age of Revolution*. Cleveland: World Publishing.

———. 1969. *Industry and Empire: From 1750 to the Present Day*. New York: Penguin.

———. 1987. *The Age of Empire, 1875–1914*. New York: Pantheon.

———. 1990. *Echoes of the Marseillaise, Two Centuries Look Back on the French Revolution*. New Brunswick, NJ: Rutgers University Press.

———. 1990a. *Nations and Nationalism since 1780: Programme, Myth, Reality*. New York: Cambridge University Press.

———. 1994. *The Age of Extremes: A History of the World 1914–1991*. New York: Vintage.

Hodges, Donald C. 1995. *Mexican Anarchism after the Revolution*. Austin: University of Texas Press.

Hodgkin, Thomas. 1957. *Nationalism in Colonial Africa*. New York: New York University Press.

Hoffmann-Nowotny, Hans-Joachim. 1997. "World Society and the Future of International Migration: A Theoretical Perspective," in Emek Uçarer and Donald Puchala, eds., *Immigration into Western Societies: Problems and Policies*. London: Pinter, 95–117.

Holt, Thomas C. 1992. *The Problem of Freedom: Race, Labor, and Politics in Jamaica and Britain, 1832–1938*. Baltimore, MD: Johns Hopkins University Press.

Hopkins, Terrence K. 1990. "A Note on the Concept of Hegemony," *Review* 8, 409–12.

Hopkins, Terence K., and Immanuel Wallerstein, eds. 1980. *Processes of the World-System*, vol. 3. Beverly Hills, CA: Sage.

Hopkins, Terence K., and Immanuel Wallerstein, coords. 1996. *The Age of Transition: Trajectory of the World-System, 1945–2025*. London: Zed Press.

Hornborg, Alf. 1998. "Ecosystems and World Systems: Accumulation as an Ecological Process," *Journal of World Systems Research* 4, 169–77.

Houtart, François, and François Polet. 2001. *The Other Davos*. London: Zed Books.

Hughes, Arnold. 1992. "The Appeal of Marxism to Africans," *The Journal of Communist Studies* 8 (2), 4–20.

Hulst, Hans van. 1995. "Op advies van de minister van Kolonien," in Hans Vermeulen and Rinus Penninx, eds., *Het Democratisch Ongeduld*. Amsterdam: Het Spinhuis, 81–115.

Hunter, Robert. 1969. *Violence and the Labor Movement*. New York: Arno.

Hytrek, Gary. 1999. "Insurgent Labor, Economic Change, and Social Development: Costa Rica, 1900–1948," *Journal of Historical Sociology* 12 (1), 29–53.

Iliffe, John. 1979. *A Modern History of Tanganyika.* Cambridge: Cambridge University Press.

Inglehart, Ronald. 1997. *Modernization and Postmodernization.* Princeton, NJ: Princeton University Press.

Isaacman, Allen. 1972. *Mozambique: The Africanization of a European Institution: The Zambesi Prazos, 1750–1902.* Madison: University of Wisconsin Press.

James, Cyril L. R. 1969. *A History of Pan-African Revolt.* Washington, DC: Drum and Spear.

———. 1989. *The Black Jacobins: Toussaint L'Ouverture and the San Domingo Revolution.* New York: Vintage.

James, Winston. 1998. *Holding Aloft the Banner of Ethiopia, Caribbean Radicalism in Early Twentieth-Century America.* London: Verso.

Jasper, James. 1999. "Sentiments, Ideas and Animals: Rights Talk and Animal Protection," in Peter Coclanis and Stuart Bruchey, eds., *Ideas, Ideologies and Social Movements.* Columbia: University of South Carolina Press, 147–57.

Jian Yu-wen. 1973. *The Taiping Revolutionary Movement.* New Haven, C

Joll, James. 1979. *The Anarchists,* 2nd ed. London: Methuen.

Jones, Gareth S. 1983. *Languages of Class: Studies in English Working Class History, 1832–1982.* Cambridge: Cambridge University Press.

Jordan, Tim. 2002. *Activism!* London: Reaktion.

Journal of World-Systems Research. 2002. Special Issue on Global Inequality (8/1).

Judt, Tony. 1986. *Marxism and the French Left: Studies in Labour and Politics in France, 1830–1981.* Oxford: Clarendon.

Kagarlitsky, Boris. 2001. "The Road to Consumption," in George Katsiaficas, ed., *After the Fall: 1989 and the Future of Freedom.* London: Routledge, 52–65.

Kamali, Masoud. 1997. "The Modern Revolutions of Iran: Civil Society and State in the Modernization Process," *Citizenship Studies* 1 (2), 173–98.

Kaplan, Steven Laurence. 1995. *Farewell Revolution, the Historians' Feud in France 1789/1989.* Ithaca, NY: Cornell University Press.

Karpat, Kemal. 1973. "An Inquiry into the Social Foundations of Nationalism in the Ottoman State: From Social Estates to Classes, From Millets to Nations," *Research Monograph No. 39.* Princeton, NJ: Princeton University Center of International Studies.

———. 2001. *The Politicization of Islam: Reconstructing Identity, State, Faith and Community in the Late Ottoman State.* New York: Oxford University Press.

Katsiaficas, George. 1987. *The Imagination of the New Left: A Global Analysis of 1968.* Boston: South End.

———. 1998. *The Subversion of Politics: European Autonomous Social Movements and the Decolonization of Everyday Life.* Atlantic Highlands, NJ: Humanities.

Katz, Mark N. 1997. *Revolutions and Revolutionary Waves.* New York: St. Martin's.

Keck, Margaret E., and Kathryn Sikkink. 1998. *Activists Beyond Borders, Advocacy Networks in International Politics.* Ithaca, NY: Cornell University Press.

Kedourie, Elie. 1993. *Nationalism.* Cambridge: Blackwell.

Kelley, Robin D. G. 1994. "Afric's Sons with Banner Red: African-American Communists and the Politics of Culture, 1919–1934," in Sidney J. Lemelle and Robin D. G. Kelley, eds., *Imagining Home: Class, Culture, and Nationalism in the African Diaspora.* New York: Verso, 35–54.

Kellner, Douglas. 2001. *Grand Theft 2000: Media Spectacle and the Stolen Election.* Lanham, MD: Rowman & Littlefield.

Keuneman, Pieter. 1976. "The Policy of the Non-Aligned Movement," *World Marxist Review* 19 (11), 61–71.

Keyder, Çaglar, and Huri Islamoglu. 1987. "Agenda for Ottoman History," in Huri İslamoğlu-İnan, ed. *The Ottoman Empire and the World-Economy.* Cambridge: Cambridge University Press.

Khagram, Sanjeev. 2002. "Restructuring the Global Politics of Development, in Khagram Sanjeev et al., *Restructuring World Politics.* Minneapolis: University of Minnesota Press, 206–30.

Kimmeldorf, Howard, and Judith Stepan-Norris. 1992. "Historical Studies of Labor Movements in the United States," *Annual Review of Sociology* 18, 495–518.

King, Russell, 1996. "Migration in a World Historical Perspective," in Julien Van den Broeck, ed., *The Economics of Labour Migration.* Brookfield, VT: E. Elgar, 7–76.

———. 1998. "The Mediterranean: Europe's Rio Grande," in M. Anderson and E. Bort, eds., *The Frontiers of Europe.* London: Pinter, 109–34.

King, Russell, and Susan Öberg. 1993. "Introduction: Europe and the Future of Mass Migration," in Russell King, ed., *Mass Migration in Europe: The Legacy and the Future.* London: Belhaven, 1–4.

Klaits, John, and Michael Haltzel. 1994. *The Global Ramifications of the French Revolution.* Cambridge: Cambridge University Press.

Knight, G. Roger. 2000. *Narratives of Colonialism: Sugar, Java, and the Dutch.* Huntington, NY: Nova Science.

Kocka, Jürgen. 1986. "Problems of Working-Class Formation in Germany: The Early Years, 1800–1875," in Ira Katznelson and Aristide R. Zolberg, eds., *Working-Class Formation: Nineteenth-Century Patterns in Western Europe and the United States.* Princeton, NJ: Princeton University Press, 279–351.

Kodi, Muzong W. 1993. "The 1921 Pan-African Congress at Brussels: A Background to Belgian Pressures," in Joseph E. Harris, ed., *Global Dimensions of the African Diaspora,* 2nd ed. Washington, DC: Howard University Press.

Kofele-Kale, Ndiva. 1978. "The Policy of Nonalignment in an Age of Alignment Politics: Africa Twenty Years after Bandung," *Civilisations* 28 (3–4), 251–66.

Köhler, Gernot. 1996. "Surplus Value and Transfer Value," *World-Systems Archive,* Working Papers, http://csf.colorado.edu/wsystems/archive/papers/kohler/svtv.htm.

———. 1998. "Unequal Exchange 1965–1995: World Trend and World Tables," *World-Systems Archive,* http://csf.colorado.edu/wsystems/archive/papers/kohlertoc.htm.

———. 1999. "A Simulation of Global Exploitation. World-Systems Archive," Working Papers, http://csf.colorado.edu/wsystems/archive/papers/kohlertoc.htm.

Kohli, Manorama. 1985. "The Non-Aligned Movement and the Super Powers in Historical Perspective," *The Quarterly Review of Historical Studies* 25 (3), 8–22.

Kohn, Hans. 1929. *A History of Nationalism in the East.* New York: Harcourt Brace.

Korzeniewicz, Roberto P. 1989. "Labor Unrest in Argentina, 1887–1907," *Latin American Research Review* 24, 71–98.

Kothari, Smitu. 2002. "Globalization, Global Alliances and the Narmada Movement," in Khagram Sanjeev et al., *Restructuring World Politics.* Minneapolis: University of Minnesota Press, 231–41.

Kovalenko, I. 1980. "Bandung: Past and Present," *Far Eastern Affairs* 3, 17–28.

Kriesi, Hanspeter, Ruud Koopmans, Jan Willem Duyvendak, and Marco Giugni. 1995. *New Social Movements in Western Europe: A Comparative Analysis.* Minneapolis: University of Minnesota Press.

Kyle, David, and Rey Koslowski, eds. 2001. *Global Human Smuggling: Comparative Perspectives.* Baltimore and London: Johns Hopkins University Press.

Lach, Donald. 1994 [1965]. *Asia in the Making of Europe,* vol. 1, *The Century of Discovery.* Chicago: University of Chicago Press.

LaChance, Paul. 2001. "Repercussions of the Haitian Revolution in Louisiana," in David

Geggus, ed., *The Impact of the Haitian Revolution in the Atlantic World*. Columbia, SC: University of South Carolina Press, 209–30.

Laffan, Michael F. 2003. *Islamic Nationhood and Colonial Indonesia: The Umma below the Winds*. New York: RoutledgeCurzon.

Lane, Frederic C. 1979. *Profits from Power: Readings in Protection Rent and Violence-Controlling Enterprise*. Albany, NY: State University of New York Press.

Lause, Mark A. 1993. "The American Radicals and Organized Marxism: The Initial Experience 1869–1874," *Labor History* 33 (1), 55–80.

Lazzerini, Edward J. 1999. *The Chinese Revolution*. Westport, CT: Greenwood.

Lerner, Gerda. 1998. "The Meaning of Seneca Falls: 1848–1998," *Dissent* 54 (4), 34–42.

Levy, Carl. 1999. *Gramsci and the Anarchists*. New York: Berg.

———. 1999. "Asylum Seekers, Refugees and the Future of the European Union," in Alice Bloch and Carl Levy, eds., *Refugees, Citizenship and Social Policy in Europe*. New York: St. Martin's, 211–31.

Lewis, David L. 1987. *The Race to Fashoda: European Colonialism and African Resistance in the Scramble for Africa*. New York: Weidenfeld & Nicolson.

Lichtenstein, Nelson. 2002. *State of the Union: A Century of American Labor*. Princeton, NJ: Princeton University Press.

Lim, Lin. 1992. "International Labour Movements: A Perspective on Economic Exchanges and Flows," in Mary Kritz, Lin Lim, and Hania Zlotnik, eds., *International Migration Systems: A Global Approach*. Oxford: Clarendon, 133–49.

Linebaugh, Peter, and Marcus Rediker. 2000. *The Many-Headed Hydras: Sailors, Slaves, Commoners and the Hidden History of the Revolutionary Atlantic*. Boston: Beacon.

Lohrmann, Reinhard. 1996. "Environmentally-induced Population Displacements and Environmental Impacts from Mass Migrations," *International Migration* 34 (2), 335–39.

Lora, Guillermo. 1977. *A History of the Bolivian Labour Movement 1848–1971*. Cambridge: Cambridge University Press.

Lorey, David. 1999. *The US Mexican Border in the 20th Century*. Wilmington, DE: Scholarly Resources.

Lucassen, J. 1991. "Trekarbeid in Europa en Europese eenwording. Enige historische opmerkingen," in W. A. F. Camphuis and Schut Wildeboer, eds., *Europese eenwording in Historisch Perspectief*. Zaltbommel: Europese bibliotheek, 158–73.

Macqueen, Norrie. 1997. *The Decolonization of Portuguese Africa*. London: Longman.

Maffesoli, Michel. 1996 [1998]. *The Time of the Tribes*. London: Sage.

Magraw, Roger. 1989. "Socialism, Syndicalism and French Labour before 1914," in Dick Geary, ed., *Labour and Socialist Movements in Europe before 1914*. Oxford: Berg, 48–100.

Magubane, Bernard Makhosezwe. 1994. *The Ties That Bind: African-American Consciousness of Africa*. Trenton, NJ: Africa World.

Makdisi, Ussama Samir. 2000. *The Culture of Sectarianism: Community, History and Violence in Nineteenth Century Ottoman Lebanon*. Berkeley: University of California Press.

Mallon, Florencia E. 1995. *Peasant and Nation: The Making of Postcolonial Mexico and Peru*. Berkeley, CA: University of California Press.

Manji, Firoze. 2006. "World Social Forum: Just Another NGO Fair?" *Pambazuka News*, January 26. Online at http://www.pambazuka.org/en/category/features/39464. Accessed January 29, 2006.

Mansouri-Guilani, Nasser. 1998. "Pour une nouvelle régulation des relations internationales," *Hommes et Migrations* 1214 (July–Aug.), 5–16.

Marable, Manning. 1991. *Race, Reform, and Rebellion: The Second Reconstruction in Black America, 1945–1990*. Jackson: University of Mississippi Press.

———. 1996. "The Pan-Africanism of W. E. B. Du Bois," in Bernard Bell, Emily R. Grosholz, and James B. Stewart, eds., *W. E. B. Dubois, On Race and Culture*. New York: Routledge.

Marcuse, Herbert. 1966. *One-Dimensional Man: Studies in the Ideology of Advanced Industrial Society*. Boston: Beacon.

Marilley, Suzanne M. 1996. *Woman Suffrage and the Origins of Liberal Feminism in the United States, 1820–1920*. Cambridge, MA: Harvard University Press.

Martens, Albert. 1999. "Migratory Movements: The Position, the Outlook: Charting a Theory and Practice for Trade Unions," in John Wrench, Andrea Rea, and Nouria Ouali, eds., *Migrants, Ethnic Minorities and the Labour Market*. New York: St. Martin's, 219–28.

Martin, Hans-Peter, and Harald Schumann. 1996. *Die Globalisierungsfalle, Der Angriff auf Demokratie und Wohlstand*. Reinbek: Rowohlt Verlag.

Martin, Pamela. 2003. *The Globalization of Contentious Politics*. New York: Routledge.

Martin, Philip. 1992. "Migration and Development," *International Migration Review* 26 (3), Fall, 1000–12.

Martin, Philip. 1997. "The Impacts of Immigration on Receiving Countries," in Emek Uçarer and Donald Puchala, eds., *Immigration into Western Societies: Problems and Policies*. London: Pinter, 17–27.

Martin, Tony. 1993. "Garvey and Scattered Africa," in Joseph E. Harris, ed., *Global Dimensions of the African Diaspora*, 2nd ed. Washington, DC: Howard University Press.

Martin, Vanessa. 1989. *Islam and Modernism: The Iranian Revolution of 1906*. Syracuse, NY: Syracuse University Press.

Martin, William G. 2005. "Global Movements Before 'Globalization': Black Movements as World-Historical Movements," *Review* 28 (1), 7–28.

———. 2005a. "The World-Economy and the Dilemmas of African State Formation," in Ricardo Larémont, ed., *Borders, Nationalism, and the African State*. Boulder, CO: Lynne Rienner, 277–313.

Martinez, Elizabeth. 2000. "Where Was the Color in Seattle? Looking for Reasons Why the Great Battle Was So White," *Colorlines* 3 (1), Spring. Online at http://www.arc.org/C_Lines/CLArchive/story3_1_02.html. Accessed June 1, 2003.

Marx, Karl. 1973. *Grundrisse: Foundations of the Critique of Political Economy*. New York: Vintage.

———. 1976 [1867]. *Capital: A Critique of Political Economy*, vol. 1. New York: Penguin.

———. 1977. *Capital: A Critique of Political Economy*, vol. 1. New York: Penguin.

———. 1984 [1852]. *The Eighteenth Brumaire of Louis Bonaparte*. New York: International Publishers.

Marx, Karl, and Friedrich Engels. 1998 [1848]. *The Communist Manifesto*. New York: Verso.

Masilele, Ntongela. 1994. "Pan-Africanism or Classical African Marxism?" in Sidney J. Lemelle and Robin D. G. Kelley, eds., *Imagining Home: Class, Culture and Nationalism in the African Diaspora*. New York: Verso, 308–30.

Masselman, George. 1963. *Cradle of Colonialism*. New Haven, CT: Yale University Press.

Masselos, Jim. 1985. *Indian Nationalism: An History*. New Delhi: Sterling.

Massey, Douglas, and Kristin Espinosa. 1997. "What's Driving Mexico–US Migration: A Theoretical, Empirical and Policy Analysis," *American Journal of Sociology* 102 (4), 939–99.

Mathews, K. 1987. "Africa and Non-Alignment," *India Quarterly* 43 (1), 40–51.

Mazrui, Ali. 1977. *Africa's International Relations: The Diplomacy of Dependency and Change*. London: Heinemann Educational Books.

McAdam, Doug, John D. McCarthy, and Mayer N. Zald, eds. 1996. *Comparative Perspectives on Social Movements*. Cambridge: Cambridge University Press.

McCarthy, John D. 1997. "The Globalization of Social Movement Theory," in Jackie Smith, Charles Chatfield, and Ron Pagnucco, *Transnational Social Movements and Global Politics*. Syracuse, NY: Syracuse University Press, 243–59.

McCaughey, Martha, and Michael D. Ayers, eds. 2003. *Cyberactivism: Online Activism in Theory and Practice*. London: Routledge.

McMichael, Philip. 1987. "State Formation and the Construction of the World Market," *Political Power and Social Theory* 6, 187–238.

McPhail, Clark. 1991. *The Myth of the Madding Crowd*. New York: A. de Gruyter.

Meeker-Lowry, Susan. 1996. "Community Money: The Potential of *Local* Currency," in Jerry Mander and Edward Goldsmith, eds., *The Case Against the Global Economy*. San Francisco: Sierra Club Books, 446–59.

Meltzer, Milton. 1967. *Bread—and Roses: The Struggle of American Labor, 1865–1915*. New York: Knopf.

———. 1991. *Bread—and Roses: The Struggle of American Labor, 1865–1915*. New York: Facts on File.

Menjivar, Cecilia, Julie Davanzo, Lisa Greenwell, and Burciaga Valdez. 1998. "Remittance Behavior among Salvadoran and Filipino Immigrants in Los Angeles," in *International Migration Review* 32 (1) Spring, 97–126.

Menzies, Gavin. 2003. *1421: The Year China Discovered America*. New York: William Morrow.

Mertes, Tom. 2004. *A Movement of Movements: Is Another World Really Possible?* London: Verso.

Meyer, David S., and Sidney Tarrow. 1998. "A Movement Society: Contentious Politics for a New Century," in David S. Meyer and Sidney Tarrow, eds., *The Social Movement Society*. Lanham, MD: Rowman & Littlefield, 1–28.

Mies, Maria. 1986. *Patriarchy and Accumulation on a World Scale*. London: Zed Books.

Mintz, Sidney W. 1974. *Caribbean Transformations*. Chicago: Aldine.

Mittleman, James H., ed. 1996. *Globalization: Critical Reflections*. Boulder, CO: Lynne Rienner.

Monthly Review Editors. 2003. "The Economy: What Recovery?" *Monthly Review* 54 (11), 1–13.

Morris, Stephen J. 1994. "The Soviet Union and the Philippine Communist Movement," *Communist and Post-Communist Studies* 27 (1), 77–93.

Moses, Wilson J. 1978. *The Golden Age of Black Nationalism 1850–1925*. Hamden, CT: Archon.

Muni, S. D. 1982. "Non-Alignment from Bandung (1959) to Colombo (1976)," *Political Science Review* 21 (2–3), 149–64.

Myers, Norman. 1993. "Environmental Refugees in a Globally Warmed World," *Bioscience* 43 (11), 752–76.

Naples, Nancy, and Manisha Desai, eds. 2002. *Women's Activism and Globalization: Linking Local Struggles and Transnational Politics*. London: Routledge.

Nelson, Daniel. 1997. *Shifting Fortunes: The Rise and Decline of American Labor, from the 1820s to the Present*. Chicago: Ivan R. Dee.

Nkrumah, Kwame. 1957. *The Autobiography of Kwame Nkrumah*. New York: International Publishers.

Nolan, Mary. 1986. "Economic Crisis, State Policy, and Working-Class Formation in

Germany, 1870–1900," in Ira Katznelson and Aristide R. Zolberg, *Working-Class Formation: Nineteenth-Century Patterns in Western Europe and the United States.* Princeton, NJ: Princeton University Press, 352–96.

Notes from Nowhere. 2003. *We Are Everywhere: The Irresistible Rise of Global Anti-Capitalism.* London: Verso.

Nugent, Daniel, ed. 1998. *Rural Revolt in Mexico: U.S. Intervention and the Domain of Subaltern Politics.* Durham, NC: Duke University Press.

Nursey-Bray, Paul F. 1992. *Anarchist Thinkers and Thought: An Annotated Bibliography.* New York: Greenwood.

Obdeijn, Herman. 1998. "De Middellandse Zee, een nieuwe Rio Grande?" in Piet Emmer and Herman Obdeijn, eds., *Het paradijs is aan de overzijde.* Utrecht: uitg. Jan van Arkel, 125–42.

O'Brien, Robert, Anne Marie Goetz, Jan Aart Scholte, and Marc Williams. 2000. *Contesting Global Governance, Multilateral Institutions and Global Social Movements.* Cambridge: Cambridge University Press.

O'Connor, James. 1994. "20th Century Limited: Capital, Labor, and Bureaucracy in the Age of Nationalism," *Capitalism, Nature, Socialism* 5 (3), 1–34.

Offen, Karen. 1999. "Women and the Question of 'Universal' Suffrage in 1848: A Transatlantic Comparison of Suffragist Rhetoric," *NWSA Journal* 11 (1).

Olson, Elizabeth. 2002. "U.N. Human Rights Official Won't Seek Another Term," *New York Times,* International, March 19, A 13.

Onwudiwe, Ihekwoaba. 2001. *The Globalization of Terrorism.* London: Ashgate.

Pamuk, Sevket. 1987. *The Ottoman Empire and European Capitalism, 1820–1913: Trade, Investment and Production.* Cambridge: Cambridge University Press.

Pantsov, Alexander. 2000. *The Bolsheviks and the Chinese Revolution, 1919–1927.* Honolulu: University of Hawai'i Press.

Parenti, Michael. 2000. *To Kill a Nation: The Attack on Yugoslavia.* New York: Verso.

Patnaik, Prabhat, and C. P. Chandrasekhar. 1998. "Notes on International Migration Suggested by the Indian Experience," in Dean Baker, Gerard Epstein, and Robert Pollin, eds., *Globalization and Progressive Economic Policy.* Cambridge: Cambridge University Press, 357–64.

Perrie, Maureen. 2000. "The Russian Revolution," in David Parker, ed., *Revolutions and the Revolutionary Tradition in the West, 1560–1991.* New York: Routledge, 151–68.

Peter, John. 2003. "Brazil's Land Rush Leads to Standoff: Poor Squatters Seize Occupied Farms, Sparking Violence, Pressuring President," *Washington Post,* Sept. 5, A 12.

Petras, Elizabeth M. 1980. "The Role of National Boundaries in a Cross-National Labour Market," *International Journal of Urban and Regional Research* 4 (2): 157–94.

Phillips, Gordon. 1989. "The British Labour Movement before 1914," in Dick Geary, ed., *Labour and Socialist Movements in Europe before 1914.* Oxford: Berg, 11–47.

Phimister, Ian, and Charles van Onselen. 1997. "The Labour Movement in Zimbabwe: 1900–1945," in B. Raftopoulos and I. Phimister, eds., *Keep on Knocking: A History of the Labour Movement in Zimbabwe, 1900–1997.* Harare, Zimbabwe: Baobab Books, 1–54.

Phiri, Kings M. 1993. "Afro-American Influence in Colonial Malawi, 1891–1945," in Joseph E. Harris, ed., *Global Dimensions of the African Diaspora,* 2nd ed. Washington, DC: Howard University Press.

Pieterse, Jan Nederveen. 2002. "Global Inequality: Bringing Politics Back In," *Third World Quarterly* 23 (6): 1023–46.

Piven, France Fox, and Richard A. Cloward. 1992. "Normalizing Collective Protest," in Aldon D. Morris and Carol M. Mueller, *Frontiers in Social Movement Theory.* New Haven, CT: Yale University Press, 301–25.

Plane, David A. 1992. "Demographic Influences on Migration," *Regional Studies* 27, 375–83.

Polanyi, Karl. 1957. *The Great Transformation.* Boston: Beacon.

Polarnet. 2005. "Features of the Nunavut Land Claims Agreement." Online at http:// www.polarnet.ca/polarnet/nunavut.htm. Accessed August 18, 2005.

Ponting, Clive. 1993. *A Green History of the World.* New York: Penguin.

Portal, Roger. 1950. *L'Oural au XVIIIe siècle; étude d'histoire économique et sociale.* Paris: Institut d'études slaves.

Portes, Alejandro. 1996. "Transnational Communities: Their Emergence and Significance in the Contemporary World-System," in Roberto P. Korzeniewicz and William Smith, eds., *Latin America in the World-Economy.* Westport, CT: Praeger, 151–68.

Post, Ken. 1999. *Revolution and the European Experience, 1789–1914.* Basingstroke, Hampshire: Macmillan.

Prasad, Bimal. 1983. "The Evolution of Non-Alignment," *India Quarterly* 39 (3), 299–309.

Preston, Diana. 1999. *Besieged in Peking: The Story of the 1900 Boxer Rising.* London: Constable.

———. 2000a. "The Boxer Rising," *Asian Affairs* 31 (1), 26–36.

———. 2000b. *The Boxer Rebellion: The Dramatic Story of China's War on Foreigners That Shook the World in the Summer of 1900.* New York: Walker.

Price, Roger. 1996. *Documents on the French Revolution of 1848.* New York: St. Martin's.

Ragin, Charles C. 1987. *The Comparative Method: Moving Beyond Qualitative and Quantitative Strategies.* Berkeley: University of California Press.

Ranger, Terence O. 1967. *Revolt in Southern Rhodesia, 1896–97: A Study in African Resistance.* Evanston, IL: Northwestern University Press.

Rasmussen, Hans. 1997. *No Entry: Immigration Policy in Europe.* Copenhagen: Copenhagen Business School Press.

Ratnesar, Romesh. 2001. "Chaos Incorporated," *Time Magazine,* July 23, 33–38.

Ray, Raka. 1999. *Fields of Protest: Women's Movements in India.* Minneapolis: University of Minnesota Press.

Read, Jason. 2003. *The Micro-Politics of Capital: Marx and the Prehistory of the Present.* Albany: State University of New York Press.

Regan, Tom. 1983. *The Case for Animal Rights.* Berkeley: University of California Press.

Reid, Anthony. 1993. *Southeast Asia in the Early Modern Era: Trade, Power, and Belief.* Ithaca, NY: Cornell University Press.

Rice-Maximin, Edward. 1986. *Accommodation and Resistance: The French Left, Indochina, and the Cold War, 1944–1954.* New York: Greenwood.

Richards, Alan R. 1987. "Primitive Accumulation in Egypt, 1798–1882," in Huri Islaoglu-Inan, ed., *The Ottoman Empire and the World Economy.* Cambridge: Cambridge University Press, 203–43.

Richmond, Anthony. 1994. *Global Apartheid: Refugees, Racism, and the New World Order.* Oxford: Oxford University Press.

Robertson, Robbie. 2003. *The Three Waves of Globalization.* London: Zed Books.

Robertson, Roland. 1992. *Globalization: Social Theory and Global Culture.* Newbury Park, CA: Sage.

Robinson, Cedric J. 1983. *Black Marxism: The Making of the Black Radical Tradition.* London: Zed Press.

Rodney, Walter. 1970. "The Imperialist Partition of Africa," *Monthly Review,* April, 103–14.

———. 1972. *How Europe Underdeveloped Africa*. Washington, DC: Howard University Press.

Rose, Fred. 2000. *Coalitions Across the Class Divide: Lessons from the Labor, Peace and Environmental Movements*. Ithaca, NY: Cornell University Press.

Rostow, Walt Whitman. 1960. *The Stages of Economic Growth: A Non-Communist Manifesto*. Cambridge: Cambridge University Press.

Rotberg, Robert L. 1963. "The Origins of Nationalist Discontent in East and Central Africa," *The Journal of Negro History* 48 (2), 130–41.

Routledge, Paul. 1993. *Terrains of Resistance*. Westport, CT: Praeger.

Rowbotham, Sheila, and Stephanie Linkogle, eds. 2001. *Women Resist Globalization: Mobilizing for Livelihood and Rights*. New York: Zed Books.

Rucht, Dieter, ed. 1999. *Acts of Dissent*. Lanham, MD: Rowman & Littlefield.

Rucht, Dieter. 2003. *Berlin, 1. Mai 2002. Politische Demonstrationen zwischen Tradition und Krawall*. Opladen: Leske & Budrich.

Ryder, Richard. 1989. *Animal Revolution: Changing Attitudes Towards Speciesism*. Cambridge: Basil Blackwell.

Sale, Kirkpatrick. 1993. *The Green Revolution: The American Environmental Movement 1962–1992*. New York: Hill and Wang.

Salter, Stephen, and John Stevenson. 1990. *The Working Class and Politics in Europe and America, 1929–1945*. New York: Longman.

Sarkar, Sumit. 1984. *Modern India: 1885–1947*. Delhi: Macmillan.

Sassen, Saskia. 1996. *Losing Control: The Decline of Sovereignty in an Age of Globalization*. New York: Columbia University Press.

———. 1998. "The Transnationalization of Immigration Policy," in F. Bonilla et al., eds., *Borderless Borders*. Philadelphia: Temple University Press, 53–67.

Schirmer, Daniel B., and Stephen R. Shalom, eds. 1987. *The Philippines Reader: A History of Colonialism, Neocolonialism, Dictatorship, and Resistance*. Boston: South End.

Schmidt-Nowara, Christopher. 1998. "National Economy and Atlantic Slavery: Protectionism and Resistance to Abolitionism in Spain and the Antilles, 1854–1874," *Hispanic American Historical Review* 78, 603–29.

Schonleitner, Gunther. 2003. "World Social Forum: Making Another World Possible?" in John Clark, ed., *Globalizing Civic Engagement: Civil Society and Transnational Action*. London: Earthscan, 127–49.

Scott, Julius Sherrard III. 1986. "The Common Wind: Currents of Afro-American Communication in the Era of the Haitian Revolution." Ph.D. dissertation, Duke University.

Selden, Mark. 1983. "The Proletariat, Revolutionary Change, and the State in China and Japan, 1850–1950," in Immanuel Wallerstein, ed., *Labor in the World Social Structure*. Beverly Hills, CA: Sage, 58–120.

———. 1995. "Labor Unrest in China, 1831–990." *Review* 27 (1), 69–86.

Sen, Jai, Anita Anand, Arturo Escobar, and Peter Waterman, eds. 2004. *World Social Forum: Challenging Empires*. New Delhi: Viveka Foundation.

Seton-Watson, Robert W. 1917. *The Rise of Nationality in the Balkans*. London: Constable.

Shefter, Martin. 1986. "Trade Unions and Political Machines: The Organization and Disorganization of the American Working Class in the Late Nineteenth Century," in Ira Katznelson and Aristide R. Zolberg, eds., *Working-Class Formation: Nineteenth-Century Patterns in Western Europe and the United States*. Princeton, NJ: Princeton University Press, 197–278.

Shepard, Benjamin, and Ronald Hayduk. 2002. *ACT UP to the WTO: Urban Protest and Community Building in the Era of Globalization*. London: Verso.

Shepperson, George. 1960. "Notes on Negro American Influences on the Emergence of African Nationalism," *The Journal of African History* 1 (2), 299–312.

Shinde, B. E. 1978. "China and Afro-Asian Solidarity, 1955–65: A Study of China's Policy and Diplomacy (I)," *China Report* 14 (2), 48–71.

Shiraishi, Takaski. 1990. *An Age in Motion: Popular Radicalism in Java, 1912–1926*. Ithaca, NY: Cornell University Press.

Short, Anthony. 1989. *The Origins of the Vietnam War.* London and New York: Longman.

Shorter, Edward, and Charles Tilly. 1974. *Strikes in France, 1830–1968*. London: Cambridge University Press.

Silver, Beverly J. 1995. "World-Scale Patterns of Labor-Capital Conflict: Labor Unrest, Long Waves, and Cycles of World Hegemony," *Review* 27 (1), 155–87.

———. 2003. *Forces of Labor: Workers' Movements and Globalization since 1870*. New York: Cambridge University Press.

Silver, Beverly J., Giovanni Arrighi, and Melvyn Dubofsky, eds. 1995. *Labor Unrest in the World Economy, 1870–1990*. [Special Issue] *Review* 18 (1).

Silver, Beverly J., and Eric Slater. 1999. "The Social Origins of World Hegemonies," in Giovanni Arrighi et al., *Chaos and Governance in the Modern World System*. Minneapolis: University of Minnesota Press, 151–216.

Simmons, Alan B., and Jean Pierre Guengant. 1992. "Caribbean Exodus and the World System," in Mary Kritz, Lin Lim, and Hania Zlotnick, eds., *International Migration Systems: A Global Approach*. Oxford: Clarendon, 94–114.

Singer, Peter. 1977. *Animal Liberation.* New York: Avon.

Skidmore, Thomas, and Peter H. Smith. 2001. *Modern Latin America*, 5th ed. New York: Oxford University Press.

Sklair, Leslie. 1995. "Social Movements and Global Capitalism," *Sociology* 29 (3), 495–512.

———. 1998. "Social Movements and Capitalism," in Fredric Jameson and Miyoshi Masao, eds., *The Cultures of Globalization*. Durham, NC: Duke University Press, 291–311.

Skocpol, Theda. 1979. *States and Social Revolutions: A Comparative Analysis of France, Russia, and China*. New York: Cambridge University Press.

Skocpol, Theda, and E. K. Trimberger. 1978. "Revolutions and the World-Historical Development of Capitalism," in Barbara H. Kaplan, ed., *Social Change in the Capitalist World Economy*. Beverly Hills, CA: Sage, 121–38.

Smith, Angel. 1995. "Spain," in Stefan Berger and David Broughton, eds., *The Force of Labour: The Western European Labour Movement and the Working Class in the Twentieth Century*. Providence, RI, and Oxford, UK: Berg, 171–210.

Snow, Nancy. 2002. *Propaganda Inc.* New York: Seven Stories.

Soboul, Albert. 1972. *The Sans Culottes: The Popular Movement and Revolutionary Government, 1793–1794*. Garden City, NY: Anchor.

Sohrabi, Nader. 1995. "Historicizing Revolutions: Constitutional Revolutions in the Ottoman Empire, Iran, and Russia, 1905–1908," *American Journal of Sociology* 100, 1383–1447.

Sorensen, Jens. 1996. *The Exclusive European Citizenship*. Suffolk: Avebury.

Spector, Ivar. 1962. *The First Russian Revolution: Its Impact on Asia*. Englewood Cliffs, NJ: Prentice-Hall.

Stalker, Peter. 2000. *Workers Without Borders: The Impact of Globalization on International Migration*. Boulder, CO: Lynne Rienner.

Stavrianos, Leften S. 1981. *Global Rift: The Third World Comes of Age*. New York: William Morrow.

———. 2000. *The Balkans since 1453*. New York: New York University Press.

Stevis, Dimitris. 1998. "International Labor Organizations, 1864–1997: The Weight of History and the Challenges of the Present," *Journal of World-Systems Research* 4, 52–75.

Stokes, Eric. 1978. *The Peasant and the Raj*. Cambridge: Cambridge University Press.

Sunseri, T. 1995. "Peasants and the Struggle for Labor in Cotton Regimes of the Rufiji Basin, Tanzania (1890–1918)," in A. Isaacman and R. Roberts, eds., *Cotton, Colonialism, and Social History in Sub-Saharan Africa*. London: Heinemann and James Currey, 180–99.

Sutcliffe, Robert. 1998. "Freedom to Move in the Age of Globalization," in Dean Baker, Gerard Epstein, and Robert Pollin, eds., *Globalization and Progressive Economic Policy*. Cambridge: Cambridge University Press, 325–36.

———. 2001. *100 Ways of Seeing an Unequal World*. London: Zed Books.

Sutton, Philip. 2000. *Explaining Environmentalism: In Search of a New Social Movement*. Aldershot, UK: Ashgate.

Tarrow, Sidney. 1994. *Power in Movement*. Cambridge: Cambridge University Press.

———. 1998. *Power in Movement: Social Movements and Contentious Politics*, 2nd ed. New York: Cambridge University Press.

———. 2002. "From Lumping to Splitting: Specifying Globalization and Resistance," in Jackie Smith and Hank Johnston, eds., *Globalization and Resistance: Transnational Dimensions of Social Movements*. Lanham: Rowan & Littlefield, 229–49.

Taylor, Bron R., ed. 1995. *Ecological Resistance Movements: The Global Emergence of Radical and Popular Environmentalism*. New York: State University of New York Press.

Taylor, Charles. 2002. "On Social Imaginary," *Public Culture*, 14 (13), 95–118.

Taylor, Peter J. 1997. "Modernities and Movements: Antisystemic Reactions to World Hegemony," *Review* 20 (1), 1–17.

Teng, Ssu-yü. 1971. *The Taiping Rebellion and the Western Powers*. London: Oxford University Press.

Thomas, Darryl C. 2001. *The Theory and Practice of Third World Solidarity*. Westport, CT: Praeger.

Thomas, Paul. 1980. *Karl Marx and the Anarchists*. Boston, MA: Routledge & Kegan Paul.

Thompson, Ruth. 1984. "The Limitations of Ideology in the Early Argentine Labour Movement: Anarchism in the Trade Unions, 1890–1920," *Journal of Latin American Studies* 16, 81–99.

Tilly, Charles. 1990. *Coercion, Capital, and European States, AD 990–1990*. Cambridge, MA: Blackwell.

———. 1993. *European Revolutions, 1492–1992*. Cambridge, MA: Blackwell.

Tilly, Charles, Louise Tilly, and Richard Tilly. 1975. *The Rebellious Century, 1830–1930*. Cambridge: Harvard University Press.

Tomich, Dale. 1988. "The 'Second Slavery': Bonded Labor and the Transformation of the Nineteenth Century World Economy," in Francisco O. Ramirez, ed., *Rethinking the Nineteenth Century: Movements and Contradictions*. Westport, CT: Greenwood, 103–17.

———. 1997. "Spaces of Slavery, Times of Freedom: Rethinking Caribbean History," in *World Perspective: Comparative Studies of South Asia, Africa and the Middle East* 17 (1), 67–80.

Topik, Steven. 1978. "Middle-Class Brazilian Nationalism, 1889–1930: From Radicalism to Reaction," *Social Science Quarterly* 59 (1), 93–104.

Trotsky, Leon. 1959. *The Russian Revolution*. Trans. by M. Eastman. New York: Doubleday.

United States. 2000. *International Trafficking in Women and Children*, S. HRG 106–705, "Hearings before the Committee on Foreign Relations of the United States Senate." Online at www.access.gpo.gov/congress/senate. Accessed Feb. 22 and April 4, 2000.

Urrutia, Miguel. 1969. *The Development of the Colombian Labor Movement*. New Haven, CT: Yale University Press.

Van Der Veer, Peter. 1994. *Religious Nationalism: Hindus and Muslims in India*. Berkeley: University of California Press.

Van Parijs, Philippe. 1992. "Commentary: Citizenship, Exploitation, Unequal Exchange and the Breakdown of Popular Sovereignty," in Brian Barry and Robert Goodin, eds., *Free Movement: Ethical Issues in the Transnational Migration of People and of Money*. University Park: Pennsylvania State University Press, 155–65.

Vandaele, John. 1999. *Op zoek naar het beloofde land. Migratie en Ontwikkelin*. Leuven: uitg. Van Halewijck and NCOS.

Vandepitte, Mark, et al. 1994. *NGO's: missionarissen van de nieuwe kolonisatie?* Berchem: Epo.

Vernez, Georges. 1996. *National Security and Migration: How Strong the Link?* Santa Monica, CA: RAND paper P-7983.

Von Eschen, Penny M. 1997. *Race Against Empire, Black Americans and Anticolonialism*. Ithaca, NY: Cornell University Press.

Waitangi Tribunal. 2005. "Latest News." Online at http://www.waitangi-tribunal.govt.nz/. Accessed Aug. 16, 2005.

Wallerstein, Immanuel. 1976. *The Modern World-System*, vol. 1, *Capitalist Agriculture and the Origins of the European World-Economy in the Sixteenth Century*. New York: Academic.

———. 1978. "Civilizations and Modes of Production," *Theory and Society* 5 (1), 1–10.

———. 1983. "Capitalism and the World Working Class: Some Premises and Some Issues for Research and Analysis," in *Labor in the World Social Structure*. Beverly Hills, CA: Sage, 17–21.

———. 1984. *The Politics of the World-Economy: The States, the Movements, and the Civilizations*. Cambridge: Cambridge University Press.

———. 1986. *Africa and the Modern World*. Trenton, NJ: Africa World.

———. 1989. *The Modern World System*, vol. 3, *The Second Era of Great Expansion of the Capitalist World-Economy, 1730–1840s*. New York: Academic.

———. 1990. "Antisystemic Movements: History and Dilemmas," in Samir Amin, Giovanni Arrighi, Andre Gunder Frank, and Immanuel Wallerstein, eds., *Transforming the Revolution: Social Movements and the World System*. New York: Monthly Review, 13–53.

———. 1991a. "The French Revolution as World Historical Event," in Immanuel Wallerstein, *Unthinking Social Science: The Limits of Nineteenth-Century Paradigms*. Cambridge, UK: Polity, 7–22.

———. 1991b. *Geopolitics and Geoculture*. Cambridge: Cambridge University Press.

———. 1995. *After Liberalism*. New York: New Press.

———. 1999a. *The End of the World as We Know It: Social Science for the Twenty-First Century*. Minneapolis: University of Minnesota Press.

———. 1999b. "Islam, the West, and the World," *Journal of Islamic Studies* 10 (2), 109–25.

———. 2002. "New Revolts against the System," *New Left Review*, 18, 29–39.

———. 2004. "The Modern World-System in Crisis: Bifurcation, Chaos and Choices," in Immanuel Wallerstein, *World-Systems Analysis: An Introduction*. Durham, NC: Duke University Press, 76–90.

Wallerstein, Immanuel, and Resat Kasaba. 1980. "Incorporation into the World-Economy: Change in the Structure of the Ottoman Empire, 1750–1839." Prepared for IIe Congrès International d'Histoire Economique et Sociale de la Turquie, Université de Strasbourg, July 1–5.

Walton, John. 1984. *Reluctant Rebels: Comparative Studies of Revolutions and Underdevelopment*. New York: Columbia University Press.

Waters, Christopher. 2001. "After Decolonization: Australia and the Emergence of the Non-Aligned Movement in Asia, 1954–55," *Diplomacy & Statecraft* 12 (2), 153–74.

Weil, Robert. 1996. *Red Cat, White Cat: China and the Contradictions of "Market Socialism."* New York: Monthly Review.

Weiner, Myron. 1996. "Ethics, National Sovereignty and Control of Immigration," *International Migration Review* 30, 171–97.

———. 1997. "The Global Migration Crisis," in W. Gungwu, ed., *Global History and Migration*. Boulder, CO: Westview, 95–115.

Weir, Robert E. 1997. "A Fragile Alliance: Henry George and the Knights of Labor," *American Journal of Economics and Sociology* 56 (4), 421–39.

West, Michael O. 1999. "Like a River: The Million Man March and the Black Nationalist Tradition in the United States," *Journal of Historical Sociology* 12 (1), 81–100.

Wignaraja, Poanna, ed. 1993. *New Social Movements in the South: Empowering the People*. Atlantic Highlands, NJ: Zed Books.

Willets, Peter. 1978. *The Non-Aligned Movement: The Origins of a Third World Alliance*. London: Pinter.

Williams, Chris. 1995. "Britain," in Stefan Berger and David Broughton, eds., *The Force of Labour: The Western European Labour Movement and the Working Class in the Twentieth Century*. Oxford: Berg, 107–36.

Williams, Eric E. 1944. *Capitalism and Slavery*. Chapel Hill, NC: University of North Carolina Press.

Wilson, Andrew. 1976 [1868]. *The "Ever-Victorious Army:" A History of the Chinese Campaign Under Lt.-Col. C. G. Gordon and of the Suppression of the Taiping Rebellion*. Edinburgh, UK: William Blackwood and Sons.

Wischmann, Lesley. 1987. "Remembering the Haymarket Anarchists: A Hundred Years Later," *Monthly Review* 39 (5), Oct., 17–31.

Wolf, Eric R. 1969. *Peasant Wars of the Twentieth Century*. New York: Harper and Row.

———. 1982. *Europe and the People Without History*. Berkeley: University of California Press.

Womack, John. 1968. *Zapata and the Mexican Revolution*. New York: Vintage.

Worthing, Peter M. 1997. "Strangers in Hanoi: Chinese, Americans, and the Vietnamese August Revolution of 1945," *The Journal of American–East Asian Relations* 6 (2–3), 125–44.

Wright, Thomas C. 2001. *Latin America in the Era of the Cuban Revolution*, rev. ed. Westport, CT: Praeger.

Young, Robert J. C. 2001. *Post Colonialism, An Historical Introduction*. Malden, MA: Blackwell.

Yuen, Eddie, George Katsiaficas, and Daniel Burton Rose, eds. 2002. *The Battle of Seattle: The New Challenge to Capitalist Globalization*. New York: Soft Skull.T: Yale University Press.

Zinn, Howard. 1995. *A People's History of the United States: 1492–Present*, rev. ed. New York: HarperCollins.

Index

About the Contributors

Tuba Agartan is a doctoral candidate in sociology at Binghamton University.

Caleb Bush is an assistant professor of sociology at the University of New Mexico, Gallup.

Woo-Young Choi is a doctoral student in sociology at Binghamton University.

Tu Huynh is a doctoral candidate in sociology at Binghamton University.

Fouad Kalouche is an assistant professor of philosophy at Albright College.

William G. Martin is a professor of sociology at Binghamton University.

Eric Mielants is an assistant professor of sociology at Fairfield University and is the author of *The Origins of Capitalism and the Rise of the West,* published by Temple University Press.

Rochelle Morris is a counselor at United Behavioral Health in Philadelphia.